# INTERPRETATIVE ORIGINS
# OF CLASSICAL SOCIOLOGY

# INTERPRETATIVE ORIGINS
## OF CLASSICAL SOCIOLOGY
### Weber, Husserl, Schutz, Durkheim, Simmel

Jules J. Wanderer

The Edwin Mellen Press
Lewiston•Queenston•Lampeter

**Library of Congress Cataloging-in-Publication Data**

Wanderer, Jules J.
  Interpretative origins of classical sociology : Weber, Husserl, Schutz, Durkheim, Simmel
/ Jules J. Wanderer.
     p. cm.
  Includes bibliographical references and index.
  ISBN 0-7734-6006-3
  1. Sociology--Philosophy. 2. Sociology--History. 3. Weber, Max, 1864-1920. 4.
Husserl, Edmund, 1859-1938. 5. Schutz, Alfred, 1899-1959. Durkheim, Emile,
1858-1917. 7. Simmel, Georg, 1858-1918. I. Title.

HM585.W36 2005
301'.092'3--dc22

                                       2005052061

*hors série.*

A CIP catalog record for this book is available from the British Library.

Front cover illustration: "an elegy: grenada mississippi," oil on panel, 48" x 96", by artist and owner I. Jennifer Wroblewski. Used with permission.

The Edwin Mellen Press
Box 450
Lewiston, New York
USA 14092-0450

The Edwin Mellen Press
Box 67
Queenston, Ontario
CANADA L0S 1L0

The Edwin Mellen Press, Ltd.
Lampeter, Ceredigion, Wales
UNITED KINGDOM SA48 8LT

Printed in the United States of America

For my mother, who very well might have invented it.

Contents

Preface

If the subject matter under study in the human sciences looks different depending on the perspective from which it is approached, then in what regard do such perspectives differ? They may of course lack congruity in many respects, however, a crucial distinction between them may be the criterion for what is real. In China we may observe surviving relatives burning cardboard miniature cars, television sets, or bogus bank notes on grave sites in order to bring their deceased loved ones into the possession of those items. In a Western setting someone very smart may obtain a piece of a host after it has been consecrated, subject it to chemical analysis and find no difference between it and hosts that have not been consecrated. What is reality to these people, orient or occident, and how do they test whether something is real or just imagined? And, most importantly, would they accept the notion that something maybe real to me yet not real to you? From William James to Erving Goffman a key question in the context of interpretation has been: Under what condition do people think things are real?

Jules Wanderer has now presented a book on these and related problems. It is – using a familiar title of a book by Susan Sontag – sociology in a new key. Wanderer admirably avoids the frequent imposition that a book may be either learned and hard to read or composed in easy access language but superficial in content. Here is a very learned book that is delightful to read because of the clarity of language use. It tells an old story, one that dates back to Durkheim, Simmel, and Weber: The subject matter of the human sciences is dramatically different from what the natural sciences study in that human persons and groups are conscious of themselves – or at least they have that potential – while planets, molecules and atoms are not. This then not only justifies but even requires an epistemology which the human sciences cannot share with physics, astronomy, chemistry, or biology.

But if this is an old story, why does it have to be told again and again? Wanderer knows, and probably experienced during his long tenure as professor, that now, as many times before, there is a distinct tendency to favor the paradigm of the natural sciences on account that it helps produce results that are reliable. The data we get from distant stars have their dignity solely on the basis of being reliable. Whether or not they are relevant would be the question only for the spoilsport to ask. But in the learned tradition of the human sciences that Wanderer presents in this book, the tension between relevance and reliability has always been a legitimate topic for concern. What good does it do if we have precise information on facts that we really do not want to know about, but at the same time excuse ourselves from studying vital human problems because the collection of hard data seems too difficult to classify and understand?

It is these and other exciting issues that the present book addresses. It is – unfortunately – a very topical book, because, alas, the human sciences are at the brink of disowning their reputable past as disciplines of interpretation. Wanderer's new book belongs in the hands of students of sociology, cultural anthropology, education, psychology, political science, social philosophy, economics and others; students who may want to share the wisdom of the past of their disciplines in order to be taken seriously in the debate about which direction to go in the future.

Dr. Horst J. Helle
Institut für Soziologie
Ludwig-Maximilians-Universität

Shanghai, February 2005

Acknowledgements

Thanks to the those skilled interpreters who educated me, Howard Higman and Ed Rose; to those who listened as I sharpened my interpretative skills, George Rivera and Megan Forsmark; to readers of early drafts, Dennis Blewitt and Jay Watterworth, and later drafts, Horst Helle, Geoffrey Raymond and Laurel Richardson; to students, too many to name. Special thanks go out to Jennifer Wroblewski for help in the preparation of this manuscript.

# Chapter One
# INTRODUCTION TO INTERPRETATIVE SOCIOLOGICAL THEORY

A STUDY OF INTERPRETATION

In a simply constructed study with far reaching implications, sociologist Harold Garfinkel shed light on the part played by interpretations in social life. He examined students' responses to mock "counselors" in counseling sessions that were represented to students as an alternative "way of giving persons advice about their personal problems." [1] "Counselors," hidden from view, would answer any question put to them, providing it could be answered with an unqualified "yes" or "no." Students asked a variety of questions: Do you feel that I should continue dating this girl? Should I change my major? Should I leave school? Unknown to the students, the counselors' replies, always "yes" or "no," had been predetermined using a table of random numbers." [2]

The "counselors'" were not motivated by traditional therapeutic considerations, including the content of the students' narratives, issues that might have come up in prior questions, any logical and ethical constraints, nor any need for consistency. Some students asked the same question twice; for example, "Should I leave school?" only to receive contradictory advice from the counselor — "yes the first time, and "no," the second. Because the "counselor's" replies to students' questions were <u>randomly</u> generated, advisories were, of course, under no constraint to be consistent.

Following each question and answer session, students recorded comments on their exchanges with the "counselor." They were asked to evaluate their "counseling" experience in general, as well as with regard to any inconsistent responses. Because the "counselors" offered no substantive advice, students were also asked whether they felt unsatisfied, puzzled, or frustrated with the "yes" and "no" answers. Students reported they were, in fact, satisfied. They had interpreted and made sense out of random "yes's" and "no's." According to the study:

> [The students] saw directly 'what the adviser had in mind.' They heard 'in a glance' what he was talking about, *i.e.*, what he meant and not what he uttered.[3]

Students "made sense of," *i.e.*, *interpreted* the meaning of unqualified monosyllabic replies. Not one student discontinued "counseling" because of frustration or lack of understanding. Their recorded comments revealed that none had problems making sense of the "advice" given them. But how did they feel about receiving <u>contradictory</u> advice, as when the "counselor" advised them first to quit, and then not to quit school? Did inconsistencies dampen their willingness to continue "counseling"? Surprisingly enough, students succeeded in making interpretative sense, not only out of randomly generated "yes's" and "no's," but also out of <u>contradictory</u> "yes's" and "no's." When answers were incongruous or contradictory, subjects speculated that the "adviser" had learned more in the meantime; that "he" decided to change "his" mind; or that, perhaps, he was not sufficiently acquainted with the intricacies of the problem. Others speculated that the fault was in the question, such that another phrasing was required. [4]

Though generally satisfied with these "counseling" sessions, the students' evaluations of their experiences <u>changed</u> when they learned about the deception. "In most cases," Garfinkel wrote, "they revised their opinions about the procedure to emphasize its inadequacies for the experimenter's purposes."[5] At first, students' interpretations of randomly generated utterances ("yess" and "no's") qualified as the stuff – the content – of satisfactory and meaningful "counseling." After the situation was redefined as deceptive, students alternatively interpreted the very same "counselors' " "yes's" and "no's" as <u>less</u> satisfactory.

Garfinkel's study employed unadorned verbal content. Yes and no responses were unaccompanied by gestures, clues, signs, facial expressions or other embellishments. Its simplicity belies how well it showed how meanings, prefigured in socially defined counseling situations, shaped individuals' interpretations of their experience of "yes's" and "no's." Even contradictory "yes's" and "no's" were sufficiently responsive to situational influences, allowing students to make <u>different</u> sense of the responses in <u>differently</u> defined situations, believing the responses to mean one thing when the "counseling" session was presumed by them to be authentic, and another when the deception was revealed. The objective status of the meaning of "yes" succumbed to social circumstances, its interpretation consistent with Bourdieu's observation that "stimuli do not exist for practice in their objective truth."[6]

The mock counselor study uncovered some essential sociological features of <u>all</u> social interactions, the contents of which, albeit usually far richer than mere "yes's" and "no's," exist less in objective truth than as grist for the <u>interpretative</u> mill. The processes of making sense --producing interpretative understandings-- animate all social relationships: between parents and children, lovers, friends, students and professors. Garfinkel's students did not face unique interpretative burdens because of an artificially constructed experimental social situation. On the contrary, as practiced participants in social life, they made sense of the restricted content of the "counseling sessions" in the very same way they would interpret and make sense out of far richer content in other social settings.

INTERPRETATION: Not One, But Many.

An entry in the Oxford English Dictionary notes that the verb "to interpret" first appeared in the 1300's, when it meant "to explain, understand, translate and expound." "Expounding" referred specifically to holy scriptures that were, of course, textual materials assembled over centuries. The particular endeavor involving the interpretation of written scriptures in order to guide people to their truths was known as biblical exegesis. Some five hundred years later, in the 1800's, another meaning of "interpretation" appeared in the English language. It referred not only to sacred written texts, but also to secular activities, such as musical and theatrical performances. The new meaning of interpretation opened the door to the possibility that texts of different sorts – not only theatrical and musical performances – could be alternatively interpreted. In matter of fact, the contents of social life might also be alternatively interpretable.

HERMENEUTICS: The Science of Interpretation

Interpretation is rooted in the idea of messages and messengers, originating in Greek literature where Hermes, son of Zeus, adorned with winged shoes, served as the gods' messenger. Hermeneutics, the art or science of interpretation,[8] takes its name from Hermes, who also served as god of science, eloquence, commerce, and the arts. The broadening of the meaning of interpretation to include secular artistic performances, introduced in the 1800's, reflected the extended tasks assigned to Hermes in Greek mythology.[9]

"Interpretations" have always suggested activity of some kind: acts of interpretation, acts of explanation and expounding, acts of carrying messages. They were employed at first in the theological realm of written texts, and later in more secular realms of written music and plays. While different from, and certainly somewhat more complicated than interpretations of randomly generated "yes's" and "no's," interpretations of biblical texts, musical performances, novels and plays all suggest, implicitly, the act of carrying messages <u>from</u> authors <u>to</u> audiences: writers of 16th century plays to present-day audiences, from the composer of an nineteenth century symphony to contemporary audiences, or, even, from "counselors'" randomly generated "yes's" and "no's" to students seeking counseling.

Acts of interpretation, in both their hermetic role and most general sense, entail conveying messages between two or more entities; in the case of Hermes, from one god, the author, to another god, the recipient. More broadly, interpretations of artistic works or biblical texts link authors to audiences – some potentially large: for example, biblical materials and the readers throughout the centuries who have interpreted those materials; as well as authors and composers of sacred and secular works and the musicians and actors who perform (and interpret) their plays and music.

Whether in the context of biblical exegesis or the arts, interpretations bridge time by linking the past and the present; space, by crossing geographical boundaries; and cultures, by bridging ethnic and language differences. Orchestra conductors, *e.g.*, convey (their interpretations of) the will of composers; just as actors and directors convey (their interpretations of) the will of playwrights. Not uncommonly, interpretations bridge historical periods, cultures, and the gap between long dead authors and contemporary audiences. When, at the beginning of this century, a female <u>American</u> conductor in Denver leads a symphony orchestra performing music written hundreds of years earlier by J.S. Bach, a male <u>German</u> composer, her interpretation bridges two cultures, several centuries, and more.

Today, popular music crosses cultural, linguistic, and geographic boundaries, as evidenced by rock and roll CD sales around the world and world tours of English and American rock and roll groups. In a nightclub in Moscow, a Russian jazz group bridges temporal and cultural boundaries by performing interpretations of "standards" written 50 or more years earlier, in the USA, by American composers such as Gershwin or Ellington. By comparison, Hermes job was relatively easy, since he carried messages from god to god – some of whom, reputedly, were difficult characters – but all of whom, at least, spoke the same language and occupied the heavenly realm at the same time.

The broadened meaning of interpretation to include secular texts such as artistic performance raised two questions with implications for interpretations in social life. In musical performances, *e.g.*, the first question asks whether a conductor's contemporary reading (interpretation) is compatible with what the composer had in mind two hundred years earlier. In the case of Garfinkel's study, curiously enough, the parallel question is whether a student's interpretation of the randomized "counselor's" response was compatible with what the bogus "counselor" had in mind. Or whether compatibility was even necessary for their ensuing interaction. What if the "counselor" were a real person? In music, critics, who are also interpreters, might argue that the composer intended the piece to be played a little slower or faster. A critic's interpretation, thus, might clash with a performer's interpretation. Few interpretations are invulnerable to criticisms, as is shown in the case of Arturo Toscanni, a world famous conductor who was criticized for the relatively "fast" tempos that characterized his interpretations of Beethoven symphonies.[10]

The second question raised by the possibility of alternative interpretations is whether it is possible to identify the "true" reading (interpretation) of a composer's score. Or, as Schutz observed, can the "proper" interpretation, in terms of an "objectively given" system of musical notation, be determined?[11] What about a "true" reading of an author's text or poem? Or the "true" interpretation of the significance of the fence your neighbor put up between your houses? In music, there appears to be little that privileges one interpretation over another; not even so-called blood ties. In the case of a recorded performance of Shostakovich's Fourth Symphony conducted by the composer's own son, one critic felt it fell short of the composer's will or intentions:

> One would like to accord this performance
> special authority because it is led by the composer's
> son. Who better to understand the emotional nuances
> of the work --and the composer's original expressive
> intentions-- than his own flesh and blood. [12]

In films or stage plays, actors present their (and their directors') interpretations of dramatic characters such as Lady Macbeth, Hamlet, or Dr. Strangelove. There are many ways to play Count Dracula: sympathetic Dracula, menacing Dracula, comic, sexy, or, even, tragic Dracula. Claims to the definitive Hamlet, or to the "true" interpretation of a piece of music, or to what the smiles of friends or lovers signify are problematic.[13] They pose the same problems as those built into the interpretation of a "counselor's" reply to the question, "Shall I quit school?"

The sociological factors that enable alternative interpretations, as well as their expressions in social theory, are discussed below. For now, one might take note of Pareto's observation linking interpretations and sociology: that "for the very reason that first hand knowledge of facts is rarely available, interpretations are indispensable, and anyone resolved to do absolutely without them might as well not bother with history and sociology."[14] It might also be noted that the "true" interpretation of Hamlet is unnecessary for the continuation of the performance of the play, just as "true" interpretations Garfinkel's "counselors" replies were unnecessary for the satisfactory continuation of counseling sessions.

INTERPRETATION: What Can Be Interpreted and Reinterpreted?

In a word, everything. Or, put differently, anything that can be regarded as a sign, something that stands for, or signifies – symbolizes – something else is interpretable. Quilts, *e.g.*, are usually thought of as handmade bed covers with artistic patterns on their top surface – common patterns include "Log Cabins," "Wedding Rings," and "Bow Ties," to name just a few. Now valued because of their designs and workmanship, quilts are considered examples of folk art and fine art.[15] Recently, another interpretation of quilt patterns has come to light, suggesting that, at one time, quilt patterns signified something more than mere design. Nineteenth century quilt designs embodied messages related to activities along the Underground Railroad.[16] The meaning of the "Monkey Wrench" or "Bear's Paw" pattern was interpretable by members of the community of slaves planning escape on the Underground Railroad. They learned to follow bear trails through the forest marking easy paths leading to water and food. The arrival of a "Monkey Wrench" quilt signaled to the recipient that it was time to assemble the tools needed to take the journey to freedom.

More broadly, in *Mythologies* (1972), Barthes, the French literary critic, alternatively interpreted wrestling, soap-powders, margarine, toys, wine and milk, steak and chips, striptease, *etc.,* by concentrating less on their content than on their cultural significance. Concerning the activity of wrestling, his readers learned that "what is thus displayed for the public is the great spectacle of Suffering, Defeat, and Justice,"[17] displayed not in moderation, but excessively, in the nature of spectacle.[18] Just as quilts, music,[19] wrestling, soap powders, and just about anything else have alternative interpretations, so has "nothing." In the following account of a neighborhood stakeout of a drug-dealing scene in which "nothing" was going on, a police officer reported how even "nothing" is something that can be alternatively interpreted.

> Even when nothing happens, there is much to interpret. Are they out of product, and will they re-up within ten minutes or an hour? Are they "raised" -- afraid we're around-- and, if so, is it because they saw our van (unmarked but patently obvious) or saw one of us peering over the roofline, or is it because a patrol car raced by, to a robbery three blocks away? Did they turn away another customer because he wanted credit, or because they thought he was an undercover, and were they right? Is the next deal worth the wait?[20]

INTERPRETATION: "Truth"?

Not surprisingly, both the potentialities and abuses associated with alternative interpretations continue to be debated among critics, artists, philosophers and sociologists. Arguments about the "truth" of one and only one interpretation, or one interpretation rather than another or others, are far from exhausted. In art criticism, the debate takes the form of a question about what appears on the canvas: images are either literal representations of objects or they are signs. If the former, then what is intended are mimetic representations of objects such as barns, flowers and landscapes. If the latter, however, then what appears on a canvas is not a literal barn, but something interpretable as standing for, or signifying, something else, *i.e.,* a figurative representation or sign. Georgia O'Keefe, according to one art critic, avoided interpretations altogether, addressing herself never to signs, but only to objects:

> O'Keefe never clutters her paintings with signs; only
> objects will do. Where the work of other artists
> might recognize the domains of language, of shop-
> ping, of domestic needs, O'Keefe keeps her world
> focused on what her inner eye sees alone.[21]

When what appears on canvas is alternatively interpreted as a sign, which is to say that the image stand for something else, any number of "something else's" – and what they signify – are possible. The painting might be said to represent the artist's inner emotions and impressions in response to the subject of the painting. Or what the portrait signifies – not a female but the artist's interpretation of her as the woman he loves, or lusts after; not merely a building, but a building endowed with signification as a political or religious statement.

In the object-sign debate, Gadamer came down on the side of objects, concluding, "hence a picture is not a sign." A picture doesn't disappear in pointing to something else. The object transcends interpretations, i.e., "it shares in what it represents."[22] Objects are not subordinated to their representations, and should be understood in their own terms.[23] Sontag distinguished between old style and modern style interpretation, pointing out,

> The modern style of interpretation excavates, and as
> it excavates, destroys; it digs 'behind' the text, to
> find a sub-text which is the true one.[24]

"Modern style" interpretations are the doctrines of Freud and Marx, the works of whom Sontag hastened to characterize as "aggressive and impious theories of interpretation."[25] As sub texts they compete with one another, with the result that the work of Kafka, for example, "has been subject to mass ravishment by no less than three armies of interpreters."[26] In contrast to interpretations that ravish stand those that convey "truth."

Taking a different tack, Gadamer argued that "true" interpretation cannot be found by making the right choice among <u>alternatives</u>, reasoning that competing interpretative subtexts cannot guarantee the rightness or wrongness of an interpretation. Choice is not compelling, but <u>arbitrary</u>. And, so far as choice is arbitrary, in the final analysis, "no one supposes that questions of taste can be decided by argument and proof."[27] In what has been termed "interpretative universalism," Ronen asserted that there is nothing "outside the game of interpretation itself," in which case, no interpretation is privileged over any other.[28] Examples of interpretative universalism are found in the postmodern claims of Fish (1980) and Rorty (1991), among others.

## ALTERNATIVE INTERPRETATIONS: Wheels Within Wheels

If <u>any</u> interpretation can be viewed as one of several possible alternative interpretations, the pros and cons of each are debatable. But, perhaps (as Gadamer pointed out) they are never resolvable. Just what did the "counselor" mean by "no"? Is the Beethoven too fast? Is the Dracula too sentimental? Was that smile authentic or merely a prop to encourage the sale of a used car? Not uncommonly, merely proposing an alternative to an interpretation represents a challenge to its claim to objective truth.

Thus the extended meaning of alternative interpretation has several unintended consequences. First, alternative interpretations, when regarded as texts or signs themselves, can be in turn alternatively interpreted, reflecting the view that there is nothing "outside the game of interpretation itself."[29]

12

## DEBUNKING

Debunking, one type of alternative interpretation, originates in doubt, in the suspicion that a prevailing wisdom is <u>merely</u> just another interpretation and not an objective truth.[31]  Possibly, the prevailing wisdom was crafted in error. Possibly, it was wittingly or unwittingly drafted in the service of a deception. Examples of deliberate deceptions include propaganda, and the work of a wide assortment of spinmeisters found in politics, public relations, commerce, advertising, and network news. Debunkers often point out deceptive interpretations that "spin" facts or events in order to cover up lies or bias, or to "pull the wool over" others who are more naive or vulnerable. Pareto wrote about one variety of interpretation that contained "an element of truth, which the shrewd use for their own ends." His example: "there are plenty of rogues, surely, who make their profit out of spiritualism; but it would be absurd to imagine that spiritualism originated as a mere scheme of rogues."[32]  More recently, a CBS insider criticized the network for presenting biased interpretations in their newscasts. He added that "real media bias comes not so much from what [political] party they attack. Liberal bias is the result of how they see the world." [33]

Not only do debunkers challenge the objectivity – the "truth" – claimed by representatives of the prevailing *status quo,* they also declare their own alternative interpretations to be more legitimate than the fallacious or deliberately deceptive prevailing wisdom. Debunkers thus seek to help the world get its head straight, with wide ranging proclamations that cover everyday <u>meanings</u> of objects, institutional arrangements, roles, norms, consciousness, and even dreams. For example, Marx, Nietzche, and Freud sought the "true" meaning of religion by stripping away its <u>false</u> meaning. Each attempted to demystify religion by <u>reinterpreting</u> it: Marx characterized religion as an opiate; Nietzche argued it made weakness respectable and was thus a refuge of the weak; and Freud saw religion as the unconscious wish for father. Each, in his own way, sought truth "by the invention of an art of interpretation."[34]

Debunkers and the alternative interpretations they bid us to consider tend to be unpopular. One reason is simply that alternatives to the prevailing wisdom are often startling. Certainly, Freud and Marx's interpretative assault on the everyday understanding of consciousness qualified as astonishing. Both raised seemingly odd questions about claims to proprietorship of consciousness and the forces that shape individual awareness. The question alone was, on its face, outrageous: is my consciousness really my "own," originating with me? Or is it, my awareness and interpretations of objects, actions, dreams, and institutional arrangements, shaped by forces steeped in the prevailing wisdom or *status quo*? And might that wisdom no longer be considered an objective reality, but simply one of many possible alternative interpretations?

FREUD: A Debunking Scheme of Interpretation

Freud's work on dreams, aptly titled *The Interpretation of Dreams,* introduced a powerful alternative interpretative scheme into mainstream Western thought. Even though Freudian theory does not qualify as social theory, the distinctions he drew between dream images and their symbolic properties illuminated analytic patterns that proved useful in social theory. Examining the taken-for-granted and ordinary content of dreams – birds, staircases, flying, top hats, getting lost, cigars, *etc.* – Freud alternatively interpreted them. He analyzed dream work (specifically, his patients' narratives about their dreams[35]) as signs or texts, *i.e.*, as materials that stand for something else. Freud believed that the alternative interpretation of dream material was not an idle exercise, but a necessary step in the successful treatments of his patients' psychological troubles. Thus Freud helped establish the now commonly accepted understanding that literal interpretations of dreams are not the only ones possible. Alternatively, the contents of dreams, when regarded as signs, may stand for something – unconscious psychological mechanisms – hidden from the dreamer's own consciousness.[36]

> In the following pages, I shall demonstrate that there is a psychological technique which makes it possible to interpret dreams, and that on the application of this technique, every dream will reveal itself as a psychological structure, full of significance, and one which may be assigned to a specific place in the psychic activities of the waking state.[37]

If dream images qualify as signs, then narratives about them can be interpreted, just as in the case of the subject of paintings (discussed above), in two ways: in terms of their literal descriptions, usually governed by the prevailing wisdom; or, alternatively, as signs or symbols, standing for something else. Literal dream images, such as flying, walking down a staircase, or getting lost – whether in the labyrinthine corridors of a massive hotel or in bureaucracy, can be interpreted to stand for something else: childhood sexual trauma, whether real or imagined, wish fulfillment, or anxiety.

Many different kinds of things that appear in dreams were interpretable as symbols. Freud included among the types of things symbolically represented in dreams the body as a whole, parents, children, brothers and sisters, birth, death, nakedness. He included, specifically, houses, emperors, empresses, king, queen, smooth walls of a house, ledges and balconies, little animals, vermin, water, the sexual life which is symbolically represented as the number three; sticks, umbrellas, poles, trees, knives, daggers, lances, steps, watering cans, pencils, Zeppelins, flying, reptiles fish, pits, hollows, caves, jars, bottle, chests, cupboards, stoves; "above all, rooms," apples, peaches, fruits, woods and thickets, pits, hollows and caves.[38] Using examples from his own dreams, Freud wrote that "behind the dream there is hidden a phantasy of indecent, sexually provoking conduct on my part..."[39]

Just how wide the net claimed by Freudian interpretation is illustrated by a story told by Wittgenstein, the philosopher. In a conversation between Wittgenstein's sister and Freud, she happened to mention Wittgenstein's interpretation of a painting showing a "bare room, like a cellar. Two men in top hats were sitting on chairs. Nothing else." Freud, after learning Wittgenstein had actually dreamt that painting scene, said to her, "Oh, yes, that is quite a common dream -- connected with virginity."[40]

However Freud's contributions to substantive psychological theory are regarded today, he forwarded interpretative theory by drawing a distinction between manifest dream-material and latent dream-thoughts. If manifest dream-materials and narratives about them are regarded as texts, then what those texts signify can be also be interpreted. For Freud, the manifest (the dream image) was produced out of the latent through the process of dream-work. His subsequent interpretations of dream-work revealed how unconscious materials from Id – unknown to, and not controlled by the dreamer – forced themselves upon Ego, albeit, often, with modifications and distortions that included "an unlimited use of linguistic symbols, the meaning of which is for the most part unknown to the dreamer."[41] The bare room appearing as manifest dream-material in Wittgenstein's dream was given by Freudian theory an interpretative significance – a symbolic appearance.

FREUD: Everyday Life

With the distinction between manifest and latent dream materials in place – between the object and its symbolic representation – Freud cast an interpretative shadow over much more than dreams and religion. He also debunked conventional interpretations of everyday life, including the conviction that we know our own minds. It was but a very short step, he argued, from the alternative interpretative processes spelled out in dream work to ordinary and reoccurring events in every day life. Recurring events included "errors," "accidents," "forgetfulness," "chance," "mistakes" in reading and writing, erroneously carried out actions, and so-called "slips" of the tongue. As with dreams, Freud's interpretations of these events were based on a distinction between what is manifest and apparent and the attending latent or hidden meaning; or, more broadly speaking, between the appearing text or object and what it can alternatively be interpreted to signify.[42]

> What is possible in the case of forgotten names must be also possible in the interpretation of dreams: starting with the substitute we must be able to arrive at the real object our search . . . [43]

When regarded as texts, even everyday events qualify for alternative interpretations. To forget someone's name, *e.g.*, is not a one time, accidental event, because, Freud insisted, it will very likely happen again and again. Slips of the tongue or breaking objects are also repeatable. Recurrent thematic texts –slips and accidents-- stand for, *i.e.*, signify, something more systematic than accidental. Accordingly, slips of the tongue and reading errors, as defined by common sense and the prevailing wisdom, are not simple mistakes. "A woman who always reads storks instead of stocks" Freud declared, is not making a simple reading error, but "is very anxious to have children."[44] His <u>alternative</u> interpretation of her reading mistake revealed that the slip was not a mistake at all. Instead, it symbolized a systematic expression of <u>unconscious</u> concerns about childbearing. Similarly, the accidental breaking of an object can be either literally or symbolically interpreted, as Freud illustrated in an examination of his own experience. At first, he interpreted breaking a marble Venus – literally – as an "accident," but upon further reflection, reinterpreted it as a grateful (and symbolic) "sacrifice" brought about by the news that someone he believed was dying, in fact, recovered.[45] Truly, one might very well not know one's own mind.

Clearly, for Freud, interpretative links between significations (or symbolic materials) and manifest content were not transparent. Governed by unconscious psychological mechanisms, such as repression, suppression, *etc.*, they served to conceal unconscious threats, feelings of anxiety, *etc.* Repressed and threatening feelings of anxiety or sexuality or resentment were free to lurk beneath the mantle of slips of the tongue, mistakes, and symbolic appearances in dreams. Therapy, in the form of alternative interpretations of what dreams and everyday life events "stand for," thus depended on uncovering the psychological mechanisms that function to conceal psychic significations in the unconscious. Whatever else he achieved, Freud helped to undermine exclusive reliance on conventional and literal interpretations of dreams and everyday life. Even though his approach is less fashionable now, and though the theoretical <u>content</u> of the interpretative schemes he developed have come under much criticism, Freud succeeded in showing how the principle of alternative <u>symbolic</u> interpretations of conventional wisdom can contribute some understanding of the human condition.

MARX: A Debunking Scheme of Interpretation

> The philosophers have only *interpreted* the world in
> various ways; the point is, to *change* it.[46]

Despite Marx's intention to be more action-oriented than interpretative, a large portion of his legacy can be found in his contributions as a debunker. Remmling wrote that with Marx's arrival on the intellectual scene, "the world experienced the full impact of systematic doubt and suspicion."[47] And, Marx maintains the position of "the master of suspicion in social science."[48] Like Freud, Marx expressed his suspicions via the establishment of a basis for the exploration and revelation of alternative interpretative schemes of, among other things, institutionalized arrangements and "consciousness" represented in everyday experience. A self-styled debunker, Marx explicitly challenged conventional wisdom and taken-for-granted knowledge, stating, in the preface to *The German Ideology*, his aim to "debunk and discredit that philosophic struggle with shadows of reality which so appeals to the dreamy, drowsy German people.[49] Unlike Freud, who stressed the part played by <u>unconscious</u> psychological forces, Marx emphasized the <u>material</u> circumstances of social productive life and the ensuing differential power and influence residing in social classes.

Marx developed an alternative interpretative scheme that debunked <u>conventional</u> interpretations of social and institutional arrangements, such as those brought to bear on interpretations of family life: the roles of husbands and wives, religious life, as well as relationships among workers and owners, students and professors. Conventional interpretations, he argued, were not merely incomplete in the sense of falling short of objective reality, they were also illusory. They were deceptive "shadows" of reality.

Tracing the path by which deceptive and illusory arrangements come into play, Marx noted that humans are different from animals by virtue of "the fact that they begin to produce their means of subsistence."[50] The distinction is significant because it is in the course of production that individuals express their lives, inwhat Marx characterized as "a definite mode of life."[51] Because individuals are what they produce, Marx concluded, their nature "thus depends on the material conditions which determine their production." To Marx, production is broadly and profoundly influential: it is not only linked to modes of life and interactions among individuals it also determines "The production of ideas, of conceptions, [and] of consciousness."[52] All of these are directly interwoven with material activity and relations of production.

Members of society experience different relations production. Imagine, for example, life among the Laplanders. Some own reindeer, some care for them; others use their products as consumers of milk. Yet, others use skins to produce shelter and clothing. Likewise, in other societies factories flourish: some own them, some work in them, some provide them with raw materials, some utilize their products in the production of other products, and some consume those products. In Marx's view, differential relations to production manifest themselves (legally) in different property relations, thus engendering different interests. The interests of owners are different from those of workers: owners want to maximize profits, for example, and workers are interested in maximizing their wages. Because of the inverse relationship between wages and profits, wherein one is gained at the expense of the other, interests of owners and workers conflict.

Social classes develop around the shared interests that are associated with relations to production. Even though they seek to pursue different and often conflicting interests, classes are not equally effective in achieving their aims. With differential access to institutional arrangements, one group is more successful in securing and protecting their interests than others, allowing it to concentrate more wealth and power. When wealth and power are unequally distributed, it follows that class interests will be unequally represented in institutionalized arrangements.

This argument led Marx to divide society by separating "social phenomena into a super structure, oscillating between symbols and adequate consciousness, and an effective substructure."[53] The super structure includes social institutionalized arrangements that are less real than the effective substructure upon which they are based, *i.e.*, the ideational significance of institutional arrangements is less real than the material circumstances on which they are founded. In everyday life, however, the relationships between substructure and super structural arrangements are not transparent, and the result is that members of disadvantaged classes tend to focus their attention on more immediate but "less real" institutional arrangements: illusions or "shadows" shaped by material circumstances of social existence. Material conditions, Marx believed, not only determined institutional arrangements, but "consciousness" as well:

> It is not the consciousness of men that determines their existence, but, on the contrary, their social existence determines their consciousness.[54]

Separating social phenomena into superstructure and substructure serves two aims: first, by pointing out and debunking the deceptions perpetuated in everyday meanings and conventions; and, second, by providing material --once class interests are recognized-- to support alternative interpretations of the forces that shape everyday life experiences. Thus super structural arrangements – conventional interpretations of the meaning of family life, education, legal relations, dietary and religious practices, forms of the state, *etc.* – are alternatively interpreted and debunked. The significance of conventional role arrangements in marriage, expressed for example in husband and wife's roles, were not what they seemed. Rather, they stood for something related to, and rooted in, class interests and the material conditions of life.

Alternative interpretations have the potential to challenge institutional arrangements founded in the *status quo.* Conventional wisdom regards educational institutions, *e.g.*, to be based on educational philosophies and ideas related to the edification and cultural enrichment of ensuing generations. Religions, conventional wisdom argues, are to be founded in the beliefs and practices related to sacred things that produce moral communities of persons adhering to them.[55] Political institutions ought to be founded in and inspired by the interests of the state, its ideals, and the well-being and protection of its citizens. Institutionalized law enforcement should be founded in the principles of service to, and protection of, community members.

Conventional interpretations help make sense – *i.e.,* understand the meaning of – what "counselors" say and do; of how teachers act toward students; ministers or priests to their congregations; and police officers to those suspected of having committed crimes. But Marx debunked conventional interpretations, arguing that social institutions, as social super structural arrangements, were *not* founded in and inspired by spiritual or educational ideas or political philosophies. Therein was the deception. As Marx saw it, conventional interpretative schemes were founded in society's material substructure – in class interests – and were not what they appeared to be. Instead, material relations of production shaped institutional arrangements.

Thus, an alternative interpretative scheme, necessary to penetrate illusions, must reflect effective class interests, taking into account the power of classes to pursue their interests and to produce private property arrangements, laws and police protection, and family and marital arrangements. All of these --and more-- are determined by substructure rather than by matters of the spirit, educational philosophy, justice, or lawfulness. The implications for the meanings of everyday

22

practices clearly follow and encompass how, where, and what food is eaten; the meaning of religious practices and beliefs; the meaning of popular music in American culture;[56] and the meaning of educational and recreational practices. These are not what conventional interpretations make them out to be. Alternatively, they are activities that serve class interests: education prepares a labor force to takes its place in profit making enterprises; institutionalized religion serves to focus the attention of laborers on the after life, thus distracting them from their exploitation in this life; and propagation of popular music serves to consolidate musical forms, reduce competitive forms (jazz and classical radio formats, *e.g.*), in order to maximize profits for the producers of an increasingly narrower range of musical offerings.[57]

Marx, therefore, posed alternatives to conventional interpretations of the meaning of institutional arrangements: why they are there, what purposes they serve, and how they are conventionally justified.

> The sum total of these *relations of production* constitutes the *economic structure of society* --the *real foundation* upon which legal and political *superstructures* arise to which definite forms of social conscious correspond. The mode of production of material life determines the general character of the social, political, and spiritual processes of life.[58]

FUNCTIONALISM: An Alternative Interpretation.

Alternative interpretations have both intended and unintended consequences. While some debunking is often intentionally designed to subvert the *status quo,* the place of functionalist thought in debunking was achieved through more indirect intellectual routes. Although functionalism was neither intended to debunk the institutionalized *status quo,* in the manner of Marx or Freud, nor intended to serve as a full blown interpretative scheme, it succeeded in both by developing what Merton called "the most promising and possibly the least codified of contemporary orientations to problems of sociological interpretation."[59]

Early functional theory in anthropology[60] was driven by an interpretatively inspired shift in perspective. Scholars, rather than concentrating solely on descriptions of the contents of exotic cultural practices, *e.g.* eagle or alligator worship, or cannibalism, shifted their attention to a more abstract interpretation of what those cultural practices contributed: first, to the satisfaction of individual needs, and then, later, to the continuity and persistence of a social system. The abstract nature of the shift from content to function bears comparison with the distinction drawn by Freud between manifest and latent content. Thus, descriptions of the content of cultural practices can be supplemented by alluding to what they stand for in more abstract terms, *i.e.*, their function.

There are two approaches to functional thought. The first frames understanding of cultural ceremonies and practices, less in terms of their contents than in the context of how they satisfied individual needs. Functional thought thus centers on so-called "organic impulses,"[61] as found in the case of the family meeting individuals' reproductive needs.[62] More generally,

> Function, in this simplest and most basic aspect of
> human behavior, can be defined as the satisfaction
> of an organic impulse by the appropriate act.[63]

Weber, who referred to functionalism as "the so-called 'organic' school of sociology," recognized and applied its interpretative implications.[64] Not surprisingly, he championed the interpretative potential of functionalism as a way to understand social interaction by relating parts to wholes. The analytical result is that an individual's acts can "then [be] interpreted somewhat in the way that a physiologist would treat the role of an organ of the body..."[65] At the same time, he urged caution in the use of functional analyses, citing dangers to be found in illegitimately "reifying" functionalism and its concepts.[66] To reify a concept is to suggest it is real, or, in the case of social systems, that concepts have "'needs' or 'reasons' of their own."[67] Such reification is very much in violation of the spirit of alternative interpretations.

Functionalist thought also developed along a second line, both in anthropology and sociology.[68] Despite Weber's effort to individualize aspects of functionalism, it came to be been identified with institutional analyses, and in so doing, reflected an intellectual shift more toward positivism than toward interpretation or hermeneutics. In the case of the family, Malinowski also pointed out that functional analysis provides "the supply of citizens to a community."[69] The transition of functional thought from its roots in individual needs to an interpretive approach couched in the context of contributions to the larger social order reconciled, organized, and classified reports of newly discovered cultural practices in the wake of British colonial expansion.

During the 18th and 19th centuries, British ship captains, missionaries, sailors, and academics sailed around the world, observing a variety of native customs quite different from their own. The expeditions of James Cook, at the end of the 18th century, *e.g.,* in the conduct of geographical researches in the South Pacific, took him to the Sandwich Islands, Australia and New Zealand, and Hawaii. He and his crews, and later travelers, returned home armed with details of a wide range of exotic secular and sacred beliefs and practices. Regarding religious practices, some native peoples, for example, believed they shared common ancestry with animals. Among tribes in the Western Sudan, some "believe that crocodiles are their souls."[70] Members of a local group among the Arunta tribe considered themselves descendants of a particular kind of plant or animal, namely, their totem.[71] Among other tribes, there was no sharp demarcation between man and beast.[72] Travelers reported instances of cannibalism, eating flesh to absorb qualities of others, as well as the consumption of hearts, hands, or sweat.[73] Service wrote that "cannibalism practices on slain enemies is widespread in Polynesia."[74] These are but hints of the scope of cultural practices that filtered back to travelers' home ports.

In a context that emphasized the <u>contents</u> of exotic appearing practices, functionalism represented an alternative interpretation. Thriving in the field of cultural and institutional analyses, it addressed several problems introduced by the intellectual fallout of British Colonial expansion. The first was classificatory. Imagine a roll top desk with many cubbyholes, so that when captain's and sailors' reports about this or that practice were filed, each was placed in a cubbyhole: cultural practices and beliefs, religious, and totemic practices here, cannibalism there, *etc*. As the number and variety of reports grew, so did questions about how many categories were needed to classify them. And then, which criteria best differentiated them: was alligator worship an instance of religious practice or animal fetish? Both? Neither? What about the "worship" of bears, eagles, *etc*. Is that really "worship"? Does each report earn its right to its own cubby hole? Clearly, it would not take long to fill all available cubby holes, especially if classifications took only the <u>content</u> of beliefs and practices into consideration, so as to accommodate separate categories for eagle worship, bear worship, plant worship. The social scientific problem is complicated by the problem of organizing a classification scheme in the face of widely diverse practices and then determining what constitutes similarities and differences among them.

But social scientists faced problems other than those of classification and storage. How were members of one culture to explain what appeared to be very different cultural beliefs and practices of another culture? How to explain differ-

26

ences and questions about the implications of cultural variability for an under-standing of the "races" of mankind?

For instance, from the standpoint of English traditions, church on Sunday meant wearing one's best clothes, polite singing, sermons, and wafers. To mem-bers of English Churches, the <u>contents</u> of native practices, so very different from their own, made little sense as "religious" practices. The examination of other in-stitutions, for example family and economic arrangements and cannibalism, under comparative scrutiny, produced similar difficulties.

Some in the intellectual community believed that animal worship and the practices of the English church were simply too disparate to represent similar hu-man religious institutions. Arguing from an ethnocentric position, they maintained that their own institutional arrangements reflected real (*i.e.,* authentic) <u>human</u> re-ligions, and, consequently, other expressions of institutional arrangements --such as those that traced common ancestry with animals -- were either not human in-stitutions, or not really religion. Going even further, some conceded that whereas eagle worship might express religious practice, it also suggested the possibility of qualitatively different practices of an altogether different species. That viewpoint raised the possibility that the world was populated by different species of human-like creatures, who succeeded in producing very different institutional arrange-ments, some of which could be said to be more human than others.

Despite markedly diverse content among cultural practices, there was scant evidence to support the hypothesis that those different cultural practices rep-resented institutional arrangements produced by <u>different</u> species.[76] Instead, the exotic practices of native peoples were alternatively interpreted in terms of their functions.

The alternative interpretation acknowledged differences in the contents of beliefs and practices but, at the same time, it supported the view that peoples with different practices and beliefs were members of the <u>same</u> species. Pritchard (1973) writing in 1847, for example, sought to establish, through comparative study, the unity of the human species. A reconciliation between views on the diversity of culture and their implications for the understanding of the relationship among peoples around the world was achieved with an interpretive shift: under-emphasizing differences among the <u>contents</u> of cultural practices, by emphasizing, instead, their <u>functions</u>. Diverse cultural contents were analyzed and compared at another level of abstraction. Just as apples and oranges are comparable when they are considered not simply in terms of descriptions of their contents -- colors, texture, *etc.*, but <u>as if</u> they were "fruit" (a higher level of abstraction), different rituals and ceremonies, very different in content, are comparable in so far as, and <u>as if</u>, they "functioned" in similar ways within their own societal contexts.

Rather than classifying the contents of this or that exotic practice, functionalists <u>interpreted</u> practices in the context of what they contributed to the continuity and persistence of the society in which they appeared. Thus, they relativized content, depriving it of its exotic qualities. English church practices <u>functioned</u> in the same way as alligator worship, and eagle totemic practices. Different familial institutional arrangements might look different if one were to regard the content of their practices alone, but functionalism side-stepped the problem of classifying the enormous variability of <u>contents</u> of other cultures by adding to their practice the contributions as institutionalized familial arrangements, asking the same question of all practices: what function does this familial institution contribute to the persistence and continuity of the society in which it appears?

The interpretative shift from content to societal function altered the significance of colonialist reports of native practices. Different rituals and ceremonies, and different institutions, could be regarded as only superficially different. What unites all peoples of the world are the similar functions served by those different institutionalized cultural practices. Subscribing to what had become known as cultural relativism, functionalists also avoided moral judgment of cultural practices, regarding them merely as parts of different wholes (societies).

WHAT MAKES ALTERNATIVES POSSIBLE? Ambiguity and the Surplus of Meaning

"Are you laughing with me or at me?"

Alternative interpretations are possible because signs and texts --words, written or spoken, actions and gestures --are ambiguous and overly rich in meaning. In natural languages, most words have more than one meaning. Polysemic words proffer what Ricoeur (1976) termed a "surplus of meaning," inviting a variety of interpretations. Dictionaries list multiple meanings even for everyday words, posing barriers to understanding:

> Hence comes the great trouble we have in understanding each other, and the fact that we even lie to each other without wishing to: it is because we all use the same words without giving them the same meaning.[77]

Complicating this issue are new meanings, continuously emerging, that signify surprisingly obscure things. For example, members of one discursive community (baseball players) find it useful to have a word indicating the direction of spin on a ball.[78]

Not only do meanings of words shift over the course of time[79] with new meanings entering the language as old ones pass out, but different meanings and shades of meanings exist contemporaneously. In some cases, the same word has exactly opposite meanings: "buckle," for one, and "cleave," for another. Buckle together and buckle, to break apart. "Cleave" means one thing when an ax cleaves an object in two, and the opposite, as when mother and child cleave together. Sentences constructed from combinations of polysemic words compound ambiguity, often necessitating such qualifiers as "I was only kidding," "Are you being facetious?" "Are you serious?" and "What is that supposed to mean?" Fortunately, meaning is not wholly dependent upon words considered as brute utterances. Students in the Garfinkel study saw what mock counselors "had in mind," not because of the words they uttered – "yes" and "no" – but because of what students interpreted those utterances to mean within the social context of advisory sessions. Social contexts, therefore, are most helpful in reducing ambiguity and the surplus of meaning.

If simple "yes" and "no" answers to the students' questions were sufficiently ambiguous to permit students to interpret and resolve contradictory advisories and to develop reasonably consistent and satisfactory narratives, then what about the ambiguities and complexities to be found in the richer content of everyday talk, action and gestures? The contents of social life – the materials that comprise social interactions, and not only talk, but gestures and actions: smiles, raised hands or fingers, and actions: pushing, shoving, teasing, and playing – signify different things in different contexts. At a party, glances exchanged between friends, or wives and husbands or, even, strangers, mean different things: "I'm bored," "Time to go," "Do you want to go?" "I'm having a good time," to name just a few. Even smiles are not unambiguous, illustrated in the famous, but enigmatic, smile of Mona Lisa. A lover's smile does not mean the same thing as the smile of a subordinate or a used car salesperson. Two thousand years ago the message contained in "thumbs up" dispatched a gladiator to his death. Today, it means "good job" or "I need a ride" or "OK." Even acts such as burning things are ambiguous. Virginia courts, as of this writing, are considering interpretations of the differences – or similarities – between the act of <u>burning</u> crosses and <u>burning</u> the American flag. One interpretation holds that burning is burning; another argues that flag burning is merely burning a symbol, whereas burning a cross is widely acknowledged among members of Southern communities to constitute a threat.

In addition to their places in every day life, interpretation and interpretative themes played an important role in the debates among the founders on sociology's method and subject matter. Giddens defined three different streams of interpretative social theory,[80] expressed in the so-called "two sociologies" debate and in the efforts of the founders to delineate a subject matter for the new discipline of sociology.[81] In their disagreement over so-called "collectivist" and individualistic influences, Simmel and Durkheim supported the idea of <u>societal</u> influences on alternative interpretative schemes, by treating expressions of <u>social</u> life as signs or texts. Weber, on the other hand, emphatically rejected "collectivistic" influences on interpretations, relying, instead, on individualistic factors with the concept of *Verstehen.*

## Chapter Two
## FOUNDING A NEW DISCIPLINE

INTRODUCTION

In the 19th century, sociology was not yet a member of the university establishment. It was considered a so-called "late arrival" and faced several challenges to its claim for a place in the university community. Advocates for the acceptance of sociology as a bona fide scientific discipline had to address two main issues, represented by the questions all scholars ask: "What is our subject matter?" and "How can we know it?"[82] Answering the first question required the delineation of a <u>unique</u> subject matter --a unit of analysis-- for sociology. The second required demonstration of an acceptable <u>method</u> of study. While the founders of modern sociology, Weber, Durkheim, and Simmel, agreed that sociology should have a place in the university, they did not fully agree as to the form the subject matter should take.[83]

Clearly sociology had to lay claim to an intellectual territory of its own. "The science of society," Simmel observed, "is in the unfortunate position of still having to prove its right to exist."[84] Established disciplines typically must protect their own intellectual territories and subject matter. Territorial concerns within the university are expressed in professorships, chairs, degrees, inclusion in core college curricula; and, outside the university, in accreditation, licensing procedures, certifications, state medical and bar examinations, and more.[85]  To validate sociology's claim for a place in the university, the founders[86] had to convince the university establishment that sociology's subject matter --its unit of analysis-- was uniquely sociological. Uniqueness defended against reductionism, showed that social phenomena were different from, and not reducible to, concepts employed in other established disciplines such as psychology, anthropology, or economics. During these early days, if sociological phenomena had been too readily explained (away), or if sociology's concepts were already in play in other disciplines, then the claims of a new social science would have been substantially weakened.

The founders, in their specification of a unit of analysis, were obliged to outline the study of something different from individuals, for that is the realm of psychology. Durkheim recognized the necessity of bypassing the pitfalls posed by studies of individuals:

> But if no reality exists outside of individual consciousness, it wholly lacks any material of its own. In that case, the only possible subject of observation is the mental states of the individual, since nothing else exists. That, however, is the field of psychology.[87]

Weber broadened the debate somewhat, arguing that a new science, sociology, would invite new scholarly perspectives. He pointed out, "A new 'science' emerges where new problems are pursued by new methods and truths are thereby discovered which open up significantly new points of view."[88]

At the same time that sociology's founders would need to avoid indulging in psychological studies of individuals, they had to be careful to avoid the appearance of advocating what some critics of sociology misconstrued as an untoward dependence on metaphysical ideas. The unique character of sociological study could neither be located in the individual nor in metaphysical entities. Each of the founders, in his own way, more or less successfully settled on a middle course.

Durkheim, especially in his later writings,[89] and Simmel[90] were led, through Kantian influences, to define sociology's subject matter in terms of <u>societal</u> <u>produced</u> <u>meanings</u> and the profound impact those meanings have on individual experience. Both were wary of psychological reductionism. Instead, they proposed concepts --at some time in their careers[91] -- that deliberately skirted individualistic factors. Durkheim often cited "social facts", which he insisted were independent of <u>individual</u> manifestations, as were his concepts of "collective representations," the "collective conscience," and "moulds."[92]

> If one can say that, to a certain extent, collective representations are exterior to individual minds, it means that they do not derive from them as such but from the association of minds, which is a very different thing.[93]

Simmel also avoided the study of individuals, and urged instead the sociological study of "societal forms,"[94] or "forms of experiencing." Forms, he asserted, were produced through <u>sociation</u>, and "cannot be defined from the individual considered in isolation."[95] According to Simmel, forms of experiencing, in their capacity as societally produced meanings, shape or form individuals' experiences of life's contents. These experiences range from the mundane to the exotic.

The interpretative refrain that found its way into Durkheim and Simmel's thinking – a refrain linked to meanings that were societally produced and shared -- was very different from that adopted by Weber in his approach to sociology. Durkheim and Simmel took pains to analytically distance their concepts from <u>individual</u> mind and individual actors. For them it was society, the <u>abstraction</u>, and its productions toward which sociologists should turn their attention. Weber[96] envisioned a very different course for sociological inquiry, and in strong language explicitly rejected "collective" concepts of the sort set forth by Durkheim and Simmel.[97] The following excerpt, drawn from a letter written just before he died in 1920, makes Weber's position on the matter of <u>collective</u> conceptions very clear:

> If I have become a sociologist... it is mainly in order to exorcise the spectre of collective conceptions which still lingers among us. In other words, sociology itself can only proceed from the actions of one or more separate individuals and must therefore adopt strictly individualistic methods."[98]

The vivid imagery evoked by the phrase "exorcising the spectre" indicates how Weber felt about efforts to define a subject matter or unit of analysis with "collective conceptions."[99] For, as Gerth and Mills noted, Weber's "point of departure and the ultimate unit of his analysis is the individual person."[100] Unfortunately, Weber's interpretation of and antipathy towards "collective concepts" is only one example of many criticisms that have plagued attempts to define a subject matter for sociology in a manner that lacks literal or metaphorical allusion to <u>individuals</u>.[101] So-called "collective concepts," as proposed by Durkheim and Simmel, became a matter of extravagant debate.

Feeding the debate over Durkheim's concepts was a shift in emphasis, that he himself set in motion, from the study of objects --sticks or stones-- to the study of "collective representations." By "collective representations, Durkheim meant the ways in which sticks or stones came to be <u>represented,</u> and subsequently experienced, by members of a specific community as "sacred" objects. Because of that shift, and the suggestion it implied about how collective ideas exercise influence on individual experience, several of Durkheim's conceptions were likened to invocations of hovering "group minds" and disembodied social facts. Corning observed that Durkheim was found "clearly guilty....[of attributing] independence and causal efficacy to disembodied social facts, the reifications created in his own mind to statistical artifacts."[102] Other writers referred to disembodied social facts that bore suggestions of mysterious entities like group minds.[103] Douglas wrote that Durkheim "seemed to be invoking some mystic entity, the social group, and endowing it with superorganic, self-sustaining power."[104] For more than 100 years Durkheim's "collective concepts" have inspired more criticism and controversy than any other sociological idea.

Durkheim made an effort to position the subject matter of the new discipline at some distance from individualistic factors by slighting "beliefs and desires of individuals" that he believed were often misunderstood.[105] Durkheim's unpopular arguments[106] were met with suspicion. They were considered unreasonable at best, and metaphysical and mystical at worst. At the same time that Durkheim insisted that "society is not a mere sum of individuals," he recognized that the social things he envisioned as sociology's subject matter were "actualized only through men."[107] The distinction he sought rested in the view that the products of human activity -- activities that Durkheim termed "associations," *i.e.*, interactions among individuals-- represented properties of social life that were both external to, and coercive of, those individuals.

An examination of the implications of those social products for interpretative theory is presented below.

It is not hard to understand why critics viewed a subject matter designed to walk the line between psychological reductionism and metaphysics, and that was defined as external to individuals, as "sociological metaphysics."[108] Curiously, at the *Ecole Normale,* Durkheim had been nicknamed "The Metaphysician."[109]

Cognizant of the pejorative characterizations of his central concepts, as "meta-physical," "mystic," or "group minds," Durkheim took pains to remind his readers,

> Despite its metaphysical appearance, this word [a "social fact"] designates nothing more than a body of natural facts which are explained by natural causes.[110]

Simmel's attempts to conceptualize a subject matter that was unique but not dependent on studies of individuals were founded on a broad conception of sociology.[111] In Simmel's vision, the new discipline of sociology was "the epistemology of the special social sciences, as the analysis and systematization of the bases of their forms and norms."[112] Whatever else might be said of Simmel's plans for an epistemological sociology, it is clear what he did *not* have in mind: Sociology was to be less about measurement and counting objects than about a concern with the societal sources and the consequences of the forms that shape social science knowledge. In sociology, Simmel saw "forms of experiencing" that serve to shape individuals' interpretations of life contents, and, consequently, the meaning of their experience. As conceived by Simmel, sociology's project was no slight burden for a fledgling discipline.

There were some writers who viewed Simmel's approach to sociology's subject matter with a jaundiced eye--especially his advocacy of forms as the unit of analysis. Objections were directed at what he conceived as "forms of experiencing" and "societal forms." Sorokin, who broadly surveyed early social thought, totally dismissed Simmel's conceptions of form and content, writing that they were "...meaningless and inapplicable to social phenomena."[113] In a recent commentary on Simmel's influence, Aronowitz wrote, "At the same time it should be noted that other key aspects of Simmel's analytic orientation have had rela-

tively little influence: in particular his conceptualization of the forms."[114] (1994)
Lesser criticisms emphasizing Simmel's ambiguity and lack of systemization have
also been offered. Oakes, for example, noted that, "As Simmel employs it the
concept of form is systematically ambiguous."[115]

Simmel articulated the abstract character of sociology's subject matter
more directly than Durkheim. At the same time that Simmel eschewed the use of
individuals as sociology's unit of analysis, he underscored the abstractness of fundamental sociological concepts. He directly confronted the question of whether
"society is a real entity or a fictitious abstraction."[116] And as troublesome as his
specifications of sociology's subject matter were --in terms of its social, "collective," or abstract character-- Simmel insisted on the abstract nature of sociological
concepts:

> Existence, we hear, is an exclusive attribute of indi-
> viduals, their qualities and experiences. 'Society' by
> comparison, is an abstraction."[117]

## A METHOD
### Two Sociologies: Terms of the Quantitative-Qualitative Debate[118]

Unlike the case that had to be made for its subject matter, sociological
methods did not have to be shown to be unique. On the contrary, strong arguments were presented to support the position that sociological methods should be
fashionably "scientific." What that meant, in the days of the founders and there-
after, was that sociological methods should emulate those employed in the positive natural sciences. The ensuing debate centered on the necessity and desirabil-
ity of following in the methodological footsteps of the natural sciences. One side
maintained that social science methods could and should copy those of the natural

sciences. On the other side were those committed to the belief that because the subject matter of the natural and social sciences were so very different from one another -- not merely in degree, but in kind -- different methods were called for.

The distinction drawn was called forth in a question: can a human fleeing from a pursuing crowd be studied in the same fashion as papers flying before the wind? The underlying methodological issue was whether human actors and papers were empirically equivalent, and could therefore be studied with the same methodological tools. Some answered, "Why not?" After all, motion is motion. But, the other side argued, motion or flight regarded as a quantity, measured in m.p.h., differs from the emotional qualities involved in flight from a angry crowd. Therefore, differences between the social and the physical world do not justify the use of the same methods because "the paper knows no fear and the wind no hate, but without fear and hate the man would not fly nor the crowd pursue."[119]

One shortcoming of the consideration of paper and human actors as methodologically equivalent is that it eliminates meanings – including fear, panic and hate -- from understanding and explanation. Human actors, the argument continues, engage in social actions, which is to say, interpretatively guided actions with attributes such as reflexivity, self-awareness, or self-consciousness. Such attributes are altogether unavailable to natural science phenomena. Different categories of subject matter necessitate different methods of inquiry, leading Weber to note that, "Whereas in astronomy, the heavenly bodies are of interest to us only in their quantitative and exact aspects, the qualitative aspect of phenomena concerns us in the social sciences."[120]

**Two Sociologies**

The principle issues of the quantitative/qualitative methodological debate, sometimes called the qualitative-quantitative distinction, have been stated in different ways.[121] Natanson discussed it in the context of the "Two Sociologies." (1962) Brown characterized it as the "positivist-romantic debate," and colorfully represented the founders of modern sociology as "astride two horses at once, each galloping off in its own direction;" one qualitative, the other, quantitative.[122]

Durkheim apparently rode both horses. Early in his career he called for the study of social causality and the study of "ecological and demographic facts."[123] These facts were quantitative, and included countable objects[124] such as death, suicide, and marriage rates.[125] Later in his career, Durkheim switched horses. He shifted his attention to "collective representations," and by so doing recommended the study of a qualitative subject matter. The aspect of the latter with which he became predominantly interested was the social determination of the meaning of things; that is, the symbolic character of "the collective representations of society."[126]

Despite an impressive list of sociologists who advocate a variety of different qualitative approaches,[127] including interpretative methods, it was the quantitative perspective that took and sustained an early advantage. Quantitative methods became the dominant methodological paradigm in sociology as a result of the influence of the positivistic philosophies of natural science that, even today, some believe cast a shadow over the social sciences. [128]

POSITIVISM AND MEASUREMENT: Follow the Leader

Measurement played a key role in the early debate over the question of whether the methods of social science should emulate those of the natural sciences. It might not be going too far to say that prestige among disciplines is linked to how well each measures its subject matter. Some psychologists, observing the work of physicists, modeled investigations along the lines suggested by the latter's scientific methods and sophisticated measurement tools. Inspired by the activities of German scientists such as Von Helmholtz, whose laboratory studied and measured sound, the optical constants of the eye, color vision, and electrodynamics, psychologists established psychological laboratories to measure psychological phenomena, *e.g.,* The Institute for Experimental Psychology, founded at Leipzig in 1875, by Wilhelm Wundt.

The argument favoring natural science methods was structured around the idea that if physicists were measuring physical phenomena -- sound and sight -- in laboratories, then why couldn't the same be done for psychological subject matter? And, in turn, for sociological subject matter? There was growing optimism among sociologists that scientific measurements were possible and desirable in their own discipline. This optimism fueled the qualitative/quantitative debate in sociology (in particular) and the human sciences (in general). Networking influences were great, since the intellectual community was small enough then that a filtering down process could take place. For instance, Weber knew Von Helmholz's *Sensations of Tone* (1892), in which he reported experiments linking the quality of tone to the quality of overtones or harmonics. Helmholtz's experimental findings appeared in Weber's book, *The Social and Rational foundations of Music* (1958).

**Positivism and the Laws of Order and Progress**

But measurement was one just one face of positivism.[129] The possibility of discovering general laws or stages of development was another. For Comte (1798-1857), the meaning of positivism was related to the three stages of development through which each branch of knowledge passed. A social physics, which

Comte reluctantly renamed sociology, would be patterned along the lines of the natural sciences and would lead, he believed, to the discovery of society's laws – "laws of order" and "laws of progress." An examination of these laws or stages would undoubtedly benefit society.

According to Comte, in the first stage, the <u>theological</u> stage, phenomena are due to immediate volition in objects, their essences, or to a supernatural being. In other words, things happen because of the will of god; political authority is based on divine right.     In the second, the <u>metaphysical</u> stage, some abstract force operates on the object, but exists independently of it. Knowledge seeks to discover the essence of this force. Political authority is based on the sovereignty of the people.

In the third and final stage, the <u>positive</u> stage, no postulation of volition or force is necessary. Relations between facts and more general facts, or laws, are sought though observation, experiment, and analysis. Positivism, for Comte, meant an understanding that the universe is not composed of throngs of individuals each of whom acts in accordance with its own volition, but instead is an ordered organism governed by necessary <u>laws</u>.[130]

Sociological inquiries, patterned after mathematics and the methodological conventions of the natural sciences, would include experimentation, observation, and comparison, and, additionally, historical comparisons. The results of sociological inquiries would permit fitting society's separate parts into the framework of the system as a whole -- a system governed by general laws and causal sequences.

**The Counter Argument**

During this era, natural science was in full fashion. Advocates of the usefulness of positivistic principles for the human sciences were encouraged by successes in the natural sciences. Despite those successes, however, some social scientists and social philosophers refused to jump on the positivism bandwagon. They remained unconvinced that the study of human behavior should follow positivistic methodological guidelines established in the study of nature. They found no compelling reason to commit sociology's future to natural science methods. They rested their arguments on the principle that the social and natural worlds were altogether different phenomena, and the difference is not so much in degree as in kind. Clearly, different phenomena necessitated the use of different methods of inquiry. Giddens summarized this position:

> But any approach to the social sciences which seeks to express their epistemology and ambitions as directly similar to those of the sciences of nature is condemned to failure in its own terms, and can only result in a limited understanding of the condition of man in society.[131]

## DILTHEY

Dilthey (1833-1911), a historian and philosopher who is characterized by some as pioneer of the human sciences,[132] provided one of the stronger philosophical justifications for seeking a different method for the human sciences. By extending the idea of biblical exegesis to historical interpretation and to the human sciences, Dilthey set the stage for a consideration of a method for the human sciences termed *Verstehen*, a method clearly different from those of the natural sciences. In sociology, *Verstehen* is now most often associated with Weber's contribution to the method. Weber was not only acquainted with Dilthey's writings, but knew Dilthey himself, as Dilthey often visited the Weber family household during Weber's youth.

As a historian, Dilthey fell heir to the positivist debate as it impacted the study of history. The aspect of positivism that was represented by Comte sought to found human studies on methods of mathematics, biology and physical sciences. With those tools in hand, ideally, investigations in the human sciences would employ causal thinking and leave nothing to chance. Thus equipped, studies of the human condition would uncover features of social life that reflected generally applicable natural <u>laws</u>.

Some advocates of non-positivist approaches reacted negatively to the call for positivistic studies of the human condition. For them, positivism represented a much too tight ideological box. Rather than accepting a view of the human condition as constrained by general natural laws, they countered with arguments in support of free will, individualism and voluntarism.

Dilthey joined the ranks of those opposed to the view that natural laws governed human behavior. To replace natural law, he fashioned an alternative basis for the study of history and philosophy (in particular), and for the human sciences (more generally). Dilthey's point of departure for a historically relevant human science rested on a modification of Kantian epistemology. Kant's "transcendental philosophy" examined the inherent structures of the mind -- the innate laws of thought. Kant alleged that the flux of raw sensations alone could <u>not</u> provide the links and the connections leading to these so-called laws of thought. Categories furnished by the intellect that were also necessary, and would in turn create conforming objects. It is through *a priori* categories that the flux of raw sensations eventuates as finished products of thought, a process by which experience is transformed into knowledge.

In lieu of Kant's *a priori* categories, through which we know nature, Dilthey suggested "categories of understanding." Dilthey's categories expanded on Kant's (which were limited to nature) so that they applied as well "to the sphere of intellect (geistige Welt)."[133] With these categories of differing world-views, Dilthey purported to describe how the human mind operated in history. The categories repudiated Comte's natural laws by differentiating the study of human conduct --how human mind operates in the understanding of "facts" -- from the study of the natural world or of the "facts" themselves. Dilthey called attention to the difference between ascertaining meanings associated with alternative interpretations linked to different world-views and ascertaining "facts." The former are "understood by grasping the subjective consciousness, while the latter can only be causally explained from the outside."[134] Later, this distinction to which Dilthey drew attention was expressed as the difference between the appearing object and the appearance of the object.

In place of Comte's fixed laws, Dilthey introduced a different, alternative interpretation, expressed in the development of a typology of world-views, by which humans perceive the world. Irreconcilably, each world-view provides a "truth." Each one, Dilthey said, is conditioned historically and therefore is limited and relative.[135] A "truth" is, in other words, a historically relative "truth" -- that is, a "truth" according to the prevailing world-view.

> (1) The first world-view is naturalism, in which "The human mind functions like a mirror, passively reflecting the natural world;"[136]
>
> (2) The second is idealism of freedom, in which the forms of human mind are imposed on the empirical world to produce an understanding of it; and

(3) The third world-view is objective idealism human, in which human intelligence partly reflects the empirical world and partly serves to mould it.

Dilthey's three <u>alternative</u> world-views stand in sharp contrast to Comte's approach to the discovery of <u>fixed</u> general laws governing social life. Dilthey also added a complicating factor that conditioned the understanding of ideas within, and relative to, each world-view: for <u>shared</u> understanding to take place, human mind must operate with similar patterns, or, as Dilthey termed them, similar categories of understanding.

With a successful repudiation of general law in place, Dilthey went on to differentiate both the subject matter and method of the natural and human sciences. Even though he argued for a scientific approach for both, Dilthey advocated a method for the study of the human sciences that was markedly <u>different</u> from what was suggested by positivism. In place of causal explanations that worked best for the natural sciences (because they reflected <u>fixed</u> natural laws), he suggested the method of subjective understanding. This method worked best and most appropriately for the human sciences, he reasoned, because it accommodated the relativism associated with different world-views. His effort was characterized as clearing a meadow of humanist social thought in the forest of positivism.[137]

Subjective understanding, however, was not designed to sacrifice objectivity. Dilthey maintained that through "psychological reenactment," or "imaginative reconstruction," the human scientist could attain direct understanding of another's experience.[138] Subjective understanding, or *Verstehen*, made the meaningful order of the world possible because that order "does not originate in the objects, but rather in the structure of the perceiving mind."[139] Thus, it was through a shared world-view that *Verstehen* facilitated direct understanding of the consciousness of the other. *Verstehen,* mainly through Weber' development of subjective understanding, then became a cornerstone of interpretative theory in sociology.

## Chapter Three
## WEBER'S DEVELOPMENT OF *VERSTEHENDE* SOCIOLOGY

INTRODUCTION

Like other founders of the discipline, Weber sought to define a unit of analysis for sociological inquiries that was neither too individualistic nor too metaphysical. Walking the fine line between those two alternatives invited certain risks. The most notable and controversial among them was associated with using collectivist notions to define a subject matter for sociology – a step Weber refused to take.[140] Weber's disdain of "collectivist notions," alongside his recognition of the shortcomings associated with reliance on individuals as a source of data, led him to call for the study of types, which he termed a "pure type of subjective meaning attributed to the hypothetical actor or actors."[141]

In his delineation of a *method* for sociology, Weber forged a compromise between the methods of the natural, positive sciences (fashionable then and now) and Dilthey's vision for the human sciences. Weber combined the properties of *Verstehen*, or "the method of explanatory understanding," based on Dilthey's work, with the causal properties of "the method of logical possibility." Curiously enough, while Weber heartily advocated the former, in practice he favored the latter.[142]

Weber's study toward a career in law at Heidelberg University was interrupted by a military tour, after which he completed legal training at Berlin and Goettingen. He entered the law while continuing to work on a dissertation that combined his interests in history and economics. As was true of many of the scholars who played significant roles in defining the direction the new discipline of sociology would take, Weber turned to sociology after a formal education in another discipline. Weber's training in law[143] and economics not only influenced his choice and treatment of sociological topics, it shaped his conception of the discipline of sociology itself. This conception, on the one hand, emphasized the role of individualistic factors.[144] On the other hand, his analyses of grand, large scale topics remain well established classics in sociology. These include *The City, General Economic History, Social and Economic Organization, The Protestant Ethic and the Spirit of Capitalism*, and a religious set including *Religion of China, Religion of India, Ancient Judaism,* and *Rational and Social Foundations of Music*. Beyond these texts, contemporary sociologists still make frequent reference to Weber's essays on stratification, bureaucracy,[145] types of authority, and, of course, *Verstehen*, to name just a few.

## A SUBJECT MATTER FOR SOCIOLOGY

Borrowing from Dilthey's view of history and the human sciences, Weber fashioned a definition of the new discipline of sociology:

> Sociology (in the sense in which this highly ambiguous word is used here) is a science which attempts the interpretive understanding of social action in order thereby to arrive at a causal explanation of its course and effects.[146]

## A Unit of Analysis For Social Action: The Individual, Most Certainly Not The Collectivity

Having articulated a subject matter for sociology – social action – Weber turned to the specification of exactly *what* was to be studied. He determined that the unit of analysis in sociological studies, *i.e.*, what sociologists study, was the subjective interpretation of actions *not of collectivities* but of individuals. He reasoned that only individuals can be regarded as agents in what he termed "a course of subjectively understandable action."[147] Weber proposed *individuals* as the unit of sociological analysis in a deliberate attempt to dismiss so-called collectivist notions. Social collectivities such as states, associations, and business corporations, he maintained, lacked identifiable agents other than the individuals who composed them.[148] The latter, alone, were carriers of "meaningful conduct." Founding the subject matter of sociology in subjective understanding was Weber's way of avoiding the inappropriateness of collective conceptions. "For sociological purposes," he observed, "there is not such thing as a collective personality which 'acts.'"[149] To Weber, collectivities were simply not viable as bases for studying subjectively understandable action. Moreover, even the ways that collectivities were organized had to be treated as resultants of acts of individuals.[150]

> Interpretative sociology considers the individual . . .
> and his action as the basic unit as its 'atom' . . . In
> this approach, the individual is also the upper limit
> and sole carrier of meaningful conduct. . .[151]

Even though it was the individual alone who bore meaning and served sociological interests as the agent engaged in meaningful behavior – as the "sole carrier of meaningful conduct" – Weber nonetheless called attention to the significance of the differences between substantive and methodological units of

50

analysis. The individual might well be the agent, the <u>methodological</u> observational unit, but for Weber the individual was not the direct subject (matter) of the science of sociology. Individual subject matter belonged to psychology. Therefore, despite his emphasis on the individual as the sociological "atom," Weber did not consider himself a psychologist. In fact, he viewed the presentation of strong arguments against psychological accounts as necessary steps in establishing sociology as a unique discipline.[152] Weber wrote that it was erroneous to "regard any kind of 'psychology' as the ultimate foundation of the sociological interpretation of action."[153] Thus, Weber first distinguished between the identification of a subject matter for sociology and the <u>non</u>-collectivist methods by which it could be studied. Then, by separating subject matter and method, Weber avoided psychological reductionism, even though, some maintained, he "might properly be termed a methodological individualist."[154]

Sensitive to the problems associated with establishing a new discipline, Weber examined the apparent tensions between what he advocated as individualistic methods versus the methods of the established discipline of psychology. While he found the former acceptable, the latter were not. This issue confronted all of the founders: the sociological project would not succeed were it dependent either upon a psychologically based subject matter or a metaphysical one. Because human conduct could be seen from a variety of scientific perspectives, Weber created both *distance* and a *difference* between sociology and psychology. He argued that an interpretative (explanatory) understanding of the rational behavior of an actor in the promotion of his specific interests did not become more understandable by taking psychological considerations into account.[155] Psychology's contribution was in furthering other types of explanation, specifically, "in explaining the irrationalities of action sociologically, that form of psychology which employs the method of subject understanding undoubtedly can make decisively important contributions."[156]

To further his goal of developing sociology as a unique area of study, Weber fashioned another compromise through abstraction. Even though individuals were the "atoms" of sociological studies – the actors and the bearers of meaning – sociological investigations began with questions not about those individuals, *qua individuals,* but instead about the typical motives of individuals-as-types – such as kings, magicians, entrepreneurs, bureaucratic officials, young mothers, and wood-choppers.[157] The typical motives of individuals-as-types, Weber argued, lead to the establishment and perpetuation of a community (of values). Sociological inquiry, therefore, sought to understand the rational behavior of individual types, insofar as these types are viewed as exemplifying the community's values, and not the individual's. Typing, therefore, occurs in the context of a larger, non-individualistic frame of reference.

> It is a monstrous misunderstanding to think that an "individualistic" method should involve what is in any conceivable sense an individualistic system of values.[158]

**What kind of behavior is considered for understanding?**

Social action, whether oriented to the present, past, or future behavior of others, qualifies as action only insofar as it is "meaningfully oriented to that of others."[159] Discussing two cyclists who collided, Weber asserted that while the mere collision was classifiable as a natural event, it was the cyclists' efforts to avoid each other that constituted social action. By the same token, people at a bus stop who happened to raise their umbrellas at the same time in response to a rain shower are not displaying actions that take others into account; therefore, according to Weber, that form of behavior would not qualify as social action. An additional qualification: action does not qualify as "social" when it is oriented to inanimate objects:

> [Action is social] in so far as, by virtue of the sub-
> jective meaning attached to it by the acting individ-
> ual (or individuals), it takes account of the behavior
> of others and is thereby oriented in it course.[160]

An individual's actions, when taken together and when presumed to take others into account, are understandable *in a causal sense* when they are rationally related to the realization of individual motives. Moreover, Weber pointed out, most of the laws of sociology are built up precisely on the basis of such rational assumptions.[161] When an individual's actions are irrationally related to their motives, then psychology, not sociology, is the proper mode of study

### How many different ways to understand?

There are two types of understanding. Weber classified the first of these as "direct observational understanding." Examples include our understanding of what students or scientists are doing when they write on the blackboard "2 + 2 = 4;" or our understanding of a person's action when she reaches for a door knob in order to open a door; or, as we look out of the window of a train passing through the countryside, our when we see a woodchopper at work.[162] We can achieve, according to Weber, direct observational understanding of the action of a wood-chopper, or someone who reaches for the knob to shut a door, or someone who aims a gun at an animal. [163]

Weber termed the second kind of understanding "explanatory under-standing." Different from direct observational understanding, explanatory under-standing encompassed individual motivation and the subjective meaning of ac-tion.[164] Explanatory understanding requires an interpretative grasp of meaning in that action. Meaning and motive are related; as Weber wrote, "we understand in terms of *motive* the meaning an actor attaches [to what he does and says.]"[165] This form of understanding does not take place as a simple observational report of someone writing down 2 + 2 = 4, but as the *explanation* of how an action rationally relates to the actor's goal(s), thus satisfying the motive attached to the act by the actor. The difference between direct observational understanding and explanatory understanding bears careful consideration. Weber indicated that when the subject writes 2 + 2 = 4, it is important to understand whether she is balancing the books as part of her bookkeeping work, taking an arithmetic exam as a student, making a scientific demonstration, or perhaps illustrating a song to a child.

## THE METHODS OF SOCIOLOGY

Parsons outlined four of the many methodological positions taken by Weber, and two are of special interest here: "the method of logical possibility" [166] and the method of *Verstehen*. Both addressed a variety of concerns, such as causality, judgment of object possibility, history, and the case of the individual. Dilthey, it will be remembered, had succeeded in differentiating a relativistic interpretative method from more general laws binding causal explanations of the natural sciences. He succeeded by establishing a unique, relative and limited method. In so doing he widened the gap between the human and natural sciences.[167] Weber's conceptual development of methodologies for sociology – the method of logical possibility and *Verstehen* -- were designed *to narrow* the breach between the sciences of nature and man.[168] He sought to combine aspects of both traditions, a reconciliation of causal explanation with the "the idealist tradition of sympathetic understanding of human action, *Verstehen*."[169] To accomplish that goal, Weber revisited causality, not in terms of strict Comtean laws, but in terms of causality's expression as a conceptual and abstract method. Then, after examining the role of causal factors in history, Weber brought the causal question to bear on understanding individual behavior. First, for historical analysis, Weber asked,

> By which logical operations do we acquire the insight and how can we demonstratively establish *that* such a causal relationship exists between those 'essential' components of the effects and certain components among the infinity of determining factors.[170]

## The Method of Logical Possibility

The method of logical possibility dealt with the causal question in the human sciences, not through observational techniques, but through conceptual and logical connections of means and ends. Weber stressed the conceptual character of logical possibility in support of his view that causal relationships could not be established through simple observation. Events, he insisted, were not accessible by "presuppositionless" observation.[171] An observation in the raw, or a "mental photograph," was not possible because observations themselves are encumbered. Thus, Weber wrote, the attribution of effects to causes takes place through a process of thought that includes a series of abstractions.[172] His position on "mental photographs" has been sustained via multiple studies of inconsistencies found among eyewitness reports of the same event.[173]

Weber's first, and perhaps decisive, abstraction introduced an alteration that permitted him to hypothetically vary or modify one of the causal components of an action, and then ascertain the difference that that hypothetical modification would have made on its outcome. Said more simply: if such and such had (or, had not) occurred, what would have been observably different?

> The first and decisive one occurs when we *conceive* of one or a few of the actual causal components as

> modified in a certain direction and then ask our-
> selves whether under conditions which have been
> thus changed, the same effect . . . or some other ef-
> fect 'would be expected.' [174]

Weber made frequent and productive use of the method of logical possibility to examine large-scale social phenomena, such the development of capitalism, bureaucracies, and even the tonal properties of Western music. (Weber 1958)
To illustrate his point, Weber raised (and subsequently answered) hypothetical
questions. In the case of music, for example, he asked, "What if the Western
world had not been caught up in its particular process of rationalization?" So that
in the case of overtones – the array of notes appearing in the vibrations of a struck
string – by dividing the string in rational subdivisions, i.e., in half, thirds and
fourths, one produces the notes appearing in a typical Western musical scale. The
hypothetical question he raised was: wouldn't Western music and Oriental music
sound more similar than it does were a musician to rationally divide overtones of
a stuck string?[175]

Having established a methodological device by which conceptual experiments could be imposed on large-scale historical events, Weber turned his attention to the study of individuals, suggesting,

> It is, however, now clear that the causal analysis of
> personal actions proceeds logically in exactly the
> same way as the causal analysis of the "historical
> significance" of the Battle of Marathon, i.e., by
> isolation, generalization and the construction of
> judgments of possibility.[176]

To illustrate how the method in a causal analysis applies in the case of individuals, Weber wrote of a temperamental young mother who was seen giving
her misbehaving child what Weber termed "a solid cuff." When the justice of her

action was challenged, she defended herself by referring to her own <u>history</u> and her own usual motives. By motive, Weber meant "a complex of subjective meaning which seems to the actor himself or to the observer an adequate ground for the conduct in question."[177] Her argument stressed the point that the event – cuffing her child – *would have been different given different conditions or antecedents*, a claim verifiable by reference to her *usual* behavior.

Weber went on to show how the method of logical possibility – causality – combined with individual motives in the case of the young mother:

> Then 'she' will, *e.g.*, expound the thought and offer it as an excuse that if at that moment she *had* not been, let us assume, 'agitated' by a quarrel with the cook, that the aforementioned disciplinary procedure *would* not have been used at all or would not have been applied 'in that way'; she will be inclined to admit to him: 'he really knows that she is not ordinarily in that state.' She refers him thereby to his 'empirical knowledge' regarding her 'usual motives,' which in the vast majority of all the generally *possible* constellations would have led to an    other, less irrational effect.[178]

Weber's point was that the logic governing historical analysis also applied in the case of the young mother who, after the fact, engaged in abstract conceptualization. Weber, however, did not claim the young mother consciously "made a causal imputation just like an historian", that is, a judgment of objective possibility, or, even, that she engaged in causal thinking.[179] In fact, as Weber wrote, she would likely be astounded to learn she had made such a causal imputation.

Weber cautioned readers that interpretations of the decisions of historical figures (then and now) such as Napoleon, for Weber, or JFK, Reagan, or George Washington, for us, only *seemed*, on the face of it, to be different from interpretations based on one's own memory of one's own actions. It was a misconception, or more pointedly a "naive prejudice," Weber argued, to assert that there is any vast difference between interpretations of historical actions from the outside – *i.e.,* from the perspective of a third party – and interpretations based on the contemplation of "inward aspects" of one's own actions.[180] The misconceived difference merely represented a difference "in the degree of accessibility and completeness of the 'data.'"[181]

But what about the interpretation of contemporaries: is access to their self-reflexive thought helpful? In an examination of the actions of a living, complicated personality, are there benefits to be derived from taking into consideration that living person's input? And does that input represent a more adequate source of data than an interpretation from the "outside"? Or is this merely another example of "naive prejudice"? Weber's answer to that question took a surprising turn when he once again directed a methodological assault on reliance on individual self-reports:

> We are indeed always inclined to believe that if we find the "personality" of a human being "complicated" and difficult to interpret, that he *himself* must be able to furnish us with the decisive information if he really honestly wished to do so. We will not discuss further at this point either the fact that or the reason why this is not so --or, indeed, why the contrary is often the case.[182]

Weber relied heavily on the method of logical possibility for several reasons. Not least of these was that it produced analyses that relied neither on data nor on insights gained from actors' reports of their "inward aspects," but instead relied on the results of a "judgment of objective possibility."[183] In these logical experiments, the causal significance of a fact – for a particular (read *relativistic*) interest – was ascertained by answering the abstract methodological question: what would have been different had that fact been modified or excluded?

If, *e.g.*, the typical behaviors of individuals, based on particular set of religious values, are causally linked to the development of capitalism, then the application of a judgment of objective possibility should examine societies similar to capitalist societies, but <u>lacking</u> their requisite religious values. What would have been different for countries without the religious values necessary for behaviors associated with the development of capitalism? Historically, one would infer, they should lack capitalism. And so it was for the young mother: had she not been provoked by the cook, she would not have acted in the extraordinary fashion and "cuffed" her child! Thus, analysis based on a judgment of objective possibility. Even though the data of history are "outside," that is, third party data, and appear to be different from "inside" data (a young mother's very own recollections), the difference is merely one of *degree*, not of *kind*.[184] Whatever their source, both first and third party data need to be subject to a causal examination in the context of "judgments of objective possibility."

### The Method of *Verstehen*

The concept of *Verstehen* – interpretative understanding — existed prior to the work of Weber, Dilthey, and Vico and Comte.[185] But despite similarities among ideas suggested by writers such as Cooley, Mead, MacIver, Znaniecki, and Sorokin, *e.g.*, Weber remains the main architect of the conceptual platform upon which *Verstehen* developed in sociology.[186]

Regarding the possibility of ascertaining objectively correct meanings of human actions, Weber took a relativistic lead from Dilthey: "True" meaning is problematic. It makes no difference whether meaning refers to the actions of a concrete case of a particular actor (or actors) or to the *pure type*, as theoretically conceived. Neither refers to "an objectively 'correct' meaning, nor to one which is 'true' in some metaphysical sense."[187] Underscoring this point, Weber asserted that it was just this absence of an objectively correct and true meaning that distinguished both history and sociology from logic, jurisprudence, ethics and aesthetics, all of which do "seek to ascertain the 'true' and 'valid' meanings associated with the objects of their investigation."[188]

### *Verstehen* and the Woodchopper

Glancing out a train window, sociological observers might directly observe someone chopping wood or aiming a gun. The observers' understanding of those actions is enhanced by a consideration of motive:

> If we know that the woodchopper is working for a wage or is chopping a supply of firewood for his own use or possibly is doing it for recreation. But he might also be 'working off' a fit of rage, an irrational case.[189]

*Verstehen,* or *explanatory understanding*, depends on a grasp of the subjective meaning of chopping wood for the woodchopper.[190] Assume for the moment that "chopping wood" is an agreed upon action in the context of a shared background of knowledge. Were it possible to stop the train to ask the woodchopper questions about what he was doing, hypothetically, the woodchopper could say any one (or additional) things in reply:

(1) "I'm recreating."
(2) "I'm exercising."
(3) "I'm clearing the forest to get rid of the
      mosquitos and contain West Nile Virus."

(4) "I'm getting ready for winter."

(5) "I'm warming myself up."

(6) "I'm working for the lumber company."

(7) "I'm venting my anger at my boss."

It would be unusual for sociological observers to know which of these alternatives guides the work of the woodchopper but not impossible. If the train happened to be passing through a lumber company's cutting area, it would be highly probable that, typically, woodchopper types would be at work cutting down trees for the lumber company. Obviously, such confidence in an interpretation of the behavior of a woodchopper in the middle of field is somewhat more problematic.

Weber's explanatory understanding requires consideration of the motive of the individual woodchopper. By considering motive, Weber ties observable individual actions to the rational fulfillment of <u>individual</u> goals! Since the act of woodcutting can be interpreted as serving a number of different goals, it is incumbent on the observer to determine, firstly, whether the action is rational; and secondly, if it is rational, the extent to which the action is related – in the sense of a means-end relationship – to the individual's motive(s).

**Relativity: The Individual Counterpart to Dilthey's Historically Based World-View**

Dilthey freed history and the human sciences from dependence on general laws. That liberation was important because Dilthey understood that general laws did not lead to understanding, for understanding was necessarily both limited and relative. It takes place within a <u>particular</u> world-view and is only made possible by the categories of understanding. Weber subscribed to Dilthey's rejection of general laws governing human conduct, but modified Dilthey's concept of world-views to suit his own purposes. Weber turned the issue around by questioning the goal of social science inquiries to objectively validated empirical knowledge. He asked whether it was the goal of human sciences to discover objectively valid knowledge, or, reflecting a more relativistic position, was the goal to find the frameworks or categories that operate subjectively to order a given reality. For Weber, inquiry in the social sciences was not designed to find and uncover reality. On the contrary, reality does not (independently) impose itself as objectively valid:

> The *objective* validity of all empirical knowledge rests exclusively upon the ordering of the given reality according to categories which are *subjective* in a specific sense, namely, in that they present the *presuppositions* of our knowledge and are based on the presupposition of the *value* of the *truths* which empirical knowledge alone is able to give us.[191]

## *VERSTEHEN:* SOME SHORTCOMINGS

### Reflexivity and Relativity

One of *Verstehen's* shortcomings relates to the subjective meaning(s) attached to the action by the acting individual and the rather strong implication of an element of reflexivity. For example, when asked what he was doing, the woodchopper reflected (like the young mother who spanked her child) and then reconstructed an objective interpretation of his past behavior. Is the woodchopper's objectification "true," or is it an interpretation *relative* to a framework, such as the one imposed or implied by the question asked by a social scientific investigator?

Weber found it problematic that the young mother's reflection on her past behavior was never fully recaptured. It never appeared as a "simple 'photograph' nor as a "repeated experience" of what was experienced."[192] Therefore, her "recaptured" experience cannot be regarded as a literal rendering – as a raw experience or as a photograph of that experience. In her thinking and talking about the experience, which is to say, reflexively, the experience was transformed "into a categorically formed 'object.'"[193] And in this regard, it would be difficult to improve on William James observation:

> Experience merely as such doesn't come ticketed
> and labelled, we have first to discover what it is.[194]

The young mother had to (re)discover her experience through a process that served to objectify it. Significantly, the objectified experience – ascertained through reflection – acquired components that might well have been overlooked – perhaps even been unknown to her – during the experience itself. For instance, in a recent investigation into allegations about improper college football recruitment practices that included sex, alcohol, and rapes, a woman who was involved in parties and sexual activities declared she had not realized she was raped until much later, when she took a class in the sociology of sex. To access an experience of one's own that has been mediated by categories transforms it into a relative, limited, and interpretative experience, in the same way that history is mediated and transformed by those who lived and recalled it, as by historians who document it.

It appears that Weber promoted *Verstehen* – an explanatory understanding of the links between an individual's motives and her social action – at the same time that he recognized the real possibility that that "complex of subjective meaning" was all but inaccessible through reflexive thought.[195] He prepared us for a double uncertainty: an actor was not only incapable of "furnish[ing] us with the decisive information if she really honestly wished to do so," but interestingly, the opposite might often be the case![196] The young mother's recaptured experience – her narrative about that experience with its acquired components – is not to be regarded as a literal photographic rendering of that experience but rather as an already interpreted narrative.[197] Weber's position on the reflexive capture of experience is reminiscent of Freud's treatment of manifest dream images: both evoke the distinction between objects and the narratives about those objects in terms of what they signify – that is, both evoke the distinction between objects and categorically formed objects.

## Unwarranted Background Assumptions

A second shortcoming of *Verstehen* is associated with taken-for-granted assumptions in its operation. Weber's example of the woodchopper assumed that we all agree about, that is, we "know," what "woodcutting" is. In making that assumption, Weber implies that we all come from a shared experience or frame of reference. In the case of the woodchopper, "we" must include the sociological observer on the train, the man swinging the ax, me, the writer, and you, the reader. Simply naming an activity – "wood cutting" – implies a frame of reference or meaning context that necessarily precedes interpretative understanding. Seen in that light, *Verstehen* shifted the burden from what is problematic in the analysis of wood chopping, namely presumed sharedness – and its social character with respect to the individual motives of the chopper! What Garfinkel calls "the background features of everyday scenes" are sidestepped or assumed.[198] Garfinkel wrote that what Weber might have regarded as part of the stock of social knowledge, or "socially approved knowledge" is not actually transparent, and therefore should not be "taken-for granted" or merely assumed.[199]

A consideration of background assumptions raises questions about what necessarily precedes so-called simple observation. It is not possible for observers, looking out of a train window, to know what the woodchopper is doing without having prior knowledge, knowledge that they share with the woodchopper. Consequently, Weber's claim that the "direct observational understanding of the subjective meaning of a given act as such" straightforwardly leads to an understanding of chopping wood makes unwarranted assumptions about shared meanings, shared cultural backgrounds, and a common conceptual and linguistic framework.[200] Levy said that even Weber's use of the term "woodchopper," *i.e.*, merely <u>naming</u> the activity, implies "a frame of reference that necessarily precedes so-called observational understanding."[201]

**Message In a Jar: Prefigured Background Assumptions**

Even relatively simple behaviors involve myriad background assumptions, most of which are not transparent features of experience insofar as they tend to be taken-for-granted. Consider the background knowledge that is required in order for the proverbial islander successfully to retrieve and read a message in a bottle floating on the tide toward the beach. The accomplishment of those tasks requires knowledge that:

> (1) Bottles are not needlessly dangerous things, to be avoided;
> (2) bottles are not merely gifts from the gods, to be venerated;
> (3) bottles can contain things;
> (4) what is inside the bottle can be extracted by pulling the cork – and knowing how, or breaking the bottle without destroying its contents;
> (5) the retrieved "something" in the bottle is paper;
> (6) the scrawling marks on the paper might be writing, not lobster

markings;

(7) what writing is;

(8) that writing contain messages; and

(9) finally, what "messages" are.

Even if it can be assumed that the paper contains a message, unless the islander has some background knowledge of the <u>particular</u> language in which the message is written, she cannot read it! Moreover, unless she recognizes what language the scrawling stuff is written in (say, French), she will not even be able to enlist the right (French speaking) person to translate the scrawling. After all, nothing would be gained by asking a Japanese person to read French writing. This process may seem to overly complicate relatively simple actions. But all the examples discussed so far, (the messages of music and quilts, the note in the bottle), illustrate problems with assumptions in what otherwise appears to be a simple question: what is the woodchopper doing? Prefigured knowledge cannot be ignored when matters of meaning and interpretative understanding are involved.

**Scientist vs. Layman**

There is a third shortcoming to *Versthen*, one that is closely related to the problem associated with assuming a shared background knowledge. Is the scientific framework available to the social scientist in the pursuit of subjective understanding – *Verstehen* – the same as, and compatible with, that of the lay actor. To what extent do scientists and laymen bring similar or different background assumptions to bear upon their experiences? Specifically, does "woodchopping" mean the same thing for the social scientist as for the man swinging the ax? For most writers, the answer is an emphatic no. Moreover, the differences between scientific and lay background knowledge raise significant barriers to understanding. Thorsten Veblen, *e.g.,* referred to a "trained incapacity." He pointed out the human tendency to frame issues in line with one's professional training, and furthermore, the tendency for that training to <u>preclude</u> framing issues otherwise.[202] In terms of sociology, not only will sociologists most often resonate to the sociological implications of situations, but they will also tend to overlook or ignore other implications – or at least, so said Veblen.

One dramatic distinction between social scientists and lay persons recommends itself to a consideration of background knowledge: for the lay person, the world is pretty much just as it appears to be: "unquestionably plausible."[203] There are few surprises for the lay person who takes for granted that what others appear to be doing is pretty much the same as what he or she is doing.[204] In contrast, the social scientific observer deliberately <u>suspends</u> belief that things and objects are as they appear to be.[205] As a direct consequence, there are clearly irreconcilable differences between those of us who take most <u>everything</u> for granted and observers who take almost <u>nothing</u> for granted. Understandings vary widely because of the application of altogether different interpretative rules.[206] After all, the social scientist is trained to be skeptical and open-minded, or, at least neutral, toward the naive notion that things are just as they appear to be.

**Verification**

A final shortcoming directed at *Verstehen* is that it does not provide for verification. Abel suggested that *Verstehen* may serve as a source of possible hypotheses, but it is a method with no mechanism for verification, and therefore adds little to the store of social scientific knowledge.[207] Subjective understanding of the meaning of the work of the woodchopper cannot be verified. You can say that my writing this book relates to making the world safe for democracy, or bringing sociology into the 21st century, or returning it to the 19th, or making enough money to get back into the stock market. All are more or less plausible, but none is verifiable. Weber himself precluded the literal rendering or photo-graphic recapturing of the raw experience of my own writing. What remains is a narrative about, and consequent transformation of, that experience into "a cate-gorically formed 'object.'"[208]

Whatever its shortcomings, Weber's individualistic *Verstehen* played an influential role in shaping interpretative theory in sociology. Curiously enough, its popularity can be attributed more to Weber's interpreters and the fact that they rooted subjective understanding in individualistic factors, than to what he himself wrote about the method of *Verstehen* and how well or often he applied it.[209]

Because of the problems that Weber understood were implicit in depend-ence upon individual accounts, he directed sociological inquiry not toward the study of individuals, *per se*, but toward individuals *qua* social <u>types</u> and <u>typical</u> behavior.

Weber's training, interests, and intellectual preoccupations led him, as was noted above, to studies of large-scale macro sociological topics, such as the links between Protestantism and capitalism; an analysis of the influence of the process of rationalization on the music of Western culture; analyses of forms of authority, the determinants of social class, and the characteristics of bureaucracy. None of his large scale social, economic, political, or religious analyses easily accommo-dated Weber's formal definition of sociology as interpretative understanding.

There have been attempts to address *Verstehen's* shortcomings by grounding it in Husserl's phenomenology instead of in Dilthey's relativism. Most successful among these attempts is Schutz's reconstruction of interpretative soci-ology.

## Chapter Four

## HUSSERL'S INTENTIONAL THEORY

INTRODUCTION

Several changes in interpretative theory were set in motion by Schutz's modifications of Husserl's phenomenology. Most notable were Schutz's treatments of intentionality, typifications, and intersubjectivity. To the extent they were successful, these changes freed interpretative theory in sociology from its dependence on individualistic and subjective explanations, initiated by Weber's development of *Verstehen*. But Schutz's contributions to interpretative theory rested on firm philosophical grounds – and on the shoulders of earlier thinkers. Not all of (nor even a representative portion of) Husserl's contribution to phenomenology and intentionality can be covered here. I will instead review only that part of Husserl's phenomenology that most directly influenced Schutz's repair of *Verstehen* and his contributions to interpretative thinking and phenomenological sociology. Consequently, much of the following material centers on *Cartesian Meditations* (1973), in which Husserl examined issues relevant to sociological interpretation, namely *intersubjectivity*, shared meanings, and standpoints.

Readers are reminded that phenomenology poses formidable intellectual challenges. [210] Neither phenomenology nor Schutz's phenomenological sociology has much to do with the study or the description of <u>objects</u> and their properties. Phenomenology does not examine countable objects, such as mountains, trees, rocks, suicide rates, Democrats, or Republicans. Instead, it attempts to untangle the complexities of how we experience those objects, *i.e.*, their "appearances" and what they mean. Consequently, not only is Husserl's technical terminology difficult,[211] but phenomenology's subject matter is said to be off-putting and, even though rewarding, counter-intuitive, warranting, as Scanlon wrote, a "zig zag approach."[212]

Husserl's phenomenology was directed toward describing *the appearing of things*, not toward descriptions or accounts of the things themselves. This distinction is summarized in an often-used phrase that focuses attention not on the object itself – the "appearing thing" – but on what it *presents to consciousness*. The meaning of Husserl's distinction between the "appearing thing" and the "appearing of the thing," and its significance for an objective theory of interpretation, occupy this chapter. The distinction is also useful in later chapters where the writings of Durkheim and Simmel are revisited.

CONSCIOUSNESS AND INTENTIONALITY

When Schutz repaired Weber's individualistic *Verstehen,* he did not rely on Dilthey's relative approach to history and the social sciences. Instead, he founded an alternative approach to interpretative sociology based on Husserl's phenomenology, at the center of which is the concept of intentionality.[213] Phenomenological intentionality is different from the psychological notion of intention, the legal concept of criminal intent, and the suggestion of individual purposeful behavior. It *exclusively* refers to a property of consciousness, or to the conscious relationship we have with objects.[214]

References to personal consciousness often employ the stream metaphor. Husserl characterized consciousness as a "flux of experience" or a "Heraclitean" flux,[215] a continuous stream, or a "Multiform and changeable multiplicity of manners of appearing."[216] Heraclitus, the Greek philosopher for whom the fundamental fact in nature was constant change, invoked the image of a river into which, he said, you cannot step twice.[217] From out of that flux, consciousness is "conscious *of* such and such"," *i.e., of* something that it is not.[218] That "something," whatever its "rightful actuality-status," is an intentional object *qua* intentional.[219] So that when one listens to a melody, views a house or regards another in interaction, or even fantasizes about a windmill, or dreams about UFO's, there corresponds to each of these mental facts – acts – an intentionality (a *noema*)[220] that is experienced.[221]

Individual "acts" of attention are accompanied by meaning endowments that constitute intentionalities. An intended "house" is not merely a "house," it is a house endowed with meaning, or signification. The house presents to consciousness "my" house, or "your" house, a "beautiful" or "ugly" house, or a house designed by the architect F. L. Wright. A "melody" is not simply a melody. It is a "pretty" melody, or "Chopin" melody, the latest popular tune, the "Star Spangled Banner," or an "easy" or "difficult" melody to sing. Each object exists, Husserl asserted, only as an object of "actual and possible consciousness."[222] The meanings or significations endowing melodies so that they are experienced as "pretty" or "memorable," houses as "mine" or "your," *etc.*, are encumbrances traceable to culture and its many and varied components. These components include science and everyday (or "vulgar") life that, most notably, contain prefigured meanings, predispositions, biases, preconceptions and a variety of unexamined "claims." Encumbrances are rarely transparent, in the sense of being recognized as such, in the moment. Said differently, the mode of appearance[223] of a house (but not the house) – instead what it signifies – is simply and unquestionably taken for granted by the experiencing subject.

> Daily practical living is naive. It is immersion in the already given world, whether it be experiencing, or thinking, or valuing, or acting. Meanwhile all those productive intentional functions of experiencing, because of which physical things are simply there, go on anonymously.[224]

Thus intentionalities – "somethings" of which consciousness is conscious – however often they may be popularly misconstrued, are not real world objects, *per se*, but rather *intentional* objects constituted[225] by the activities of individual mind.[226] The mode of appearance of an object is "the object as meant,"[227] from which one can draw the conclusion, as did Giddens, that "the so called "objective" has no significance except in so far as consciousness is directed upon it."[228] Consciousness is engaged in forming meaning and constituting its own intentional objects.[229] Intentionalities are thus properties of consciousness, while the object perceived is transcendental to consciousness. What this means in a practical sense, is that intentional objects are not reducible to sensations, for while sensations change, intentional objects do not.

No matter whether the correlate of the (encumbered) intentional object is founded on an environmental or social object, *e.g.,* a mountain or a person, it "[turns] out to be an unreal or ideal entity which belongs to the same sphere as meanings or significations."[230] What an intentional object signifies – that is, the manner of its encumbrance – is not a property of the object upon which it is founded. That someone's raised thumb, along a highway, signifies a request for a ride is a matter of meaning endowed or bestowed upon the thumb, or "attached" to it.[231] Physical objects, like thumbs, and social objects, are animated by meanings but do not necessarily share or contribute to any of the nuances of meanings.[232] What the object or expression presents to consciousness – its "appearance" – is, according to Husserl, a product of several syntheses.

SYNTHESES:  All of Conscious Life Is Unified Synthetically

**Meaning and Acts of Consciousness**

First, constitutive[233] intentionalities require syntheses of (1) meanings and (2) <u>acts</u> of consciousness. <u>Acts</u> of consciousness refer to remembering, turning attention to, fantasizing, expecting, contemplating, envisioning, dreaming, futurizing, *etc*. Husserl uses the example of a dice game.

> Now the same die ... can be intended in highly diverse modes of consciousness – simultaneously, or else successively in <u>separate</u> modes of consciousness – e.g., in separate perceptions, recollections, expectations, valuations, and so forth.[234]

Here are some illustrations: at the dice table, I *anticipate* the meaning of the outcome of a throw of the dice by calling for "my point." Later, *recalling* the experience, I tell my friends about the disappointing "craps," or, I *invent* an entire evening of alternative outcomes. That night, I *dream* about making eight "points" in row and "breaking" the bank. Mental acts – the intentional objects of acts of consciousness – and the objects upon which they are founded warrant separate attention. The former are a "real part of consciousness," the latter are not.[235] For instance, the dice are transcendent to consciousness, while "craps" – that is, the meaning or significance of the outcome – is immanent. In Husserl's view, objects exist for the experiencing subject "only as objects of actual and possible consciousness."[236] Thus to regard intentional objects as anything other than facts of synthetic structures misses the point and impedes their descriptions *qua constitutive* intentionalities. Said differently, phenomenological descriptions do not emphasize the *appearing* object. They emphasize the appearing of the die, and not the die itself, which exists, Husserl argued, only in perception.[237]

> I, the transcendental phenomenologist, have objects (singly or in universal complexes) as a theme for my universal description: solely as the intentional correlates of modes of consciousness of them.[238]

When the experiencing subject *thinks, dreams,* or *fantasizes* about something, that something presents an intentional object to consciousness, *i.e*, an object with meanings attached to it. The meanings or significations that endow intentional objects possess two notable properties: value and/or usefulness. As a result, intentionalities tend to be experienced in terms of their value or usefulness. And even though it seems obvious, in the example of the dice table, "making a point" is valuable and useful, and to "crap" out, is not.

> Therefore this world is not there for me as a mere world of facts and affairs, but, with the same immediacy, as a world of values, or goods, a practical world. Without further effort on my part I find the things before me furnished not only the qualities that befit their positive nature, but with value –characters such as beautiful or ugly, agreeable or disagreeable, pleasant or unpleasant, and so forth.[239]

**Meaning and Unification**

Husserl's second synthesis combines the "unifying" property of consciousness and meaning. Unification addresses the issue of successive acts of perception – glimpses of someone's face, rolling dice, *etc.* – that present the experiencing subject with continuously changing aspects of that face or those dice. This flow of sensory evidence raises the question of just what constitutes presumptions of identity from evidence of the senses?[240] How do I know (and based on what evidence) that I am seeing the same thing – the same person's face or the same die – from different perspectives, when each glimpse has been obtained from a different angle or perspective, in what Husserl termed a multiplicity of manners of appearing?[241] Why do I not presume that I'm seeing several different things from similar perspectives? Unification refers to how each intentionality presents not a continuous stream of impressions, but <u>one</u> and the <u>same</u> thing:

> For example, if I take the perceiving of this die as the theme for my description, I see in pure reflection that 'this' die is given continuously as an objective unity in a multiform and changeable multiplicity of manners of appearing, which belong determinately to it. These, in their temporal flow, are not an incoherent sequence of subjective processes. Rather they flow away in the unity of a syntheses, such that in them 'one and the same' is intended as appearing.[242]

Showing itself in a "multiplicity" of perceptions, a die is always shifting because of changing visual perspectives: rolling over, changing light, or the blinking of an eye. In its temporal flow, however, it is not an incoherent sequence of subjective processes, but as Husserl insisted, it flows into "the unity of a syntheses, so that in them 'one and the same' is intended as appearing."[243]

> Each cogito, each conscious process, we may also say, "means" something or other and bears in itself, in this manner peculiar to the meant, its particular cogitatum. The house-perception means a house – more precisely, as this individual house – and means it in the fashion peculiar to perception; a house-memory means a house in the fashion peculiar to memory; a house-phantasy, in the fashion peculiar to phantasy.[244]

Examples of portrait painting illustrate the character of this synthesis. Conventional portraits synthesize into a unity hours and days of an artist's continuous varied perceptions: blinks of the eye, ever changing light and shadows, changes in the model's mood and pose, *etc*. This unity is represented by the finished image -- a single face or figure. While on most canvases, the model appears unified, as a synthetic composite,[245] several Picasso portraits depart from conventional syntheses of meaning and unification. They depict, instead, a "multiplicity of manners of appearing." In "Women with Pigeons" (1930) and "Marie-Therese with a Garland" (1937), the artist painted a single <u>profile</u> of his subject showing <u>two</u> eyes; in "Woman at the Mirror" (1932) the subject's full face and profile are juxtaposed; and there are two examples – "The Coiffure" (1954) and "Reclining Nude with a Bird" (1968) that show (with the help of creative twists of the subjects' torsos) in a single glance, the subjects' breasts, their profiles and their buttocks. In these portraits, Picasso painted not a representation of "appearing" objects (models), but the manner of their "appearances" to the experiencing subject (Picasso, himself), as an amalgamation of many blinks of the eye, many appearances, perceptions, views and recollections, over many formal sittings.

**Meaning More**

Consciousness engages in an even more subtle and intriguing undertaking: it "*intends* beyond itself."[246] Each *cogito*, each glimpse of a perceived object in one of its multiform manners of appearing, is <u>not</u> accompanied by its own particular meaning. It is, instead, accompanied by a uniform meaning of its *meant*. <u>Always</u> something <u>more</u> <u>than</u> what is meant in the moment, it "is, and must be, a 'meaning more.'"[247] Each glimpse of the dice, or of another's gesture, is endowed with the meaning of its (the intentional object's) meant: the fall of the dice <u>means</u> "craps," "boxcars," or "I win." The house is <u>my</u> house or yours. Every glimpse of another's gestures signifying "joy" or "anger" bears in itself "significance," and does so, as Husserl insisted, "in its own fashion."[248]

> And, the same considerations apply of course just as well to the man and beast in my surroundings as to "mere things." They are my "friends" or "foes," my "servants," or "superiors," "strangers" or "relatives," and so forth.[249]

For sociologists, the implications of "meaning more" in terms of interpretative understanding of social interaction are far-reaching. Social typing, stereotyping and profiling – associated with race, sex, ethnicity, occupation, age, *etc.* – all illustrate how intentionalities influence interactions, either positively or negatively, by endowing the talk and actions of others with meaning ("more") or significance. Just as houses are intended as "my" house, or a "beautiful house," the talk and actions of "friends" are received easily as friendly actions, whereas similar actions by "foes" are experienced as threatening. A discussion of the sociological implications of "meaning more" is reserved for later chapters.

**APPRESENTATIONS: Constituting  Intentional Objects Reflects Their Use and Value**

The manner of apprehension of an experienced object, its "appresentation," refers directly to what it signifies (stands for), and the usefulness and/or value it embodies. The 2000 US presidential election provides a good example: disputed ballots – "hanging" or "pregnant" chads – meant different things – and were therefore more or less useful and valuable – to Republicans and Democrats. In turn, Republicans and Democrats can be considered members of "subuniverses of meaning." Each subuniverse is carried by a "particular collectivity," the group that "ongoingly produces the meanings in question and within which these meanings have objective reality."[250]

As correlates of constitutive activities, intentional objects are experienced *qua* appresentations – *i.e.*, they are represented by what they stand for or signify: mountains that enter someone's perceptual sphere are valuable or useful objects for climbing, worshipping, skiing, or as places in which to find refuge. They are not, however, "representational" in the same sense as images of that object! Objects are not constitutive parts of consciousness; the die, the mountain, the professor, the Democrat, *etc.*, are perceived, but are transcendent. So that while the intentional object "*is* the transcendental, external object,"[251] my experience of it -- its appearance to me – is an immanent content of my consciousness.[252] We do not perceive the "appearance" of the thing – the "myness" of my house or the meaning of "craps" in the fall of the dice – but rather the thing itself. The "appearance" of a thing is lived experience, the awareness of which is consciousness. This distinction calls attention to conceptual differences between realms of experience and what gets properly classified within them. Mountains, dice, objects, therefore, *remain* outside my consciousness of them, but their appresentations, the manner and meaning of my experience of them, are properties of consciousness.

More generally, appresentation, as Levy wrote, means something is "taken to stand for something else, *i.e.*, Robinson Crusoe's experience of a footprint on the island stood for another human being."[253] Note that Crusoe did not regard "the footprint" as merely a scuff or hole in the sand. Curiously enough, although constituted in mental processes, what the holes in the sand signify "are not at all to be found in them."[254] That is, the experience of "friendliness" of a gesture of a "friend" is not to be found in the gesture itself!

Appresentations are unified as valuable or/and useful composites. They serve to underscore the experiencing subject's awareness of them, as opposed to something else. An example, perhaps apocryphal, from the career of the great Negro League pitcher Satchel Paige: even though Paige admitted he never remembered the names of opposing teams' hitters, he did know the hitting tendencies of each and every one of them. Players' names, perhaps useful and valuable for sports writers, were clearly not useful for him, at least from the baseball standpoint, in the context of his extraordinary pitching performances.

> Things in their immediacy stand there as objects to be used, the "table" with its "books," the "glass to drink from," the "vase," the "piano," and so forth.[255]

The properties of usefulness and/or value aid the in the constitutive work undertaken by individual mind and therefore guide constitutive activities. Objects are appresented to the individual as useful and/or valuable because of social context. The meanings relied upon by the perceiver reside in particular standpoints. When a hitter on the opposing team entered Paige's perceptual sphere, that hitter stood for not merely a cluster of (relatively useless) personal attributes, but useful and valuable knowledge about hitting tendencies: low ball hitter, sucker for a high ball, *etc.*

Every conscious process is "consciousness of this objective such-and-such," not so far as the objective such and such appears, but in its appearance to the experiencing subject.[256] Appresentations, however, are not abstractions, so that one does not ordinarily experience love or fear in the abstract,[257] but, necessarily, love of someone, or fear of something: heights, or failure, persons or situations, *etc.* Even as President Roosevelt's famous World War II speech indicated, when there was nothing to fear but fear itself, there was still something to fear.

One writer's recollection illustrates how the mind always wanders in search of "something."

> When awake, you try to remember your mother, as you do now, and you remember nothing, and since no mind can picture nothing, you remember Mr. Allan and the tobacco warehouses, the canal alongside the James River, your cousin Virginia and her mother. . .[258]

When we think, dream, remember, contemplate, fantasize about others, as constitutive intentionalities the subjects are others who are "strangers," "relatives," "friends," "sex objects," or "foes." Their gestures, talk, and actions (also constitutive intentionalities) are also appresented, signifying different things or "meanings meant:" the appresented "friend's" raised hand is intended as "friendly," just as the "foe's" is interpreted as "aggressive" or threatening. Said differently and perhaps counter-intuitively, first, "friends" are constituted – *i.e.,* others are interpreted as "friends" – and then their talk and actions are typically experienced as interpreted as friendly.[259]

What makes this view of talk and actions counter-intuitive is that we, as experiencing subjects, frequently – naively and readily – take for granted that intentional objects are the same as the objects upon which they are founded. Or, as Giddens observed, "what other people appear to do, and who they appear to be, is usually accepted as the same as what they are actually doing and who they actually are."[260] In so doing, experiencing subjects overlook both their own constitutive activities and the aid afforded them by communities of meanings on which they depend. Intentional objects are not necessarily any more identical to the objects upon which they are founded than maps are to the territories they represent. An intended "friend," for instance, has no ontological status as "friend" just as an intended "stranger" in one context may well be an intended "intimate" in another, that is, for someone else. It is often overlooked that "strangers" have no set of common personal attributes but rather, as Simmel reminded us, represent a "specific form of interaction."[261]

## Phenomenological Reductions:  The Disinterested Observer

After describing constitutive intentionalities and their encumbrances, Husserl raised the question of how it would be possible to cast off – or set aside – preconceptions, conventions, and prefigured meanings. His answer was that phenomenological reduction(s) served "to lead us back from cultural world of science to primordial world of life."[262] Through reductions, one discovers the Transcendental Ego that, when freed from bias and prejudice, is sufficiently disinterested to grasp something in terms of what "it refers to beyond itself."[263]

Husserl described several reductions that led to transcendental subjectivity, including eidetic reductions – from the realm of facts to general essences – for which he claimed a validity simultaneously independent of experience and beyond experience. Eidetic reductions begin with a sample of this or that. Then the sample is changed as much as possible without making it cease to be what it is. The invariant appears and must be intuitively seized. Bearing some similarity to Weber's "Ideal Types," eidetic reductions resonate for sociologists who, by following similar procedures, search and uncover the invariant in ideal typical "bureaucrats" – drawn from a variety of activities and organizational settings – or the ideal typical "professor" – drawn from a variety of capacities in large and small educational settings.

Husserl referred to the disconnection or bracketing of [being] with another reduction, termed phenomenological *epoche*, or "bracketing."[264] "Bracketing" is characterized by abstention from preconceptions, and represents not so much a

82

denial as a *suspension* of judgment about the validity of experience and explanations of that experience. Bracketing, *i.e.,* inhibits the acceptance of "objectively apperceived facts."[265] Consequently, the resulting world and the objects associated with it then exist <u>for</u> me, and derive their "whole sense" <u>from</u> me as Transcendental Ego, having come "to the fore" because of phenomenological epoche.[266] Through <u>epoche</u>, by "bracketing" all empirical particulars, "it seems as if we are able to penetrate to the essence of consciousness."[267] Among so-called empirical particulars, Husserl included abstention from judgments about causation, space and time. These abstentions are not to be denied, but simply disconnected without any use made of their standards.

> But I use the "phenomenological" [epoche] which
> *completely bars me from using any judgment that*
> *concerns spatio-temporal existence.* [268]

Husserl's phenomenology aimed to describe experiences of phenomena unencumbered with cultural, everyday, or scientific meanings. Phenomena would then derive their whole sense from the experiencing subject *qua* Transcendental Ego. Without the advantages of reduction, however, experiencing subjects, considered observers, must be seen as <u>interested</u> or <u>biased,</u> and are therefore much more interesting to sociologists than to philosophers. Interpretative theory in sociology benefits in two ways from a consideration of the biases uncovered by phenomenological intentionality. The first emphasizes the manner in which human beings experience their world, not so much as a world of objects, but as a world of <u>meanings</u>. The second suggests the possibility of tracing these meanings to their social origins through an examination of three issues: (1) the implications of phenomenological reductions for an understanding and description of standpoints; (2) significations and meanings contained in standpoints; and (3) the implications of phenomenological intersubjectivity, or shared meaning, for a sociological based interpretative understanding of social life.

STANDPOINTS

Whatever their claims to the contrary, members of discursive communities, *i.e.,* "systems of common or social meanings,"[269] do not experience the world as Transcendental Egos – as disinterested or objective observers. By virtue of <u>not</u> having executed *epoche* or phenomenological reduction, they occupy, albeit naively, one of a variety of available standpoints.[270] Standpoints are ubiquitous and compelling, but not transparent,[271] and, in the final analysis, are anonymous sources of bias and prejudice. Standpoints consist of meanings or significations, and find expression in personal occasions that include dreams or fantasies, or in social occasions like spelling bees, arithmetic contests, debates, scientific work, political work, *etc.* Even in everyday life, experiencing subjects have availed themselves of meanings or significations resident in a standpoint and therefore cannot lay valid claim to being unbiased "disinterested onlookers."[272] On the contrary, occupying a particular standpoint (with all of its attendant significations and meanings) implies baggage that envelopes the individual's constitutive intentionalities. Experiencing subjects encounter an already "cooked" or prefigured world of meanings, represented by "the natural standpoint" from the very start:

> Our first outlook upon life is that of natural human
> beings, imagining, judging, feeling, willing, *"from
> the natural standpoint."*[273]

In Husserl's view, the processes of abstaining from preconception, and the results of abstention, distinguish philosophy from non-philosophy, and the philosophic from the non-philosophic sciences. Non-philosophic sciences, including positive science, share a particular "naiveté" and a cluster of <u>attitudes</u> toward the world that refers to the manner in which attention is focused upon something.[274]

Preconceptions prevail not only in everyday life, but also in science and culture. Causality is one of those preconceptions. Another, found in the positive sciences, is taking the existence of objects of study for granted.[275] Yet another preconceived notion asserts that the mind can roam through the world and any of its parts "without changing the objective nature of what we consider."[276] Within that notion is the assumption that the world exists objectively – is simply out there -- and may be fully explainable and understood through the discovery of exact and objective laws.

The "natural standpoint" – with its associated attitudes and postures toward the everyday world – as well as the sciences and ideologies that flow from it, is based upon claims and assumptions that lack transparency. Assumptions about cause and effect, to take one example, bear upon scientific examinations of the world and color them accordingly, by imposing certain prejudices relative to the objectivity of experiences. Alternatively, Husserl advocated treating all cultural assumptions and the assumptions of positive science as *claims* rather than as *givens*, suggesting that "the idea of science is better treated as a claim to be uncovered and apprehended."[277] Philosophy, in order to achieve absolute presuppositionlessness, must be "free from all theory," and must, accordingly, set aside the trappings and conventions of science, or, at least, treat them as claims rather than as truths.[278]

But denying acceptance of all that the sciences give us – regarding all as inadmissible prejudice – is not enough. "Their universal basis (the natural standpoint), the experienced world, must also be deprived of it naive acceptance."[279] Ambrose Bierce defined "effect" with tongue in cheek, so as to suggest the need for an open mind in matters of claims:

> Effect, n. The second of two phenomena which always occur together in the same order. The first, called a Cause, is said to generate the other – which is no more sensible than it would be for one who has never seen a dog except in pursuit of a rabbit to declare the rabbit the cause of the dog.[280]

Scientists, feminists, Democrats, Republicans, or students, as members of discursive communities, act toward intentional objects, *i.e.,* toward appresentations. In the context of a spelling bee, one occupies the "spelling standpoint," wherein the utterance "regurgitation" signifies what is to be spelled out. It means something altogether different at the "party standpoint," where people are drinking. And yet, still something else after dinner at a greasy spoon restaurant, namely, as a response to food poisoning. Moreover, the spelling contestant acts toward the word by spelling it, an absurd action for someone at the party who acts toward the utterance by trying quickly to back away. What the utterance "regurgitation" signifies is shaped by the relevant and timely standpoint invoked by social circumstances. *"The arithmetical world,"* Husserl wrote *"is there for me only when and so long as I occupy the arithmetical standpoint."*[281]

In what might be likened to a cascade of embedded windows on a computer screen, a variety of standpoints are potentially available to experiencing subjects. A particular standpoint – and the meanings contained within – is activated by pragmatic circumstances in the "here and now,"[282] and following the computer screen analogy, it becomes the active window. The ubiquity and pervasiveness of the natural standpoint remain *"undisturbed* by the adoption of new standpoints," and the natural standpoint is there for us in the absence of more specific standpoints.[283]

Correlative objects and their appresentations are unquestionably obvious and taken for granted: for some, valuable oil lies in the ground waiting to be tapped; for others, the environment is valuable and in need of protection. Presuppositions and prefigured meanings, with which intentionalities such as "oil" or "environments" are constituted, are themselves not explicated within the boundaries of the standpoints. Rather, they are prefigured in discursive schemes. How is "value" ascertained? Are there reasonable alternatives? Meanings contained in standpoints go unrecognized as background knowledge.

INTERSUBJECTIVITY: Shared Meaning

After describing the manner by which individual mind constitutes intentional objects, with the indispensable aid of the meanings or significations residing in "standpoints," Husserl turned to the question of intersubjectivity. How do two or more individuals share meanings? How does shared usefulness and value produce harmony among individually produced intentionalities? When one person asks for the salt, *e.g*, why does another not pass the sugar; or when a driver stops on the highway in response to a hitchhiker's raised thumb, why does the hitchhiker not say, "Oh, I didn't want a ride, I just wanted to say congratulations on doing a great job driving the highway"?

Whereas the constitutive work of individual mind in the syntheses of intentionalities is elegantly described by phenomenology, Husserl's description of transcendental intersubjectivity remains more controversial.[284] His development of a model of community consciousness that paralleled individual consciousness posed many vexing problems.[285] Arguably, "the root problem" was how to describe in phenomenological terms what happens between individuals within so-called transcendental communities of transcendental "we"s.[286] In the "Fifth Meditation," Husserl shifted his attention from descriptions of individual consciousness to questions about transcendental intersubjectivity – *i.e.,* descriptions of what takes place <u>between</u> individuals. He called the phenomenon the "Community of Monads."[287]

Sociology justifiably avoids a heavy dependence on descriptions of <u>individual</u> constitutive activities, preferring, instead, to connect intersubjectivity with <u>socially</u> based, shared meanings. To found an understanding of intersubjectivity on social phenomenological principles suggests that the meanings attached by <u>individual</u> members of discursive communities are meanings that they share with other members of that community. Even though each individual is separately engaged in her own constitutive activities, she is aided in those activities by meanings resident in a community of meanings that she shares with others. In that way, intentionalities complement one another. Typically, objects, talk, and gestures mean the same thing to members of the same discursive community. When members of different discursive communities attach different meanings to objects entering their perceptual fields, the result is often less than fully harmonious interaction, as was shown in judges' disputes over the meaning of some ballots in the 2000 US presidential election.

From the sociological standpoint, intersubjectivity addresses two pertinent issues. First, it describes how individuals come to attach <u>shared</u> significations to intentional objects in the course of their <u>individual</u> constitutive activities. It accounts for how members of the same discursive community agree more often than not about the meaning of "things" – the flag, the Pledge of Allegiance, the right to life or the right to choose, the environment, SUV's, and global warming. Second, intersubjectivity illuminates the manner in which shared significations lead individuals to <u>act</u> <u>towards</u> shared appresentations so as to produce harmonious interactions with others.

Harmony manifests itself when members of discursive communities compose an internally consistent system that exhibits joint, shared meaning. If appresentations are shared, then intentional objects --mountains, ballots, talk, actions and gestures – mean the same or, at least, sufficiently similar[288] things to members of the same community. Figuratively speaking, they are on the same page: they ski the mountain, or they climb it to make sacrifices to the volcano god; on environmental issues, they exhibit concern about global warming and act accordingly. The proof of the pudding is expressed in interaction; specifically, in whether or not individuals who "cointend" act harmoniously toward their environment and one another. Just as members of the same discursive community experience and act towards a world so as to suggest some degree of "'harmony' of the monads", members of *disparate* discursive communities, not surprisingly, do not.[289] It is not unusual to find interpretative disagreements among discursive communities – based on politics, geography, sex, social class, religion, race, environmental issues, *etc.* – over the significance or meaning of SUV's, the better football team, welfare programs, affirmative action, and so forth.

Aware that his use of the phrase "harmony of monads" might suggest to some an indulgence in a metaphysic, Husserl articulated an individualized conception of intersubjectivity. He founded it "among particular constitutions in the particular monads."[290] Intersubjectivity, *i.e.,* was not superimposed upon individuals; its origin was to be found with them. Thus monadic harmony was "no more speculative, phantastic or hypothetical than the monads themselves." [291]

Husserl's writings about abnormal behaviors were also of interest to sociologists. Even though others (*qua* subjects) generally experience the world "as the same world belonging to my appearance-system," there are exceptions, abnormalities, and differences for some.[292] Abnormalities are also constitutive intentionalities, insofar as they are possible only on the basis of the constitution of prior normality -- a background, so to speak, against which deviations can be contrasted (as in the case of dualisms like "up" and "down," and "good" vs.

"evil"). Minor deviations and disagreement may result from imperfect socialization, or sub cultural differences. Excessive dissonance, however – situations where subjects constitute objects incompatibly, markedly differently, or non-harmoniously -- evidence the fact that subjects belong to different communities of meanings: for example, when Republicans understood "chads" hanging on ballots in the 2000 presidential election differently than did Democrats. Members of the different political parties "saw" the usefulness and value of "chads" – holes (or partial holes) differently, and then acted differently toward those intentional objects, by judging them as "votes" or as "mistakes," *etc.* Clearly, "if the meaning which constitutes an object is, in fact, multiple," as was certainly the case with ballots in the 2000 elections, "not only will a given entity manifest itself differently to different subjects, but it will also evoke different reactions."[293]

Introduction of "facts" is not likely to reconcile situations that are inhabited by non-harmonious intentionalities. "Facts" rarely resolve so-called frame conflicts because individuals experience them as already "cooked" and interpretatively endowed with significance and meaning, and not merely as raw "facts." It follows that members of discursive communities display a variety of reactions to the "constituted" transgressions of others, ranging from mild bemusement to incredulity to shared moral indignation to violence. This range of reaction is amply demonstrated by the "hanging chad" controversy of the 2000 US election.

Husserl's treatment of constitutive intentionality was sufficiently rich in detail to permit Schutz to lay the foundation for a sociological approach to intersubjectivity, an approach that avoided many of the pitfalls of individualized monadic communities and transcendental intersubjectivity. With the sociological implications of phenomenology and its main ideas "in hand," Schutz shaped an interpretative theory that stood in stark contrast to Weber's individualistic founded *Verstehen.*

# Chapter Five

## SCHUTZ'S REPAIR OF WEBER'S *VERSTEHENDE*

INTRODUCTION

Alfred Schutz modified Husserl's phenomenology to introduce a different interpretative refrain into social theory. Schutz directly addressed several questions raised by Weber's individualized *Verstehen*, in particular those about differences between subjective and objective meanings, between meanings and actions, and between acts and actions. Schutz's answers shifted sociological interpretation from a subjective to a more objective platform. At the same time, he clarified many of the sociological issues involved in interpretative theory that had appeared, as fragments, in earlier classical theories of Durkheim and Simmel.

We must be quite clear as to what is happening here. Schutz abandoned the subjective meaning-context as a tool of interpretation. He then replaced it with a series of highly complex and systematically interrelated objective meaning-contexts. [294]

### The Question of Motives and Subjective/Objective Meaning

Weber discussed two kinds of understanding, and termed them "direct observational" and "explanatory." In Schutz's view, Weber's single term for the latter – explanatory, that is, how an action is interpreted according to its "intended" meaning – actually included two different ideas about meaning: first, the subjective meaning for the actor; and, second, the broader framework of meaning in which a socially scientific interpreted action belongs. [295] For interpretative sociology, the main issue is not direct observation of (literal) acts, or words as brute utterances, but a consideration of those acts and words as signs, *i.e.,* what they stand for. Of central concern is what those words and acts signify or mean. "If you love me why did you . . .?" or "What is the significance of that?" or "What message does sending military tanks to the city center deliver?" or "What message is the Supreme Court sending to American universities and colleges by its decision on affirmative action?"

Schutz's point was that even though another's actions are observable, an observer cannot know what those actions mean to the actor.[296] Recalling Weber's examples of the woodchopper and the young mother: were they simply blowing off steam? Frustrated? Working? Crazy? Angry? Making a point? Schutz noted several differences between the meaning context in the mind of the observer and the subjective meaning in the mind of the producer.[297] First, for lay actors, the world is as it appears to be.[298] Schutz used the phrase "unquestionably plausible" to characterize lay actors' acceptance of knowledge of certain states of affairs as non-problematic. These actors "take for granted"[299] the meanings of things, of objects, or of events that have been shaped by their social world. The attitude of social scientific observers, however, is just the opposite. As supposedly disinterested observers of the social world, their observations necessarily involve the suspension of belief that things are as they appear.

Second, lay actors, in their biographical situations, occupy the center of their own social worlds. In contrast, for social scientific observers the situation they are observing is not the "theater" of their activities. They do not act therein.[300] Lay actors are observed by the social scientist as immersed in a meaningful biographical continuity that links their past, present and future. That continuity is different from that of observing social scientists. For them, of course, social scientific work is their theater.

Finally, lay actors respond to the pragmatic demands of a "here and now" associated with their participation in everyday social contexts – such as the spelling bee, the dentist's office, the seduction, etc. "Everyday Life," Berger and Luckman observed, "is dominated by the pragmatic motive. . ."[301] The corresponding "here and now" does not exist for the social scientist, for whom the context of meaning is "social scrutiny," rather than native interpretation of lived experience.302 The social scientist occupies a different "here and now," one related to the social scientific inquiry rather than the spelling bee.

Thus, according to Schutz, because Weber failed to deconstruct "motives," he overlooked the distinction between (1) the context of meaning which the "actor subjectively feels" is the ground of his behavior; and (2) the "context of meaning which the observer supposes is the ground of the actor's behavior."[303] These contexts "are quite incommensurable," because, "behavioral clues are mere indications," not assurances.[304] A smile might be wry, enigmatic or sardonic; it does not always indicate joy or happiness. Weber's discussion of the young mother touched on a related issue: her actions, he noted, were different from her recall, and, moreover, her recall was not a photo of the event itself. It was, instead, an invoked category within which to interpret past events. The mother's interpretative narrative about her actions is not unlike narratives about dream materials. Essentially interpretative, narratives help make sense out of both dream materials and, in the case of the young mother, her past actions toward her child.

## The Question of Meaning and Motive: Because and In Order To

Any consideration of the interpretative explanation of behavior – whether as an ideal logical experimental possibility or a hypothetical reconstruction of motivated action – must take into account the distinction Schutz drew between actions taken "in order to" and actions taken "because of." This distinction is rooted in temporal considerations, and, according to Schutz, Weber mixed them up. Events that actors propose to bring about in the future are markedly different from present behavior that is presumed to be a "result of past experiences."[305] The former pertains to a project in anticipation of "future events," while the latter contends that present behavior follows from past experiences that reflect bad companions, abuse, imperfect socialization, or poverty. The question might be asked of Weber's woodchopper: was he at "his regular job or just chopping wood for physical exercise," in order to pursue a project: building a perfect body?[306] On might say of a youthful offender, on the one hand, that he committed an offense for money – for future gain. This would be a reasonable "projection" of his action.[307] On the other hand, the offense might be interpreted as something that happened because of the offender's past experiences with bad companions or abusive parents.[308]

Schutz distinguished between "pseudo because-statements" and "genuine because-statements," using an example of Weber's.[309] Individuals at a bus stop opened their umbrellas, not because it was raining, a "pseudo" motive. According to Schutz, they opened them in order to keep from getting wet! When Willie Sutton, the bank robber, said, when asked, why do you rob banks, "because that is where the money is," he articulated a "pseudo motive." He robbed banks in order to get that money out!

> First I see that it is raining, then I remember that I
> could get wet in the rain and that that would be un-
> pleasant. I am then ready to plan any appropriate
> preventive step, whether this be running for shelter
> or spreading my umbrella. [310]

## The Question of Acts and Action

In the context of phenomenological sociology, "action" has two different meanings: action-in-progress and the completed act.[311] According to Schutz, "action" refers both to something already completed, "a finished product," and to the action as it is being constituted, "an ongoing sequence of events."[312] In English, the ambiguity associated with the passive voice underscores this distinction: "the door is closed" can be taken to mean it is in the process of being closed by someone, or, it can mean that it is not an open door, it is closed.

Schutz examined acts and action in three contexts. All three are more fully discussed below in the section on intentional theory. First, for intentional descriptions, it is the act alone that is of concern to the intentional glance.[313] Remember: action-in-progress, in the Heraclitean flow, has yet to be endowed with meaning. Only the act intended by an act of consciousness means something.

Second, *action-in-progress* and *completed action* qualify for different interpretations. Here Schutz revisited the distinction between subjective and objective meanings. The meaning of action will be primarily known by "reference to the subjective intentions of the actor." The meaning of the fulfilled and completed act, however, will be known by "reference to the public intersubjective system of meaning-patterns operative in society."[314]

Finally, Schutz divorced *acts* from *acting subjects* in noting that acts are performed anonymously. Whereas every (completed) act presupposes subject bound action and refers to subjective experiences formed in individual consciousness, the meaning of the completed act is arrived at independently.[315] As an example, when a truck of mine was rear ended, the significance of that act – not the assignment of its liability, the cost or repair, the loss of time at the repair shop, nor the now ugly rear end – was unrelated to the subjective experience of the offending driver and/or her motives or intentions. The anonymous character of completed act is also illustrated by a friend's car. It had a dent in the front fender made by a bear that had either leaned or fell on it, adding to the car's intrigue; but the dent could have been made by anyone or anything.

## The Question of Individualistic Bias

Weber's *Verstehen* made individualistic factors – not so-called "collectivist" factors – central to the sociological understanding of social behavior.[316] In so doing, he raised two questions. First, "how we identify the meaning which the act has for the individual."[317] The second, and more fundamental question is whether or not the individual ought to be the unit of sociological analysis.

> The meaningful act of the individual – the key idea of interpretive sociology – by no means defines a primitive, as he [Weber] thinks it does.[318]

Weber was wrong, Schutz argued, when he broke off his analysis of the social world with the assertion that "the meaningful act of the individual" could stand alone in a sociological interpretation of another's actions. By so doing, Schutz denied "the act of an individual" its status as a primitive, i.e., as an idea requiring no further study, no further definition.[319] Schutz, however, neither ignored individuals nor excluded them from the interpretative process. The individual remained the acting agent, as Weber insisted, the so-called "atom" of inter-pretative sociology.[320] But, importantly, due to Schutz's contribution, individuals were relieved of the responsibility of authoring the meanings of environmental and social objects. Phenomenological sociology, through constitutive intentional-ity, unburdened us of the unending task of inventing and formulating our own meanings and interpretations. No longer individualistic, as suggested by Weber, interpretations would be based on socially constructed meanings.

THE REPAIR: An Interpretative Theory Based On Phenomenological Sociology

Schutz's sociological repair of individualistic *Verstehen* clarified "Max Weber's basic concept of interpretative sociology," by shifting the philosophic foundation of sociological interpretation from Dilthey's relativism to Husserl's phenomenology.[321] Avoiding the individualistic bias[322] in *Verstehende Soziologie*, Schutz placed interpretation on a firmer sociological footing, while, at the same time, advancing principles of phenomenological sociology.[323]

Husserl's phenomenology sought descriptions of phenomena that, when unencumbered with derived meanings, could be expressed as disinterested and unbiased descriptions. Phenomenological reductions – *epoche* or [bracketing] – furthered such descriptions of originary experience, but were of less interest to sociologists than descriptions of the encumbrances themselves. Schutz's innova-tion was that he did not attempt, as Transcendental Ego, to "bracket" out derived meanings. Instead, he set an alternative course and examined the encumbrances themselves, their social origins, and their intentional implications.

Encumbrances, or meaning endowments, Husserl showed, reside in "standpoints."[324] Standpoints are associated with a cluster of postures or attitudes toward the world. When Ego occupies a "standpoint," she adopts its accompanying "attitude," and employs the meanings they contain in her individual constitutive activities. "The natural attitude," "the scientific attitude," and the "feminist attitude," all contain prefigured meanings, views of the world from a particular perspective.[325] Husserl's *epoche* underscored the importance of "standpoints" and "attitudes" in their capacity as interpretative schemes, becoming the source of materials – the encumbrances – with which individual members of discursive communities endowed objects with meanings.

> The phenomenological investigation does not have
> to do with the objects themselves but their meaning
> as constituted by the activities of the mind.[326]

Husserl's *epoche* of the "natural attitude," through [bracketing], setting aside prefigured meanings, transformed Ego from an "interested" into a "disinterested onlooker."[327] Schutz turned, instead, to descriptions of standpoints and their systems of meaning for insights into the interested (or biased) onlooker and his constitutive activities. Schutz turned the epoch about, inverting it to show that when Egos occupied "standpoints," as Democrats or Republicans, or scientists or lay actors, they did not suspend their belief and interest in material and social reality.[328] What they did suspend was "doubt that [reality] is anything other than how it appears" to them from that specific vantage point or "attitude."[329] Schutz cast a wide net, articulating the principles of a method explaining all social phenomena in relationship to the intentional meaning actors connect with their action.[330] His method to grasp meaning achieved two purposes: it facilitated an analysis of the "meaning structure of the social world," and it anchored the "methodological apparatus of interpretive sociology."[331]

**Constituting Intentionalities: The Experiential Flow**

In order "to determine the precise nature of the phenomenon of meaning" through the constituting function, Schutz adopted a conceptual platform established earlier by Brentano, James, and Husserl, among others. Accordingly, an individual's inner life, his personal consciousness, was "sensibly continuous and changing."[332] Not uncommonly, the stream/river metaphor appears in phrases like "stream of consciousness," "streams of experiences," or "a flowing continuum." In a slight variation, Einstein employed the phrase, "whirlpool of personal experience." Everyday phrases also use metaphors to capture the sense of that flow: the ecstatic moment; in the sports vernacular, to be in the "zone;" or to be caught up "in the moment." Moments are characterized by undifferentiated experiences, by experiences with blurred boundaries shading off, one into the other, or by experiences marked by the absence of self-consciousness. Examples include athletic competitions, meditation, sexual activity, fly-fishing, or rock climbing.[333] While in the "zone," experiencing subjects are unaware of conceptual thought: they neither conceptualize nor intellectualize. Conversely, conceptual thought fixes certain portions of the continuous stream, so that, out of "flowing experience," consciousness is "conscious of something." That something is an intentionality,[334] or an intentional object, or objects with-meaning-attached-to-them,[335] i.e., objects "through the activities of consciousness" that have "acquired a structure and a meaning."[336] The conception of consciousness operative here is that its very essence "is to form meaning and to constitute its own objects."[337] Simply speaking, that is what consciousness does.

**Acts of Consciousness**

Meaning, not found in the continuous stream of experience (but only outside of it), requires that experiencing subjects get out of the flow through an act of consciousness, or "a reflective act of attention."[338] There are many such acts: looking back upon, attending to, dreaming of, reflecting upon, remembering, fantasizing, fearing, or contemplating something. Only then, can one contemplate past actions, consider future projects, rehearse, or fantasize about ghosts, dragons, phantoms, or UFO's. Because a requisite of consciousness is that it is always conscious of something, thinking, fearing, fantasizing, and remembering do not occur in the abstract: "Every fear is fear of, every remembrance is remembrance of the object that is thought, feared, remembered."[339]

When Ego is no longer "in the moment," but, instead, contemplates the moment as elapsed lived-experience, discrete discontinuous images in the space-time world replace flux.[340] Then, Ego experiences objects not as continuously changing world objects,[341] but as she intends them, constituted as intentionalities, rendered as objects of inspection and interpretable as objects-with-meaning-attached to them. No longer in the moment, Ego also acquires self-consciousness: the consciousness of self, a constituted intentionality, whereby self becomes an object of inspection.[342] "The real and ideal objectifications of the world surrounding us are called 'meaningful' as soon as we focus our attention upon them" and direct our gaze at "an item of our own experience."[343]

**Out of the Flow: Intentional Objects**

Intentional objects are different from the "so-called 'real' objects of the outer world" upon which they are founded.[344] The former, as Husserl suggested, are experienced in terms of their significance, namely, what they present to consciousness.[x] Schutz argued that because meaning "can only be applied retrospectively, to elapsed acts," it can not be comprehended in the flow, but glimpsed only from outside of it. The intentional object's "appearance," is endowed with "attached" meanings: it is "good" or "bad," "right" or "wrong." The mode of appearance of an object can also be thought of as "the object as meant," so that humans and beasts are experienced in terms of what they stand for, or signify, as "friends" or "foes."[345]

Real world objects, upon which intentionalities are founded, are communicated only by signs and symbols.[346] By way of emphasis, Schutz wrote, "The symbol alone is present, whereas that which is symbolized is only appresented."[347] "Appresentation" means something is "taken to stand for something else."[348] Robinson Crusoe experienced a footprint as standing for another human being, not merely a hole in the sand. Curiously, what holes in the sand stand for "are not at all to be found in them;"[349] what they stand for is something not necessarily given "in immediacy to the experiencing subject." [350]

Context, of course, is important, so that footprints in the sand mean something different from footprints on a newly waxed floor. In a craps game, two dice that constitute "craps" are not merely two round dots, showing one dot on each die: they signify "I lose." The raised thumb presents to consciousness not a real world thumb, but, in its stead, an intentional object typically experienced by hitchhiker and driver alike in terms of its meaning: a raised thumb on the highway, a request for a "lift;" coming off an athletic field, an indication of a job well done; on the way to a difficult task, "good luck;" or in Roman gladiatorial combats, the crowd's displeasure, tantamount to a death penalty – send him to "heaven." [351]

That a thumb stands for "luck" or "death," for members of a community, is clearly not a property of thumbs, nor "thumbness." It is a property of an "attachment" to thumbs, as meaning found in a discursive community.[352] Underscoring the property of shared meanings, Schutz again questioned the role of individualistic factors. He pointed out that it was neither necessary to know who first made the sign nor the original maker's intention.

> It should be noted that in interpreting a sign it is not
> necessary to refer to the fact that someone made the
> sign or that someone used it. The interpreter need
> only 'know the meaning' of the sign.[353]

When individuals think, dream, recall, or fantasize about an object, they experience it, typically, as a world-object with-meanings-attached. The significance of intentionalities – appresentations – represents something as useful or "with value – characteristics such as beautiful or ugly, agreeable or disagreeable, pleasant or unpleasant, and so forth."[354] Because usefulness and value are attached to objects, they are properly regarded properties of attached meanings, not properties of real world objects,[355] which, Husserl argued, are experienced solely in terms of what they signify or symbolize.[356]

"Intentionalities and their significance are apprehended by an act of attention. . . to something already passed-away."[357] Arguably, the necessity of "looking back" helps clarify the often banal character of interviews with athletes after the game: what were you "thinking" or "feeling" when you scored the game winning basket, hit the game winning home run, or scored the winning goal? But, of course, they were not thinking or feeling during their immersion in "the flow of duration."[358]

> Meaning ... is not a quality inherent in certain expe-
> riences emerging within our stream of conscious-
> ness but the result of an interpretation of a past ex-
> perience looked at from the present.[359]

But it hardly makes a compelling sound byte to report athletes saying, repeatedly, "Nothing, I wasn't thinking at all, I was in a zone." Because "meaning is merely an operation of intentionality, what the goal "signified" was attached later, and, in most respects, lacks the drama and color of the actual moment in which the goal was scored.[360] Young athletes often reply to questions about what they think about in championship games by saying, "I don't think about anything, just go out there and have fun." It can be said of lovers, creative workers, and athletes in the zone, and others caught up in some moment, that while *in the flow* they necessarily act without thinking and reflecting. In a basketball game or in a bar, the time spent in contemplating whether to make a pass, to whom and how, might very well make it unnecessary.

## Metaphors and Constitutive Intentionalities

For Schutz, "attaching" meaning was metaphorical.[361] Metaphors facilitate shifts of meanings from one domain to another depending on where they have the capacity to shape experience. Time, when shaped by the "resource" metaphor,[362] is experienced, figuratively, as something that can be saved, wasted, set-aside, or spent.[363] The metaphor does not invite considerations of time literally "saved" or "wasted" (as accumulated ticks of a clock's minute hand). At stake in metaphorical utterances "is the appearance of kinship where ordinary vision does not perceive any relationship."[364] Analogous, perhaps, to how one experiences, and hopefully survives, broken hearts or promises. Thus, meanings are not literally attached to objects in the same way price tags adorn objects. Instead, the metaphor bestows on intentional objects "the accent of reality." Animated by metaphors, intentional objects remain real "after [their] own fashion," Schutz wrote, "until they clash with counter evidence."[365]

## Societal Sources of Attachment: Discursive Communities

Even though meanings are "attached" to objects by individuals in their constitutive activities, individuals do not author those meanings. Meanings and significations originate, and are replayed, in the circumstances of social life; scientists in interactions with other scientists, students in interactions with other students, corporate directors in interactions with other corporate directors, and, even, restaurant cooks in interactions with other cooks.[366] In short, significations originate and are replayed among individuals in the processes of interaction and socialization.[367] Meanings are occasioned – and then reinforced – by interactions among communities of individuals who respond to social and physical exigencies: giving directions – the meaning of north or south, in order to tell others where to find where food; or where to find water; distance, as in the meaning of yards or miles, in order to meet others at the box canyon where the buffalo herd buffalo is located; time – the meaning of hours or minutes, or numbers of sunsets necessary to coordinate arrivals at the corporate meeting at 5:30 PM, or at the box canyon to hunt buffalo; space and time, as in the meaning of the corner of Pearl and Broadway at 6:00 PM in order to meet someone for dinner. Those experiences of time, space, distance, etc., and their meanings are socially organized and come to stand for (symbolize) something that stems directly from individuals' dealings with each other, i.e., their joint behavior.

Schutz explicitly linked meanings – what objects stand for – to discourse, which he defined as "a kind of meaning-context."[368] Discursive schemes contain organized schemes of interpretation or "meaning potentials."[369] Thus conceived, organized interpretative schemes facilitate descriptions and comparisons among discursive communities, signaling differences among meanings in political party discourse, scientific discourse, feminist discourse, and in everyday discourse. Scientists, *e.g.*, use scientific discursive schemes to "attach" scientific meanings to world objects that, when thus adorned, present to consciousness constituted objects cloaked in scientific, not political or everyday meanings.

Differences and similarities among discursive schemes interest sociologists. One reason is that members of different discursive communities (scientists, feminists, Republicans) not only attach different meanings to objects, but also, typically, act differently toward them, not *qua objects*, but as they interpret them. The typical Druid, environmentalist, and lumber man experience forests and trees differently, and subsequently they act toward them differently: marrying or hugging them, protecting them, or cutting them down. Their actions, intentional theory informs us, are not directed as much towards objects, *qua objects*, as towards what those objects signify!

Not surprisingly, interpretative schemes often replace one another. A 1959 film, *Some Like It Hot*, told a relatively unsophisticated tale of two male musicians who, after witnessing a gangland killing, had to leave town. Fearing for their lives, not their identities, they dressed up as women and joined a touring "all-girl" orchestra. Adventures followed, including chase scenes and romances in the style of the fifties. Recently, an alternative interpretation, informed by political correct discourse, described the film in markedly different terms:

> When Joe tries to assert his masculinity with Sugar, Jerry insists he maintain his female identity. Aware of their dilemma, our pleasure becomes dependent of the ramifications of gender identification and sexual exposure.[370]

Many factors influence changes in interpretative landscapes, including personal influence, trauma, changing fashion, and consciousness raising experiences, to name just a few. Some music fans report lyrics of popular songs "changed" their lives, allowing them to "see" life, love, relationships, and, particularly, politics, differently. Recovery programs, Narcotic Anonymous is one example, provide alternative meaning-contexts that help addicts redefine and reinterpret what their past lived experiences "stood for." N.A.'s aim is to persuade addicts that past lived experience can "stand for" something else – can be reviewed and reinterpreted in a manner that supports recovery.[371] For decades, *Playboy* magazine enjoyed a reputation among some as the embodiment of the worst that could be said about male chauvinist attitudes. A recent research suggested an alternative interpretation. Beggan and Allison reported that *Playboy*, rather than emphasizing male dominance, had actually been introducing feminine components into masculine identity, serving as a "source for women's perspective."[372]

CHOICE AND SELECTION: Multiple Meaning-Contexts and Alternative Interpretations

When several interpretive schemes avail themselves at the same time, or from time to time, what governs choice among them? Or to use a computer analogy, when interpretative schemes are stacked like cascaded windows, what "activates" one rather than another? Many meanings are "attached" to foods and eating habits.[373] Different foods have been experienced as rewards, punishments, as forming part of rituals, as culturally prescribed or proscribed (when meat, shell fish, or pork is prohibited in the diet.) What obesity signifies has also been subject to alternative interpretations. When regarded as a sign, obesity represents, for one discursive community, a qualitative matter of nutritional concern with medical implications; for another, a quantitative matter of counting calories in/calories out; for others, it represents a cultural matter of concern involving bad diets, fast foods, and lack of exercise; and yet another, it represents what overeating means to the eater: depression, compensation, anger, attention seeking, and so forth.

William James shows that there are several, probably an infinite, numbers of orders of realities, each with its special and separate style of existence. James calls them "subuniverses," and mentions as examples the world of senses or physical things, the world of science, the world of ideal relations, the worlds of mythology and religion, the world of idols of the tribe, the various worlds of individual opinions, and the world of sheer madness and vagary. Each world whilst it is attended to is real after its own fashion; only the reality lapses with the attention.[374]

Schutz adopted a different terminology, preferring "provinces of meaning" over "worlds."[375] By stressing meanings, he underscored the view that phenomenological sociology should concern itself with the "meaning of our experiences" and not with the ontological structure of objects constituting "reality." That is, not with diet schedules, or lists of foods, the pyramid, or comparative anthropology. "Provinces of meaning," meaning-contexts, refers to meanings that reside in standpoints, whether the natural, scientific, naturalistic, arithmetic, or personalistic. To occupy a standpoint invites a biased posture or "attitude" toward the world, seeing it from an "interested" point of view. Standpoints also objectively indicate the inclination of members of discursive communities to attach particular meanings or significance to diets, persons, objects and events.

**Choice: To Choose or Not to Choose**

Every lived experience is open to numerous interpretations[376]

The question of choice among meaning-contexts does not ordinarily begin with deliberations about whether I should choose meanings resident in my political affiliation, my family, the laboratory, or my association with the Girl Scouts. One reason is that individuals, faced with the pragmatic exigencies of what Schutz termed a "here and now," find themselves in situations already prefigured. [377] Paradoxically, the first choice – whether to choose or not to choose – is bogus.

Human responses to social and environmental objects are neither automatic nor instinctive. Reactions are directed toward intentional objects. An individual constitutes intentional objects, with the indispensable aid of a symbolic order, a discursive scheme, comprised of prepredicated meanings. Actors negotiate multiple realities – as professor, friend, sibling, student, scientist, or Republican – through preconstructed meanings. They act not toward objects, *per se*, but toward intentionalities, toward what mediated objects present to consciousness: not the tree, but what the tree stands for – shade, wood for a house, or a hanging; not the mountain, but what the mountain stands for – obstacle, home of the gods, or a place to climb and ski; not persons, per se, but what they stand for – professor, mother, friend, nice, kind, helpful or unhelpful, or stockbroker.

## Interests

Given alternatives, none of which fully exhausts lived-experience, what activates one of the cascaded interpretative scheme rather than another? At the most general level, Schutz proposed interests.[378] Not interests restricted to economic interest, but interest in its relationship to intentionality. Specifically, interests refer to what Husserl's Transcendental Ego seeks to bracket out in order to become a "disinterested onlooker." Contrariwise, without benefit of *epoche*, onlookers remain "interested," occupying a standpoint by virtue of which their constitutive activities shape both what they take as their thematic problem and its solution (a choice).

## Themes, Choice, and Selection

Choice is necessitated when Ego takes up a theme,[379] so that "the focus of interest" is caught up with concern about what Schutz characterized as the next step.[380] Choice is then brought about by interruptions in the sequence of doing.

With Grandma's house taken as her theme, Little Red Riding Hood journeyed through the forest without reflection. Choices were necessary only when the wolf interrupted her "next step." Schutz further clarified "interest" by employing the distinction between "in order to" and "because" motives. A rational actor who is "interested" in a project[381] chooses, pragmatically, from among alternatives, the interpretative scheme most likely to achieve the best results. Actors choose from appropriate means, means that exist as recipes in the social stock of knowledge.[382]

Choice, different from selection, takes alternatives into account; it represents some deliberation and preference.[383] But not every human action involves considerations of alternatives. Selection neither implies an acknowledgment, nor any knowledge, of alternative schemes. It does not consider preferences, representing, instead, a singling out without comparison, as in the example of Little Red Riding Hood, walking through the forest turning left or right along the path to Grandmother's house, before her encounter with the wolf. Turning implies selection, no choice, and no preference.

> Interest is nothing else than selection, but it does not necessarily involve conscious choice between alternatives which presupposes reflection, volition, and preference.[384]

On the one hand, typically, one does not choose to choose. On the other hand, one might be asked to "see things" from a different point of view, or to approach a theme in a different way. Accepting that invitation activates a different "window," a different interpretative scheme, and alters what had previously and unselfconsciously been "seen" as unquestionably plausible. Through "consciousness raising" experiences, it is possible, with tutoring, to contemplate elapsed experience from alternative perspectives, to convert and "wear a different hat." Given interruptions in the pursuit of a project and presented with alternatives, I don't have to see the situation from a different point of view, but I might – choice and reinterpretation is then implied in the constitutive act itself.

### Other Factors in Choice: The Here and Now: Pragmatic Exigency

Choice involves another factor. Interpretive schemes "bear the mark" of particular "here and now's."[385] The active window – the dominant interpretative scheme – is the one that has been found to have "worked" or had "value" for members of a community facing typical situations. The world, after all, is not simply a matter of facts, as Husserl pointed out, but a matter of intentionalities reflecting value and usefulness.[386]

Interpretative schemes and the significations they contain are importuned by pragmatic exigencies. In the pragmatic moment – the "here and now" – of a family dinner, intentional objects include those sitting around the table, constituted by others, but not uniformly useful or valuable, as "friends," "foes," "helpers," "mothers-in-law." Also in that pragmatic moment are a variety of animals and vegetables on the table, in the kitchen, and in the news (mad cow disease), presenting to consciousness "eatables,"[387] such as animals bearing French rather than Anglo Saxon names: not pigs, but ham, not baby cows but veal, not cows but beef.

"Here and now's" are socially defined, so that they evoke, when the situation is appropriately "read," interpretative schemes associated with the "arithmetic attitude," in the pragmatic moments of an arithmetic test; the "spelling attitude" in the pragmatic moment of spelling bee, the "romantic attitude" in the "here and now" of a romantic encounter. Whatever the "attitude" summoned by the exigencies of a "here and now," the activated meaning-context assures that intentional objects, even in the case of pain, will be "experienced" from a particular interested and biased perspective.[388] Now, while it is possible for some intentionalities to transcend particular situated "here and now's," many do not. A good example of the latter is shown in the bittersweet recognition among military friends that when their tours are over, so, very likely, are their friendships. Intentional "friends," constituted useful and valuable in the "here and now" of military life are one thing, yet become another in the context of the "here and now" of a civilian life. And it is not merely a matter of geographical proximity.

To complicate matters further, "attached" meaning also has "something of the context in which it is used."[389] The meaning of an event or an encounter between two people in the middle of a novel depends upon its location in the overall narrative, just as the overall narrative is furthered by and gains meaning from that event or encounter. Reflecting the hermeneutic circle, the part informs the whole as the whole informs the part. A first time visit to a classroom, a club meeting, or the witnessing of a family squabble has the same character: the class laughs at something the professor says that does not seem funny in and of itself; and to outsiders, heated family arguments appear to be centered on rather trivial issues.

> Paradoxically it could be said that the lived experience itself decides the scheme into which it is to be ordered, and thus the problem chosen proposes its own solution.[390]

## Other Factors in Choice: Power

Discursive schemes can produce different and possibly conflicting interpretations. Activities like drilling for oil in a wildlife refuge signify different things to members of different political parties and different environmental groups who tend to "attach" to drilling different value and usefulness. "Here and now's" not only reflect pragmatic exigencies, cultural fashions, and political correctness, they also reflect power relations. The dominant meaning-context indicates how effectively a discursive community brings "differentials of power" to bear.[391] Power can be political power, media power, economic power or physical intimidation.

Members of communities learn about differential power relations, already prefigured in the stock of social knowledge, in the course of their interactions with others. On the street, one soon learns who is street wise and who is not; in academic departments, one discovers the differential significance attached to suggestions by those wielding decision making power and those made by others; in corporate board meetings, one learns when and with whom to agree and vote. Failing to acknowledge the power of some groups to activate the window and thus impose a meaning scheme entails risks. In the American Colonies, *e.g.*, the "activated window" that provided meanings for everyday life was substantially less secular than today, encouraging a view of life glimpsed in religious attitude. Dancers were insufficiently powerful to have their expressive and artistic meanings prevail over more powerful, religious based ones. Consequently, dancing was interpreted as sinful, not artistic, and dancers were punished.

**Choice and Exhaustiveness**

Expressing a counter intuitive notion, Schutz wrote that whatever particular meaning-context is chosen, it never fully exhausts any lived social experience. In other words, it is always possible for other meaning-contexts to produce alternative interpretations of the same lived-experience. As commentaries on present day TV news shows reveal, "expert" talking heads present different – possibly incompatible – interpretations of current events. In December 1997, curvy multicolored configurations appeared on glass windows of a modern office building in Clearwater, Florida. Crowds, adopting the "religious attitude" in sufficiently large numbers to disrupt traffic along a six-lane highway, U.S. 19, stopped to view images of the Virgin Mary. Others, occupying a secular attitude, interpreted the meaning of colored curved configurations not so much as inspired images, but as ordinary discoloration in glass caused by manufacturing faults, too much sun, and the overzealous watering of nearby lawns. Both in private and public life, whatever the choice from among alternative meaning contexts, the possibility remains that another, or, perhaps, many others could have been seamlessly substituted.

## Attitudes are Biased and Observers are not Disinterested

Attitudes – and the prefigured useful and value biases they contain – even though always present, are typically overlooked by experiencing subjects. Despite their protests to the contrary, members of discursive communities do not qualify as disinterested onlookers. They are interested and biased. With a community of meanings at their disposal, they wittingly or unwittingly attach taken-for-granted[392] meanings to elapsed lived experiences, limiting choice and alternative interpretations. Not surprisingly, members of the same discursive community typically experience environmental and social objects in the same way and then interact harmoniously, which is another way of saying that their actions embody shared meanings.

If phenomenological reductions enable Transcendental Ego to glimpse objects "disinterestedly," by bracketing out preconceptions, then the opposite holds for those occupying standpoints. Even everyday life involves a biased state of affairs.[393] Sports fans, as Red Barber the sports announcer observed, saw events on the ball field emotionally, not physically. Said differently, they viewed unfolding events not objectively, but as events with significance from a fan's viewpoint. In the case of soccer riots, emotions attached by fans in constitutive activities producing "foes" overflow the field of play onto the opposing team's supporters.

THE NATURAL ATTITUDE

Because of their place in individual constitutive activities, standpoints – and the attitudinal schemes of interpretation they contain – represent unavoidable components of consciousness and individual constitutive activities. Among myriad attitudes, one warrants special attention. Husserl and Schutz termed it "the natural attitude."[394] A similar idea, according to James, occupies us as the paramount reality, as the "subuniverse of the senses."

The natural standpoint (by whatever name it is known), as a fundamental structure of social life, contextualizes meanings in the production of dependable narratives in everyday life. It contains its own attitudes and postures toward the world, and consists of meanings that reflect both interests and biases. The natural attitude not only dominates the social landscape of everyday life, it also spills over to influence other attitudes; science is one example. Walsh asserted that "the glosses of positivistic sociology are actually commonsense glosses," both sets of which take the objective character of the social world for granted.[395] It is easy to recognize how, under dramatic circumstances, onlookers find themselves in an interested or biased attitude. Students spell words in dramatic "here and now" moments of spelling contests, or solve arithmetic problems at the blackboard; religious persons contemplate spiritual matters; and officers of the law write speeding tickets. More difficult to grasp is how biased "attitudes" present themselves in the absence of dramatic circumstances, in the unfolding of everyday, prosaic, mundane circumstances that characterize so-called routines of everyday life.[396]

But even in everyday life, objects and the acts, talk, and gestures of others embody meanings resident in a standpoint, the natural standpoint. These meanings assure lived experience will be glimpsed from within the natural attitude and that it will be interpretatively familiar. Constitutive intentionalities are largely taken for granted and experienced as "unquestionably plausible."[397] Doubt about the reality of the world is suspended because much of that everyday life is organized so as to "allow us to be unreflective." [398] The natural attitude, the residual meaning-context, does not have to be recognized as such to maintain itself as the active window in the mundane circumstances of everyday life. Schutz noted four factors, usually unnoticed, that sustain meanings in everyday life.[399] First, "The outer world of everyday life is a paramount reality," since we are always participating in it – and by "always" Schutz included dream work. Second, objects in the everyday life world offer resistance that establishes boundaries to our free action, as when the auto strikes the telephone pole. Third, it is a realm in which "we can gear our bodily activity." And, finally, it is the only realm within which "we can communicate with our fellow-men."[400]

The natural attitude shapes the meanings, and consequently, interpretations of intentionally inspired transactions among contemporaries. One need only to think here of the different meanings attached to objects – and proposed actions toward them – by members of different discursive communities: Are ancient forest owls more valuable than the forest to be cut for new homes? Is netting tuna fish more useful than what is required to protect dolphins? Is the environment threatened by human activity or simply a reflection of natural changes? Is the scientific evidence brought to bear on the issue compelling? Sufficiently compelling? Will the environment surrounding oil exploration and drilling sites be damaged or protected? What to do about the homeless? Or welfare programs? Or snowmobiles in the National Parks? One issue addressed by phenomenological sociology is that despite a failure to regard ourselves in a biased attitude toward world objects when occupying the natural standpoint, or any standpoint, we take sides on these issues. And we do not do so as "disinterested onlookers." Elapsed lived experience is not "objective," Schutz observed, in accordance with "scientific rules of procedure or scholarly canons of objectivity."[401] Constituted intentionalities, endowed, encumbered, and embellished with meaning(s), will oftentimes represent conflicting values and usefulness.

Unquestioned and unnoticed, "attitudes" change and shift, sometimes rapidly. As I sit and write this, I hold less than practical meanings in the "sociological attitude." They combine with pragmatic exigencies associated with my constitution of the very practical demands of the word processor – why did the screen freeze up? – only to be repeatedly interrupted by the telephone company installer asking different "here and now" questions: Where's the ladder? Where do the telephone jacks go? And then, what for lunch? Fortunately, typically, I do not invent the meanings of such practical (or esoteric) questions, nor their answers, nor struggle to make my replies to the installer's questions understandable.

TYPIFICATIONS AND INTERSUBJECTIVITY: Shared Meanings

> Only a very small part of my knowledge of the world originates within my personal experience.[402]

Intersubjectivity addresses related, but somewhat different, questions from those discussed thus far. Why do the driver and hitchhiker apparently agree on the significance of the hitchhiker's thumb and, then, act harmoniously toward their shared interpretation? The car stops and the hitchhiker gets in.[403] Whereas stand up comics deliberately switch, or breach, taken-for-granted meanings for punch lines, most of us, in the conduct of everyday activities, do not. Not wanting to disrupt interactions with others, we typically act in a manner that embodies shared meanings. One comic, Steven Wright, provides a good example of a comic switch, a turnabout or breach in common understanding. Stopped by a policeman who asked "Didn't you know the speed limit was 45 mph?" Wright replied, "But I didn't have that much time." Imagine a hitchhiker saying to the driver who stops for him, "Congratulations on doing a great job driving down the highway," and then walking away. Comic license is worth paying attention to because it highlights what is typically involved in the production of harmonious social relationships with others, namely shared understandings. Breaches, funny on stage, are often troublesome and disruptive in everyday life, as Garfinkel explored in his examination of the "routine grounds of everyday activities."[404]

Schutz's developed a sociological approach to intersubjectivity, shared meaning, in response to Husserl's effort to place it in transcendental subjectivism. His reasoning was that whereas phenomenology elegantly described the constitutive activities of each individual, transcendental intersubjectivity only inadequately described what obtained among individuals. Schutz asked how Transcendental Egos, having executed *epoche*, satisfied the conditions for a transcendental "We." Furthermore, were it even "conceivable to speak of a plurality of transcendental egos," when that plurality required monads to perform individual transcendental acts with Others?[405] That notion suggests the oxymoronic situation of being alone, together. Finally Schutz, harkening back to a concern of Weber's, asked whether the properties of individuals can be said to be encountered in higher level abstractions, that is, among so-called "personalities of a higher order."[406]

His answer to these questions was "no." As a property of originary experience, "no transcendental community, no Transcendental We, is ever established." In Schutz's view, Husserl failed to account for the establishment of a community "in terms of operations of the consciousness of the transcendental."[407] As Schutz saw it, if you and I each (and apart) constitute for ourselves a world and our own sense of it (transcendental subjectivity), then, intentionality, "constituted as it is within the unique stream of consciousness of each individual, is essentially inaccessible to every other individual."408 Inaccessibility is incompatible with the idea of shared meaning and shared experience, without which, of course, there is no intersubjectivity. Therefore, in order to reflect phenomenological and sociological principles, intersubjectivity had to be founded in something other than Husserl's monadic communities composed of Transcendental Egos.

As a foundation for interpretative understanding, "intersubjectivity" required some analytical distance from both the individualistic bias built into Weber's *Verstehen* and Husserl's transcendental communities of monads.[409] Sociology was justifiably loath to depend either on the vagaries of what one individual may or may not do, or on concepts that arbitrarily organize individual transcendental subjectivities into such communities as Husserl's "community of monads."410 With those broad guidelines in mind, Schutz founded intersubjectivity in a community of an altogether different kind: not one composed of objects – individuals – but one composed of socially based meanings. Schutz's solution shifted the problem of intersubjectivity from philosophy to sociology.

> It is to be surmised that intersubjectivity is not a problem of constitution which can be solved within the transcendental sphere, but is a rather a datum (Gegebenheit) of the life-world.[411]

Because of that shift, individuals members of discursive communities were no longer isolated in Husserl's stream of world appearances, only to find themselves continuously challenged by the necessity of inventing their own meanings, or their own interpretations.[412] Intersubjectivity had become a datum of the life-world. And because little of an individual's knowledge originates within his own personal experience, "the greater part is socially derived,"consisting, he wrote:

> . . . of a set of systems of relevant typifications, of typical solutions for typical practical and theoretical problems, of typical precepts for typical behavior, including the pertinent system of appresentational references.[413]

Intersubjectivity, constituted in typicalities, also preserved for individuals both a sense of belonging and a sense of distinctiveness. Shared understanding was not tantamount to total self-abandonment. "In the intersubjective experience of 'we-ness,'" Lengermann wrote, each individual employs the shared understandings linking her with Others, and, at the same time, is aware of the Other as "an independent subjectivity." [414]

## Typifications or Social Recipes

The concept of typifications rescued intersubjectivity from where Husserl had left it languishing in a "Community of Monads," allowing Schutz to examine the shared interpretative schemes with which individuals defined everyday life. Phenomenological descriptions show that the world is not experienced as discrete bits of information, as separate powdered chalk marks on a board, separate dots of paint on a pointillist painting, or a flag as a mere aggregate of different colored stripes and stars isolated in a dark background on textured cloth. They are not experienced as "a sum of sense data, nor as an aggregate of individual things isolated from and standing in no relations to one another."[415] Instead, these objects present to consciousness synthesized types of intentional composites that, Schutz maintained, were "experienced from the outset in terms of types."[416]

> There are mountains, trees, birds, fishes, dogs, and
> among them Irish setters; there are cultural objects,
> such as houses, tables, chair, books, tools, and
> among them hammers; and there are typical social
> roles and relationships, such as parents, siblings,
> kinsmen, strangers, soldiers, hunters, priests, etc.[417]

The intersubjective world, the "typified world," is a "shared world of sig-nifications."[418] Prefigured or prepredicated recipe-like typifications comprise so-cially approved knowledge, "helping each member of the group to define his situation in the reality of everyday life in a typical way."[419] Awareness of typifi-cations is handed down to the child by his parents and teachers, and "the parents of his parents and the teachers of his teachers."[420] It is with the indispensable aid of typifications that individuals negotiate their "taken-for-granted" social worlds.

One thing to note about typifications is that Schutz represented them as recipes, not as rules, specifically, as "cook-book knowledge."[421] Not following a recipe exactly might produce a spoiled dish, or a bad chocolate cake – to dry or too hard – but a chocolate cake nonetheless. Failing to follow rules, however, has somewhat different consequences: "If you follow rules other than those of chess you are playing another game."[422] For social life the distinction between altering a recipe and not "playing another game" is crucial. Minor verbal and behavioral variations in typically formulated social recipes do not transform an interaction from a street handout to a stock exchange transaction. When dancing, conversing, making love, hitchhiking, chopping wood, or teaching, one can follow the recipe faithfully or not, and still be said to be do those things, albeit well or badly. To fail to follow the rules of dance, conversation, lovemaking, or teaching means a different (social) "game" is being played. And those departures from rules of the games, and what they signify, have their own names: assaults, rapes, abuse, de-bates, insults, or proselytizing.

What this means, practically speaking, is that the significance of Others' talk and actions is experienced in the context of socially based typical relationships, such as "appresented" parents, siblings, kinsmen, students, patients, strangers, soldiers, hunters, priests, etc. These typifications belong to prepredictative thinking, whereby agreement on "the 'meaning' of experiences" is achieved because members of discursive communities employ the same "frame of interpretation which sees them as behavior."[423] Harmonious interactions follow on the heels of shared understandings and interpretations of the meaning(s) embodied in typical talk and actions of typical Others.

## Constitutive Typicality: Horizons

In the natural attitude, objects are not merely experienced as types of trees, animals, friends or foes. Typifications also contain a "horizon" of possible further experiences. If an encounter with a typical bureaucrat is taken as the main theme, one anticipates (rightly or wrongly) the meaning of what she says and does, and the meaning of her response to this or that administrative or budgetary request. The apperception of the bureaucrat-objectivity in *her* horizon evokes in us recollections of similar bureaucrats, and, of course, what they typically said and did. This is the inner horizon.

> Moreover, what is typically apperceived carries along a horizon of possible further experiences in the form of a pre delineation of a typicality of still unexperienced but expected characteristics of the object. If we see a dog we anticipate immediate his future behavior, his typical way of eating, playing, running, jumping, etc.[424]

Different from inner horizons, outer horizons refer to how constituted typicalities contrast with what they are not, *i.e.*, how they are different from the background against which they contrast. The meaning of a university bureaucrat's typical responses to situations and requests contrasts to responses of intimates, friends, students, staff, faculty, maintenance personnel, campus police, etc. The outer horizon of a particular typicality points to differences from other typicalities, not unlike how the meaning of "up" makes sense when contrasted to its outer horizon, what it is not – "down," or how the meaning of "evil" emerges against the background of "good."

Schutz observed that, from the very outset, humans find themselves in already "mapped" out surroundings that are "'premarked,' 'preindicated,' 'presignified,' and even 'presymbolized.' We thus anticipate the typical dog will go about typically "eating, playing, running, jumping, etc."[425] And then, even as far as our own dog is concerned, it will get sick and tremble in its typical fashion. We anticipate how typical students will employ typical excuses as they provide accounts of how and why they missed the midterm exam with the typical grandmother ploy!

## Typifications and Intersubjectivity

Typifications, and their inner and outer horizons, make five contributions to an understanding of a socially based intersubjectivity: they aid the interpretative understanding of others; they are both classificatory and constitutive; they serve to guide one's own behavior; they help create the illusion that social life is simpler than it is; and they aid in understanding the whistle-blower and the team.

First, typifications advance interpretative understanding of Others' conduct by shedding a different light upon the "subjective grounds of actions." Typifications succeed in transforming "unique individual actions of unique human beings into typical functions of typical social roles, originating in typical motives aimed at bringing about typical ends."[426]

By avoiding many of the problems raised by an individualistic and sub-jectively based *Verstehen*, typifications changed the character of sociological in-terpretations. Every social type "is plainly a group product and group prop-erty."[427] Bypassing subjective barriers that serve to conceal an individual's sub-jective meanings and motives, typifications emphasize instead shared intersubjec-tive systems of meaning, recipes, and social types. What Others do and say are interpretable as typical functional activities associated with typical roles directed to typical aims and goals. Objective meaning-contexts, according to Schutz, can be examined phenomenologically as a process of typification, whereby actors ap-ply learned interpretative schemes to shape their glimpses of others and to grasp the meanings of what they do. Individuals are experienced "like others of a desig-nated type."[428] Thus, I understand the meaning of what the "loser," or someone behind the desk at the bank, are "doing" and "saying." Just as I make sense of what is going on when dealing with postal clerks, poker players, etc.[429] Intentional social objects, Schutz wrote, such as "stranger types," "friend" types, or "foe" types, are "given to the apperceiving consciousness not merely as an objectivity as such, but as an existent of a particular type."[430] Consider the remark, attribut-able to Cary Grant: "Everybody wants to be Cary Grant; even I want to be Cary Grant."

Even in face-to-face encounters, Others are apprehended by "means of typificatory schemes."[431] One soon learns to interpret differences in the typical behavior of "friends" and "foes," such as the school bully: the raised hand of a "friend" stands for something quite different from the raised hand of a "foe." These interpretations are different from interpretations inspired or influenced by an individualistic *Verstehen*,[432] typifications avoid speculations about individual or subjective motives or intentions. Instead, they invite a consideration of the pragmatic exigencies of socially defined "here and now's," that is, situated actions such as family dinners, department meetings, classrooms, etc., as well as the prevailing discursive scheme(s).

> We must be quite clear as to what is happening here. The subjective meaning-context has been abandoned as a tool of interpretation. It has been replaced by a series of highly complex and systematically interrelated objective meaning contexts." [433]

Second, typifications contribute more to interpretative theory than mere descriptions or classifications of types of world objects.[434] Because of their capacity as "appresentational references," typifications aid in the constitution of intentional social objects. Many popular social types, e.g., are constituted in metaphor.[435] Examples include figurative "pushovers," "suckers," "pussy cats," "wimps," "ass kickers," "ass kissers," "jocks," "nerds," "Goths," and as Klapp, in a lengthy discussion of social types, indicated, "brains," "lady-killers," "highbrows," "eggheads," "crackpots," "pigs," "boy scouts," "trigger men," "bad apples," "bloodsuckers, "heart breakers," "gold diggers," "loan sharks," "fat cats," "sponges," "chickens," "jackasses," "blockheads," "small potatoes," "softsoapers," "apple polishers," "apes."[436]

The talk and actions of socially-typed individuals are experienced as if they were the talk and actions of "sucker" types, embodying the meaning of what typical suckers say and do. Until further notice, the actions of "hero" types are interpreted as heroic, without reference to their motives or intentions. Puzzling is the possibility that the same act interpretable as exploitable, on the one hand, might be interpreted as foolish or heroic, on the other. The difference is rooted in the typification, not in the particular act it shapes. The sibling typed as the "goody-goody," e.g., never does anything wrong in the eyes of parents, despite ample "evidence" to the contrary.

Typifications raise several curious questions. Should "friends," "foes," "strangers," and, even, "relatives" be considered as constituted intentionalities, namely, as products of discourse and the pragmatic exigencies of here and now's, as objects. That is, as Natanson wrote, "grasped in [their] intentional characters, grasped as being this or that."[437] Or, should they be regarded as are persons costumed for Halloween, *i.e.*, as known "real" persons hiding behind a disguise as "friend" or "foe"? If every intentional object presents to consciousness an object-with-meaning-attached, then the constituted typicality (the "friend" or "foe") is necessarily different from the social object upon whom it is founded. As Berger and Luckman noted, even in face-to-face situations "I apprehend the other by means of typificatory schemes."[438] Thus, aloof from the objects they symbolize, intended social objects, "appresentations" are no more identical to the objects upon which they are founded than maps are to the territories they represent. The intentional "friend" has no ontological status *qua* "friend," and is, obviously not everyone's "friend," just as a "stranger" to one might be someone else's intentional "lover." Types, such as "friends" and "strangers" are intentionalities, meaningful products of social interaction. Simmel took that distinction into account characterizing the "stranger" as a "specific form of interaction." Strangers, *i.e.*, "are not really conceived as individuals, but as strangers of a particular type."[439]

Third, typifications not only help make sense out of the typical behavior of others, they also provide the guidelines, recipes, or "typical precepts for typical behavior" guiding one's own behavior. That is how we know, more or less, how to "fit in", *i.e.,* how to interpret a doctor's request and then how to act toward that request as a typical patient; how to act toward school principals in typical student fashion; toward grocery clerks, toward a blind date, and toward future in-laws. Prefigured typifications and their inner horizons prepare the way for what is typically likely to be happening, at once expediting harmonious participation and insulating against unnecessary breaching. In typical fashion, one understands that routine physical exams may entail the invasion of private parts, but, even at that, they do not, typically, signify that anything sexual is going on.[440] Or, as reported in other transactions involving sexual parts, the goal might not be sexual gratification, but money.[441] Recipes, however, do not guarantee intersubjective harmony. How individuals act toward intentionalities will, in any instance, prove more or less true to the recipe. One might simply lack knowledge of the recipe. One might know the recipe, but execute it poorly. One might simply misread the situation, interpreting another shopper as a typical store clerk.

Fourth, typifications help smooth interactions for everyone who goes about practical affairs, typically, with recipes in hand. These recipes, just like other constitutive intentionalities, are taken for granted. Because they and the interpretations they shape are accepted as "unquestionably plausible," recipes help create the illusion that social life is much less complicated than it is. Thus, recipes foster simplified views through the capacity of discourse to reduce what Ricoeur characterized as a "surplus of meaning," namely, richness and ambiguity in the meanings of words, actions, and gestures.[442] Discursive schemes in general, and typifications in particular, arbitrarily limit alternative interpretations of the meaning of the typical talk and actions of Others.

Fifth, intersubjectivity describes the circumstances by which members of discursive communities come to act harmoniously: stopping at red lights; passing the salt; "admiring" the Emperor's new clothes; saluting the general, holding the door open for someone with packages; and interpreting actions of leaders and team members as moral or not. Figuratively speaking, intersubjectivity suggests they are all not only on the same team, but they are also on the same page of the playbook.

What does an intentionalist approach have to say about teams? And "whistle-blowers"? Team members, whether on athletic, corporate, military, or academic department teams, harmoniously constitute intentional objects with the help of shared prefigured meanings. They typically "see" things – typifications and their horizons – in the same way. As interested onlookers, they tend to interpret their own and others' talk and actions similarly: in terms of their value and usefulness to the team. Aided by an interest and an "attitude," in their constitutive activities, they share the meanings embodied in their own and others' actions.443 "Whistle blowers" march to a different drummer. Their constitutive activities, rooted in different interpretative schemes, produce different meanings and as we have seen, different interpretations. Above all, for team members, the interpretations of most non-team players are of doubtful value or usefulness.

Schutz's sociologically inspired modification of Husserl's intersubjectivity de-individualized interpretative understanding. Schutz replaced an individualized subjective platform with one founded on public, shared, objective schemes of interpretation. Schutz's development of intentional theory – and its concepts, significations, symbols, shared meanings, intersubjectivity, meaning-contexts and discursive schemes – makes it possible to revisit writings of Simmel and Durkheim to uncover the thread of a common interpretative refrain: the part played by meaning, experience, intentionality[444] and interpretative schemes in their vision of a subject matter for sociology. Although their terminology differs from that of Husserl and Schutz, portions of Durkheim and Simmel's writings support their "collective," symbolic, socially constructed, objective and theories of interpretation.

Durkheim and Simmel's emphases on the social construction of meaning and interpretation is not something to be exorcised, as Weber suggested. If it is true, as Silverman noted, that "we know very little, despite decades of sociological research, about the social construction of reality," then reality is something to be examined directly.[445] Durkheim and Simmel, for whom the origins of the meanings that shaped individual experience resided not in individual psychology, but in a symbolic order, began that examination. Durkheim's "collective representations" and Simmel's "forms of experiencing," founded and replayed in society and social life, re-present the world, Others, and interactions in the light of their societal meanings. We are engaged, as Durkheim pointed out, by a vast symbolic order, within which the meanings of things are social constructed.

## Chapter Six

## DURKHEIM'S SOCIOLOGISM: SOCIAL CONSTRUCTIONS

## OF REALITY

INTRODUCTION

Weber developed the concept of *Verstehen*, or interpretative understanding, in the context of Dilthey's relativistic historical approach. Schutz, aiming to replace Weber's subjective *Verstehen* with more objective interpretative schemes, based his approach to interpretative theory on Husserl's phenomenology. Shutz's modifications of Husserl's intentional theory placed sociological interpretations on more objective grounds, as well as providing the foundation of phenomenological sociology.

There is one distinction drawn in phenomenological sociology that warrants special attention: the distinction between "appearing things" and their "appearances." That is, the distinction between world objects and the experience of such objects as societally determined meanings and interpretations. The distinction helps illuminate Durkheim's efforts, in his <u>later</u> writings, to define sociology's subject matter and re-examine his view of a society – that is, social life – made possible by what he termed a "vast symbolism."[446] Even though Durkheim never used the word "appearances" in the same context as intentional theorists, he expressed the same idea with his own terms, e.g., "collective representations" and "moulds." Symbols, for Durkheim, were not "hard facts," but "collective representations" and "social facts." These facts had, according to Mestrovic, "to be deciphered and interpreted."[447] Within such a conception of society, Durkheim laid the foundation for a new and unique subject matter for sociology.

> Society is a reality *sui generis*; it has its own peculiar characteristics, which are not found elsewhere and which are not met with again in the same form in all the rest of the universe.[448]

## FROM KANT TO SOCIOLOGY'S SUBJECT MATTER

Durkheim relied on Kantian philosophy, which focused on the problem of knowledge by attending to the conditions necessarily involved in any fact of knowledge. In those terms, the stuff of experience is never raw, but has already been worked upon by mind, so that mind prescribes to the world the forms and conditions under which it shall appear. No surprise, then, that "nature" conforms to "laws" and is intelligible, since those laws were put in place by mind. Thus, through Kantian epistemology, "Indubitable truths are based upon our own, ultimately arbitrary rules, habits of using words and symbols and give no information about the world."[449] Essential conditions of sense perception, space and time, forms of intuition, *e.g.,* are not data inherent in things but are instead universals of the intellect into which all data of sense must be received.

Toward the end of his professional career, Durkheim turned his attention to the venerable debate over categories of thought, their origins, and how they shape both knowledge and individual experience. After reviewing explanations of how the world is made knowable to us, he concluded:

> Up to the present there have been only two doctrines in the field. For some, the categories cannot be derived from experience: they are logically prior to it and condition it. They are represented as so

> many simple and irreducible data, imminent in the
> human mind by virtue of its inborn constitution.
> For this reason they are said to be *a priori*. Others,
> however, hold that they are constructed and made
> up of pieces and bits, and that the individual is the
> artisan of this construction.[450]

Dissatisfied with both doctrines, and reluctant to accept Kant's notion of individual mind as the source of the categories of thought, Durkheim fashioned a third alternative: he connected the sources of knowledge and understanding, based on *a priori* categories, to social life. Socially based categories, such as "collective representations" and the often-overlooked concept of "moulds"[451] shaped the Kantian ideas of "time, space, class, or personality."[452] Durkheim also included force, personality and efficacy, number, causes, substance, and concepts, that "before all else ... are collective representations."[453] All of these, Durkheim contended ambitiously, were "like the solid frame that encloses all thought." But clearly, despite their social origins, Durkheim did not limit the influence of these categories to knowledge of the social world alone. Thus, "collective" categories cast a wide net that embraced "all known reality."[454]

> Not only is it society which has founded them, but
> their contents are the different aspects of the social
> being: the category of class was at first indistinct
> from the concept of the human group; it is the
> rhythm of social life which is at the basis of the
> category of time; the territory occupied by the society
> furnished the material for the category of space;
> it is the collective for which was the prototype of
> the concept of efficient fore, as essential element in
> the category of causality. However, the categories
> are not made to be applied only to the social realm;
> they reach out to all reality.[455]

Durkheim sidestepped the problem of psychological reductionism by abandoning the Kantian notion of an <u>individual</u> mind that prescribed to the world the form under which it shall appear. Durkheim maintained that the categories of knowledge shaping our experience originated in the circumstances of <u>social</u> life. Through this radical departure, Durkheim rooted Kantian epistemology – the foundations of the forces shaping our experience and all knowledge – squarely in social life. "Durkheim's sociologism," Hund wrote, "establishes a framework for exploring the social foundations of *a priori* knowledge."[456] Hilbert continued, "society is also in Durkheim's most radical commentary equivalent to objective reality as known and recognized by societal members."[457]

By the time of *The Elementary Forms* (originally published in 1912), Durkheim had formulated sociology's subject matter in epistemological and sym-bolic terms, rather than in ontological ones. Sociology was not to be concerned primarily with the study of objects. For Durkheim, Bordieu observed, "it is a question of defining a mental attitude and not assigning an ontological status to the object."[458] Durkheim argued that the intelligibility of the world was not a matter of its intrinsic organization, but a direct consequence of <u>societal</u> forces and tendencies, driven by a <u>symbolism</u> that originates in associations. Durkheim spelled out sociology's task as "a task of interpretation" that obliged it to "give a true account of the systems of meanings by which men in society make sense of their lives."[459]

In outlining the boundaries of the new discipline, Durkheim had to stake out a scientific and intellectual territory and tender legitimate claims to it. He had to persuade other scholars – and not necessarily friendly ones – that sociology was grounded in a sophisticated epistemology, and that it possessed a subject matter not previously covered by established academic disciplines, *i.e.*, not ex-plained away by the worldviews, concepts, vocabularies, or methods of other dis-ciplines. He had to show "the scholarly world that social causality was, in truth, a central causality in human motivation."[460] While some writers believed Durkheim was not totally successful in establishing sociology's autonomy,[461] he did repeatedly address the problem of psychological reductionism and maintained that sociology's unit of analysis could not and should not be <u>individual</u> behaviors. "Every time that a social phenomenon is directly explained by a psychological phenomenon, we may be sure that the explanation is false."[462] In articulating the roots of a solidly conceived social constructionist position, he reasoned that explanations of phenomena produced by the whole (society) should be based upon "the characteristic properties of the whole," or on "explanations of the complex by the complex," *i.e.,* "by the *sui generis* combinations from which they result."[463]

"Collective" life – what Durkheim termed "associations" among individuals – effectively produced the meanings of objects and their "representations" as "social things." "Collective representations," originated in (and subsequently were replayed in) every day associations and activities – hunts, meals, parties – and in episodic activities such as religious rituals and ceremonies. "Collective representations" shaped or "moulded" the meanings of objects and actions, for example, what "social things," such as pieces of wood, or places or acts signified, what they stood for, and whether they were "criminal," or not, or "sacred," or not.

Thus it was the symbolic order that expressed <u>sociologically</u> interesting differences between "appearing things" and their "appearances," *e.g.,* between pieces of wood: the sacred "appearance" of one, but not the other. Socially based meanings were superimposed on "appearing things" to produce their "appearances." Individuals alone and apart from one another neither cause nor produce "social things," but the *associations* among them did. Sociology's subject matter, however, was not merely a sum of individuals, nor was social life reducible to individual minds; it was something not only new, but *sui generis*.[464] As a "thing" in its own right, society constituted its own agency; it did not exist to serve another! Social life, a "vast symbolism," was made possible by associations among individuals in their joint endeavors. The products of associations were symbolic materials – communities of meanings – that were added to raw objects and acts.

> At the same time that it sees from above, it [the collective consciousness] sees farther; at every moment of time, it embraces all known reality; that is why it alone can furnish the mind with the moulds which are applicable to the totality of things and which make it possible to think of them.[465]

The role played by communities of individuals in the establishment of meaning has often been noted.[466] In distinguishing between sounds and words, Dewey, *e.g.*, wrote that a sound is not a word, but becomes a word by having meaning added to it. (1939) Without meaning, words might be regarded as "brute utterances."[467] Words come into being and gain meaning in the course of the establishment of a community of action, so that, as Perinbanayagam asserted, "meaning, of course, exists as a public phenomenon."[468] Durkheim's sociology similarly emphasized the precedence of social or community forces over individuals in the social construction of "social things," *i.e.*, what those things mean. For Durkheim, the products of "associations" efficaciously "mould" how members of a community experience, interpret, and subsequently act toward, this or that "social thing." They act not toward the "appearing thing," but toward the meaning it embodies. Symbolic or collectively represented "appearances," termed "social things," were essentially social in nature, and were, according to Durkheim, sociology's subject matter. So-called raw, uninterpreted *"appearing* things" were not!

## Metaphors

In his early writings, Durkheim employed traditional and organic metaphors, likening parts of society to parts of the body. These metaphors permitted him to draw similarities and distinctions among structures and functions.[469] Durkheim's later writing displayed a different strategy. He inverted conventional thinking: instead of using what were then popular metaphors to introduce ideas about society, he suggested that the world – nature itself – should be understood in terms of societal metaphors:

> But, if the categories originally only translate social
> states, does it not follow that they can be applied to
> the rest of nature only as metaphors.[470]

Just as the resource metaphor (discussed in Chapter V) shapes our experience of time as something that can be spent, saved, set aside, or wasted; and just as cooks come to understand food through the construction of "a range of metaphors," societal metaphors shape our experience of social and natural things.[471] "The ideas of time, space, class, cause or personality," Durkheim asserted, "are constructed out of social elements."[472] Consistent with his "first rule for sociology," namely, to escape the realm of lay ideas, Durkheim insisted on a social constructionist approach, modeling even religious exuberance, e.g., on social collective exuberance.[473] Exuberance originates in social life, in associations such as the march, the hunt, celebrations, in cooperation and agreements with regards to both means and ends, and then spills over into other domains of experience. Thus exuberance serves , e.g., to shape the experience of exuberance in the religious domain. And, more generally,

> Religious representations are collective representa-
> tions which express collective realities.[474]

Not only did "religious representations" express collective realities, so did everything else! Representations of space, time, categories, rites, rituals, *etc.,* are all collectively represented, expressing collective realities. With the concept of collective realities, Durkheim cast a wide net. One might misinterpret the significance of Durkheim's assertion that "categories," *e.g.,* and the criteria employed in defining their boundaries, are socially constructed, in the belief that interpretations or "identifications" of "large" trees and "small" trees are based on inherent distinctions between them; or that flowers are unambiguously different from weeds. Durkheim did not subscribe to inherent distinctions. His social constructionism left precious little out. As Hilbert noted, "Cosmologies, ontologies, plus all of their derivatives – that is to say, entire system of thought, including those of the natural sciences – are socially derived."[475] Furthermore, even though "collective representations" have social origins, they do not lack objectivity; to the contrary, "a collective representation presents guarantees of objectivity by the fact that it is collective."[476]

CRITICISMS

The autonomous and "collective" nature of Durkheim's approach to sociology's subject matter – that is, its epistemological and interpretative implications – remains controversial. Criticisms that accuse him of advocating something like a "group-mind,"[477] stand out as most unforgiving. Douglas, whose comments on "disembodied social facts," were cited earlier, noted that "Durkheim's sociological epistemology ran into considerable opposition and has remained undeveloped to this day."[478] Even though Durkheim never suggested that external and coercive hovering group-mind-like presences directed human affairs, he was aware of the misinterpretations of his critics.[479] On various occasions he set out, not completely successfully, to "correct a false interpretation that has been put upon our thought."[480]

False interpretations of Durkheim's work led to criticisms that his terms were enigmatic, ambiguous, or metaphysical, and that they described disembodied social facts. "Durkheim was clearly guilty," Corning wrote, of attributing "independence and causal efficacy to disembodied social facts, the reifications created in his own mind to statistical artifacts."[481] Durkheim's descriptions of "collective representations" and "social facts" as <u>external</u> and <u>coercive</u> did little to mitigate the controversy. Durkheim's comments on these criticisms are classic understatement: "When this book appeared for the first time, it aroused lively controversy."[482]

That the meanings of "social facts"[483] (and his other terms) are still debated illustrates both the potential of alternative interpretations of classic theories and their usefulness.[484] Durkheim's articulation of a unit of analysis that was based not upon the actions of individual actors but on something abstracted from <u>associations</u> among them also led to controversy. Unfortunately, the term "association" and its symbolic and interpretative products, "collective representations," were misinterpreted as "collective conceptions that acted." When Weber argued that collectivities did not act, only individuals did, he sought to disqualify "collectivities" as sociology's unit of analysis.

But not all commentaries on Durkheim's "collective conceptions" were negative. Arguably, least controversial, *e.g.,* were "social facts" in the context of social surveys.[485] Some writers placed great stock in the moral implications of Durkheim's formation of sociology's subject matter. Hilbert, *e.g.,* discussed equivalencies between morality and society on the one hand, and morality and objective reality on the other.[486] Vogt took the position that, for Durkheim, society was the source of the mental and moral at the same time, and that society, itself, was essentially mental or moral in nature.[487] Still others reinterpreted Durk-heim's terms in a manner that preserved their "external and coercive character," but at the same time sheltered them from the stigma of "hovering group minds." Hund, *e.g.,* defended the view that social facts are real and constraining, noting that the question of the existence and reality of social facts is identical to the question of the existence and reality of social rules. "Constitutive rules," he wrote, "make group life and society possible" by creating "the very possibility of form-ing social relationships, obligations and social structures."[488]

**The Shift**

Durkheim shifted both in focus and terminology over the course of his ca-reer. He changed his focus from countable objects to their meanings, a shift which roughly paralleled the shift from quantitative to interpretative and qualitative thinking, or from "appearing objects" to their (socially constructed) "appear-ances."

In *Rules* (1938), Durkheim devoted more than two chapters to "social facts." He wrote that social facts "far from being a product of the will ... deter-mine it from without; they are like molds in which our actions are inevitably shaped."[489] In *Suicide,* he made early use of social-fact-like notions, writing, "the suicide-rate is therefore a factual order, unified and definite, as is shown by both its permanence and its variability."[490] He stressed that even though individuals commit suicide, "each society is predisposed to contribute a definite quota of vol-untary deaths."[491] Societal predispositions or tendencies, "whatever they are called" – external to individuals – are nonetheless objective "social facts," a matter, he noted, that he had taken up and proved in Chapter II of the *Rules.*[492] Collective tendencies were more than mere metaphors or manners of speech, *i.e.,* for Durkheim they were not "without real signification."[493] The sociologist, he advised, "must establish himself in the very heart of social facts."[494]

In *Sociology and Philosophy* (1953), Durkheim examined "moral facts," noting morality was, first of all, (and not surprisingly) associated with group membership.[495] In the chapter entitled "Individual and Collective Representations," he took the position that "representations" have all the properties appropriate to the subject matter for sociology: they are exterior to individual minds although they do derive from relationships among them – associations).[496] He also alluded to "social facts," by identifying them with the attributes they shared with "representations," namely, externally, coerciveness, independence, *etc.*[497]

By the time of *The Elementary Forms of the Religious Life* (1965), Durkheim had achieved a conceptual blend of "social facts" and "representations." Both were fully imbued with symbolic and epistemological implications, and both were enlisted as components of the "vast symbolic order."[498] Mestrovic observed that in this idea, Durkheim "regards the other varieties of social facts, from religion to suicide, as similar representations of social reality."[499] Across an extended range of topics, Durkheim's fundamental notion remained consistent: "Collective representations," or "moulds," although external to individual minds, effectively shaped the "appearances" of things, namely, what they meant to, and how they were experienced by, members of society. Enjoying a life of their own, "facts" and "representations" expressed collective tendencies – shared meanings – and most importantly, were categorically and objectively knowable! Most ambitiously, "all the World" fell within the boundaries of shared meanings and society's influence.

> Since the world expressed by the entire system of
> concepts is the one that society regards, society

alone can furnish the most general notions with which it should be represented.[500]

## THE SYMBOLIC ORDER

Finally, interpretations of "social facts" and "collective representations" emphasized their symbolic properties and their relationship to meaning and signification. Commenting on links between Durkheim and Schopenhauer, Mestrovic, *e.g.,* noted that the "intellectual's new task was not the discovery of order in the universe, but the decoding, deconstruction, and interpretation of human culture conceived as a human product."[501]

Various sociological phenomena have been analyzed in the context of "symbolism." Turner noted that Durkheim, among other early theorists, recognized that a community was not a place, so much as a relationship to systems of symbols.[502] Perinbanayagam tied "social facts" to meaning, writing that "in their exteriority and constraint, [social facts] exist and function in the meanings and actions of individuals."[503] Likening "social facts" to our use of money or language, Stone and Farberman observed that "for Durkheim, a collective representation was a social 'fact' – a thing – which, in its symbolic form, existed outside of man and constrained him ... into using it, like money or language."[504] The epistemological implications of Durkheim's conception of the subject matter of sociology,[505] namely its role in constituting social reality, was recognized by Mestrovic who wrote that "representations" and "social facts" were symbols that do not merely mirror social reality, "but also objects constitutive of it."[506] But some underestimated the strength and scope of the significance of symbolic materials in Durkheim's approach. Levi-Strauss, *e.g.,* criticized Durkheim's use of symbolism on anthropological grounds, and, for the wrong (sociological) reason:

> Society cannot exist without symbols, but instead of showing how the appearance of symbolic thought makes social life altogether possible and necessary, Durkheim tries the reverse, *i.e.*, to make symbolism grow out of society.[507]

Durkheim stressed two themes: human associations and their shared symbolic and epistemological products. Thus armed, he addressed questions about how "collective representations" shaped and "moulded," for members of a community, their experiences (*i.e.,* their "reality" worlds) and their interpretations the natural and social world – for example, not things *per se* but their "appearances."[508]

Durkheim emphasized several points about so-called "collective conceptions," the terms that referred to sociology's subject matter, such as "moulds," "frames," "social facts," and "collective representations." First, they were abstract, referring not to attributes of individuals, but rather to something uniquely social. Second, although social and broadly influential, and although they expressed "collective tendencies," they were not metaphysical. Third, Durkheim made no ontological claims for sociology's subject matter.[509] His subject matter indicated (or represented) some "thing" added to "appearing things," as well as sense experience. Fourth, whatever was added then effectively "moulded," framed, mediated, or transformed "appearing things" into "social things," then finally into what is loosely termed today as "socially constructed" reality.[510] Durkheim, *i.e.,* located the subject matter of sociology in the recognition of differences between "appearing things" and their *shared* "appearances."

**Abstract, not concrete.**

> It is an abstract and impersonal frame which surrounds, not only our individual existence, but that of all humanity.[511]

That sociology's subject matter was abstract meant that individual concrete behavior, motives, and intentions were <u>not</u> sociology's <u>unit</u> <u>of</u> <u>analysis</u>. Durkheim maintained that individual psychological predispositions should be studied by psychologists. Things that were uniquely sociological had a place "outside of and above individual and local contingencies."[512] Therefore, the ascertainment of "social facts" or "collective representations" – abstracted from associations among individuals – necessarily proceeded from "an aspect that was independent of their individual manifestations."[513]

Sociology's subject matter was abstract, but, nonetheless, <u>objective</u>. Such a notion, Durkheim admitted, "offends common sense."[514] By objective, he meant that all things, including actions of others, were experienced by individual members of a community as "social things." "Social things" were embodiments of socially based meanings. The shared significance of a "social thing" was expressed, *e.g.*, in how and why the "appearance" of an otherwise ordinary "appearing" piece of wood or rabbit's foot was interpreted as if it were "sacred," and why deference was shown to "sacred" objects, a particular piece of wood or stone, or a sacred place. Deference is an indication of what that object means to members of a community and can be abstracted from how they act toward it. It is of profound sociological interest that community members act *as if* a piece of wood or stone, or an alligator or eagle, possessed "sacred" properties, while, at the same time, act toward similar "appearing" objects, animals, or places as if they were ordinary.

> If men did not agree upon these essential ideas at every moment, if they did not have the same conception of time, space, cause, number, *etc.*, all contact between their minds would be impossible, and with that, all life together.[515]

Durkheim extended this idea to a consideration of others and social roles. The shared significance of males and females, as "appearing things," finds expression, *e.g.,* in typical gendered "appearances," role behaviors, and what they meant to members of a community: who hunted, who gathered, who prepared food, and who suffered and needed to recover from child birth (*couvade*).[516] These behaviors, residing in a vast symbolism, embody social and not "innate" meanings.

**Not individual but social.**

> When, then, the sociologist undertakes the investigation of some order of social facts, he must endeavor to consider them from an aspect that is independent of their individual manifestations.[517]

"Collective representations," Durkheim asserted repeatedly, originated in social, not in individual circumstances. Moreover, "representations" were something more than a "mere sum of individuals."[518] Consequently, Durkheim argued, sociology should avoid preoccupying itself with individual mind or individual consciousness.[519] Nor should it take a functionalist approach, as outlined by Malinowski, that would be based upon the satisfaction of individual needs.

> But if no reality exists outside of individual consciousness, it wholly lacks any material of its own. In that case, the only possible subject of observation is the mental states of the individual, since nothing else exists. That, however, is the field of psychology. From this point of view the essence of marriage, for example, of the family, or religion, consists of individual needs to which these institution supposedly correspond. . . [520]

The alternatives were clear: if the subject matter were individual consciousness or the mental states of individuals, then the study belonged in the field of psychology. If it were based on associations among individuals and symbolic materials produced in the *circumstances of social life*, then it belonged in sociology. In the latter case, individuals could be seen experiencing and acting not toward things in the raw, but to "social things," things as they were cooked, symbolically mediated, or "moulded." With such guidance, Durkheim directed sociological study away from countable objects, *per se*, such as pieces of wood or places – simply as "appearing things" – and toward "representations," meanings embodied in the "appearances" of things.

> Another reason explains why the constituent elements of the categories should have been taken from social life: it is because the relations which they express could not have been learned except in and through society. If they are in a sense immanent in the life of an individual, he has neither a reason nor the means for learning them, reflecting upon them and forming them into distinct ideas.[521]

This uncompromising social constructionist position led Stone and Farberman to conclude that, for Durkheim, "man has, in his collective existence, become the source of reality."

> Since the universe does not exist except in so far as it is thought of, and since it is not completely thought of except by society, it takes a place in this latter; it becomes a part of society's interior life, while this is the totality, outside of which nothing exists. The concept of totality is only the abstract form of the concept of society. . . [522]

Durkheim mounted another assault on attempts to individualize sociology's subject matter. He noted a methodological <u>imperfection</u> in the discipline that served to minimize the significance of societal tendencies. That imperfection specifically consisted of mistaking effect for cause, blinding "most sociologists to the inadequacy of a method" in which – and I paraphrase here – religious sentiments are considered innate in man, as is sexual jealousy, paternal love, *etc.* The error that confuses cause and effect was made in an attempt to explain social institutions such as religion, marriage, and the family, with inherent individual sentiments, rather than as they truly were – results of collective organization.[523] Innate individual needs and sentiments did not, for Durkheim, play a part in the shaping of institutional arrangements.

The same was true for concepts which, Durkheim asserted, did not originate with or belong to individuals. Writing that "a concept is not my concept," he pointed out that concepts often indicate something an individual has never directly experienced or witnessed.[524] Today, for instance, one can conceive of a herd of elephants or giraffes, intergalactic aliens, worm holes, eleven dimensions or, even, compassionate bureaucrats, without having ever encountered one.

Finally, because of the advantages he gained by concentrating on the symbolic order and the meanings contained therein, Durkheim <u>never</u> had to claim that "collectivities" acted.[525] Nor did Durkheim empower or reify abstractions, such as "collective representations," as some critics alleged. He carefully distinguished between collectivities and individuals, acknowledging, just as Weber had, exactly who did the "acting" in social affairs:

> Indeed, social things are actualized only through men; they are a product of human activity.[526]

## Not Metaphysical but Social Things

A social fact existed "in it own right."[527]

As a branch of philosophical and theological study, metaphysics, referring to Aristotle's work of that name, examines transcendental principles that are presumably beyond the physical. Metaphysical reasoning is abstract reasoning. It is often perplexing, subtle, and sometimes fantastic. Because the term is sometimes used pejoratively to derogate positions and arguments, the founders of modern sociology were careful to outline a subject matter for sociology that would successfully avoid the metaphysical label. Advocating what later was termed a social constructionist position, Durkheim was especially susceptible the charge that his work was metaphysical. His outline of sociology's subject matter, however, was not at all metaphysical – despite his critics' allegations. "Collective representations" and "social facts," among the many terms he introduced to indicate the societal forces that shape the meaning of individual experience, were as natural as were trees and mountains.

Thus he clarified the <u>empirical</u> origins – *i.e.* associations – of the widely cast socially based, symbolic net that moulded individuals' experience of time, categories, classifications, space, *etc.* As examples, he cited calendars, that, when regarded as "social things," represented "the rhythm of the collective activities," such as rites and feasts. "Space" he noted, "is conceived – in particular societies – in the form of an immense circle, because the camp has a circular form. . ."[528]

"Collective representations" shaped individuals' interpretations of some sticks and stones as "sacred" things, but not others. Representations also shaped people's interpretations of their own and others' actions as "criminal" or not. But even though Durkheim described "representations" in terms of exterior and coercive social forces, *"hav[ing] an existence of their own. . . "* he made clear that that "existence" referred to nothing metaphysical.[529] It referred to a symbolic order produced in the circumstances of social life. "Collective representations," as parts of nature, did not reside outside of nature.

> But the problem concerning them is more complex, for they are social in another sense and, as it were in the second degree. They not only come from society, but the things which they express are of a social nature.[530]

Whereas, *e.g.,* individuals compose part of the natural order of things, "father-in-laws" and "mother-in-laws" suggest something different. They are not found in the state of nature, instead, are socially produced. What the term "mother-in law" means, and how that person is experienced by community members, is shaped by "collective representations." Newly married couples find a community of meanings already in place and, then, for the most part, replay those meanings. When the "appearing thing," a man, *e.g.,* takes on the *collectively represented* "appearance" of an in-law, that is, a role informed by social meanings, something symbolic is added by way of matrimony to what is said and done by someone else's father. Similarly, sacred objects represent the "sacred" significance added to the piece of wood, stone or clearings in the forest. Neither Jane Doe, "the mother-in-law," nor a piece of wood, the "churinga," enjoy ontological status. They are natural facts also, in spite of the social meanings that have been added to what they say and do, even if these meanings are pre-figured with properties that are external, obligatory and constraining.

The social symbolic material added to "appearing things" efficaciously "moulds" or transforms them into "social things." The significance of Durkheim's insight is that "appearances" of *collectively represented* "appearing things" shape

148

how members of a community interpret and subsequently act toward those "appearing things," namely, toward the <u>meaning</u> of the ("appearing") man, now father-in-law in "appearance." Hence, Durkheim's terms referred to nothing metaphysical:

> Despite its metaphysical appearance, this word designates nothing more than a body of natural facts which are explained by natural causes.[531]

The mountain's "appearance" (whether signifying something to worship, something evil, an opportunity for fun, *etc.*) represents an aspect of, and is therefore an embodiment of, some aspect of the symbolic order. An individual's experience of the mountain – what it means to her, or her interpretation of it, and how she acts toward it – is "moulded" by shared collective "representations." And not without consequences: for then the mountain is worshiped, played upon, climbed, drilled in, tunneled through, *etc.*

Despite a proclivity to take "social things" and the world for granted, *i.e.,* to assume that "appearances" are objectively given, "the individual," as Hilbert wrote, "is obliged to experience the world in certain ways and not others, even though such obligations seem to the individual to arise from the objectively arranged nature of reality as such."[532]

**Associational, not ontological. Something added.**

> If one can say that, to a certain extent, collective representations are exterior to individual minds, it means that they do not derive from them as such but from the association of minds, which is a very different thing.[533]

"Associations" include both prosaic and uncommon activities that individuals undertake jointly. Among these, Durkheim cited "every summons to a celebration, a hunt or a military expedition."[534] These, as well as other activities, imply "fixed and established dates, and consequently that a common <u>time</u> is agreed upon . . ."[535] Further emphasizing societal tendencies, Durkheim insisted that "joint activity takes place outside each one of us." It is helpful to recognize that "collective representations" originate directly in negotiated, shared, social activities in order to celebrate at the same time and in the same place; to meet at an appointed time to confront the invading enemy; or successfully to trap and kill the buffalo. Negotiations as to where and when to meet, what to slay, pick, or fish for, necessitate spatial and temporal organization and agreements as to a host of categories. Neither metaphysical, nor inherent in nature, nor in the nature of human nature, categories were social "things" necessarily negotiated and replayed in associations. Clarifying the category of direction, *e.g.*, Durkheim argued that "by themselves there are neither right nor left, up nor down, north nor south, *etc.*"[536] Even the identification of "enemies" or "buffaloes" or, more generally, what is "eatable," requires <u>shared</u> <u>categories</u>, *i.e.,* identification of socially constructed similarities and differences among plants and creatures. Social life in ongoing associations and interactions established "patterns of behavior," symbolic frames, "moulds," or "collective representations," that, for Durkheim, were specific realities of their <u>own</u>, having their own characteristics. [537]

> From the actions and reactions between its individuals arises an entirely new mental life which lifts our minds into a world of which we could have not the faintest idea had we lived in isolation. [538]

Durkheim posed another challenge to common sense by pointing out that the "entirely new mental life" was not a direct product of sense experience.

Meanings that originated in the circumstances of social life and that were contained in a shared symbolic order were added to sense experience itself so that when Durkheim mandated the sociological study of "collective representations," he was most assuredly not staking out ontological territories. He was not defining sets of objects that were directly accessible through sense experience.

> Therefore, the sacred character assumed by an object is not implied in the intrinsic properties of this latter: it is added to them. The world of religious things is not one particular aspect of empirical nature; it is superimposed upon it.[539]

When a community's "sacred" meaning has been added to a thing, it then becomes "sacred" in the minds of the community members. The object is *moulded sacred*. It comes to signify something "sacred" because something external that is superimposed on it.[540]

> Now in themselves, the churinga are objects of wood and stone like all others; they are distinguished from profane things of the same sort by only one particularity: this is that the totemic mark is drawn or engraved upon them. So it is this mark and this alone which gives them their sacred character.[541]

Even a sacred idol "is often, however, nothing but a block of stone or a piece of wood, things which in themselves have no value."[542] Flags are bits of cloth that "a soldier will die to save," a postage stamp lacking artistic character may be worth a fortune. "Obviously," Durkheim noted, "it is not the intrinsic nature of pearls, diamonds, furs or laces that make the value of these different articles of dress vary at the caprice of fashion."[543] Underscoring the significance of the vast symbolic order by virtue of which meaning is added or superimposed, Durkheim wrote that "the images of totemic beings are more sacred than the beings themselves."[544] Not only abstract or inanimate objects were thus transformed. Animals were also constituted by societal tendencies: "even the most useless or harmless animals... have been worshiped."

The relevance of "representations," and their impact on interpretations, extends to studies of families, domestic relations, clans, matriarchy and patriarchy, crime, *etc*. In a tone reminiscent of what was later termed "secondary deviation," Durkheim maintained that acts were criminal not because of any intrinsic property of the act itself, but because of the reactions of members of a community to the <u>meaning</u> of the act thus deemed criminal. The act, the "appearing thing," was not "criminal." Its criminal "appearance," however, was indicated by peoples' response to it. For Durkheim, the meaning of the act – its symbolic property – was superimposed. One can only imagine how Weber, trained in the law to consider individual intention as an indispensable element with regard to criminality, would have reacted to Durkheim's disregard for individual motives or intentions in favor of an approach fashioned along social constructionist lines.

> We note the existence of certain acts, all presenting
> the external characteristic that they evoke from so-
> ciety the particular reaction called punishment.[545]

In a sharp departure from common sense thinking, Durkheim maintained that "crimes," "sacred" objects, *etc.,* in so far as they were "moulded" by "representations," were founded on, but different from, objects and acts naively revealed by sense experience. "Social facts" and "representations" <u>added</u> something to sense experience, organizing and mediating it. Moreover, "representations" also <u>substituted</u> for the world revealed to us by our senses.

> In this way collective thought changes everything it
> touches. It throws down the barriers of the realms
> of nature and combines contraries; it reverses what

> is called the natural hierarchy of being, makes dis-
> parity equal and differentiates the similar. In a word,
> society substitute for the world revealed to us by our
> senses a different world that is the projection of the
> ideals created by society itself.[546]

In full accord with the tradition of writers who characterized personal experience as flow, Durkheim employed the stream metaphor to characterize sensation as something in perpetual flux.[547] Sensations follow upon each other like
waves, and, even during the time that they last, they do not remain the same. Each
is an integral part of the precise instant when it takes place. Echoing Heraclitus,
Durkheim wrote, "We are never sure of again finding a perception such as we experienced it the first time."[548] Presaging what might be said today about the reliability and accuracy of eyewitness reports, Durkheim remarked:

> It is true that when our sensations are actual, they
> impose themselves upon us in fact. But we are free
> to conceive them otherwise than they really are, or
> to represent them to ourselves as occurring in a dif-
> ferent order from that where they are really pro-
> duced.[549]

That which is added to sense experience is not merely incremental, it is
transformational: "Thinking by concepts is not merely seeing reality on its most
general side, but it is projecting a light upon the sensation which illuminates it,
penetrates it and transforms it."[550] Collective thought, founded in a vast symbolic
order, embraces concepts and "moulds" raw sense experience. Collective thought
thus transforms raw experience – substituting for it – to produce shared experiences, interpretations and knowledge.

**A Vast Symbolism**

> Thus social life, in all its aspects and in every period of its history, is made possible only by a vast symbolism.[551]

Several writers noted the symbolic implications in Durkheim's approach to sociology's subject matter – a subject matter that evidenced, shared, and mediated, meanings that were symbolically embedded in "social facts," "collective representations," or "moulds." [552]

Meaning originated in associations[553] whenever individuals negotiated what categories of plants and creatures were eatable, the time and place for ceremonies, marches, and hunts. These negotiations produced and organized time, space, *etc.*, into categories: which direction means "north"? How long does it take? What "four-mile" canyon means; when to turn "left" or "right." Sociology's subject matter was not this or that object or act, but something symbolic that was external to, superimposed on, or added to, and subsequently transformed. "appearing things" into "social things."[554]

> We are now able to understand how the totemic principle, and in general, every religious force, comes to be outside of the object in which it resides. It is because the idea of it is in no way made up of the impressions directly produced by this thing upon our senses or minds.[555]

Not only were objects endowed with significance and meaning, assuming socially originating "appearances," so were acts of individuals toward each other! Acts are "criminal" when they are interpreted as criminal. Said differently, an act is an "appearing thing." Its "criminality" resides in its criminal "appearance."

> [It] is not [their] intrinsic quality... but that

definition which the collective conscience lends
them.[556]

Durkheim's later terms emphasized symbolic materials, or frames of meaning:[557] not the immediate sense experience of "appearing objects," but what those objects stood for; not how the senses encounter the raw contents of life, but how those contents were mediated, or "moulded." Not sounds as raw brute utterances, but as words. Not raw actions, but mediated actions: actions as they are socially defined "criminal," "innocent," "sacred," "profane," "moral." The scope of the symbolic order is such that, because "sacredness" is socially produced, any object or act can be "collectively represented" as "sacred," i.e., be transformed into a "sacred thing." Durkheim paid scant attention to objects as raw sense experience. The mountain, e.g., set apart from the background of sense experience, presents itself to us as a mediated object. Thanks to its "collective representation," the mountain signifies the home of the gods, a place to ski, an obstacle, a source of bounty, cragginess, hostility, etc. A stand of trees will not represent – that is symbolize – a sacred sanctuary unless its meaning is "moulded" as "sacred;" alternatively it may be interpreted as a place to have a picnic, a source of raw material for the lumber man, a good, shady place to build the farm house, etc. "Durkheim had by time of his latest writings," Lukes wrote, "come very close to maintaining that symbolic thought is a condition of and explains society."[558]

By de-individualizing and de-psychologizing sociology's subject matter, Durkheim identified society with a vast symbolic order, an unlimited social container of meanings and significations. For sociology, he advocated the study of "social things" – "representations," "facts," or "moulds," etc. – not "appearing things," or objects in the raw, but their "appearances," their shared meanings as interpreted by members of a community. Thus, one strand of Durkheim's social theory[559] repeats a, by now, familiar interpretative refrain. Whereas Husserl used the phrase "meaning endowments," and Schutz, "attached meanings," Durkheim used terms like "added" and "superimposed" to indicate societal mediation of the meaning of objects and actions found in "collective representations." "Representations" that represent symbolic materials shape interpretations of sticks of wood (or people, animals, or places) as "sacred" or not, just as they do the meanings embodied in "yes" and "no" replies in "counseling" sessions.

Just what were social "things"? For Durkheim, they included "all objects of knowledge that cannot be conceived by purely mental activity, those that require for their conception data from outside the mind. . ."[560] That which acts and objects "stood for" was founded in the circumstances of social life – in human associations and societally-based meanings – and therefore exist outside individual mind. Because they are social and shared, these meanings produce harmonious and shared interpretations of all things among members of a community. But should one expect "collective representations" to be the same for all groups within a single society, or the same among different societies? Should one expect Republicans and Democrats to interpret objects such as ballots, bills, and boycotts similarly? To the extent to which their circumstances of life differ, Durkheim's answer is no.

> So, at bottom, it is the unity and diversity of social life which make the simultaneous unity and diversity of sacred beings and things.[561]

# Chapter Seven

# SIMMEL'S "FORMS OF EXPERIENCING"

## INTRODUCTION

The founders of modern sociology understood the problems they faced in outlining the boundaries of a new discipline. They needed to delineate a subject matter that was unique, that was scientific, and that avoided reductionism – especially any undue dependence on individual, psychological behavior. Simmel saw that nothing new was to be gained, except the new label "sociology," by throwing – actually, he said dumping – "all historical, psychological, and normative sciences into one great pot labeled 'sociology.'"[562] Unlike other already established sciences,[563] the science of society was "in the unfortunate position of still having to prove its right to exist."[564] Advocating that right, Simmel defined a unit of analysis that was unique, that avoided any hint of a metaphysic, and that clarified the problematic issue of concrete vs. abstract, a problem represented in the question Weber had already posed: in sociological analysis, who or what is the actor? Collectivities do not act; but, at the same time, sociology should not concentrate on particular individuals and their psychological states. In response to these conflicting criteria, Simmel proposed the study of societal forms.

> I understand of the task of sociology to be description and determination of the historico-psychological origin of those forms in which interactions take place between human beings.[565]

Ubiquitous "forms" apply analytically in many different social contexts.[566] Arguably, and perhaps because of their variety, Simmel's forms remain controversial to this day. To shed a softer light on that controversy, I will examine "forms of experiencing" in some detail because they are particularly rich in interpretative and symbolic implications.[567] The interpretation of "forms of experiencing" presented here is guided by the phenomenological distinction Husserl drew between the "appearing object" and the "appearing of the object,"[568] or to use Morrison's terminology, the distinction between the "appearing object" and its "appearance."[569]

Simmel did not use these terms, but evidence points to his recognition that at least one aspect of sociology's potential subject matter could be found in the distinction between them. Simmel knew Husserl,[570] corresponded with him,[571] and was acquainted with his work.[572] Although Simmel never mentioned Husserl, similarities in their thought have been found. Weingartner speculated that Simmel might "very well have been influenced by" Husserl. Backhaus noted affinities between Simmel and Husserl,[573] as did Oakes.[574] Kaern placed Simmel in "Phenomenological and Constructionist sociology,"[575] and Owsley and Backhaus viewed Simmel's historical investigations as constituting a phenomenological oriented philosophy of history.[576]

Phenomenological ideas peppered Simmel's writings. Discussing chalk marks (or ink marks) in the context of content and form, *e.g.,* Simmel noted that no matter how crude and imperfect the drawings, figures will be regarded not as mere chalk or ink marks ("appearing things") but in terms of their "essential significance" ( *i.e.,* their meaningful "appearances").[577] Simmel acknowledged this distinction via the terms he employed in the analytic separation between life's contents and the forms that shaped their meaning. Seen this way, "forms of experiencing" symbolically represent, to the experiencing subject, life's contents – not simply as they appear *qua* content, but as they are symbolically re-presented, as "appearances."

Because established sciences had already claimed much of the content of human experience, *e.g.*, political, economic and cultural life, as their own intellectual territory, Simmel believed that what remained for sociologists to study were the forms that shaped those experiences. Just as Durkheim examined the part played by societal forces in "moulding" individuals' experiences of objects and acts, namely, their "appearances" or "representations" as "sacred" or "criminal," Simmel described the social processes by which life – its contents or "appearing things" – were symbolically shaped and subsequently experienced by individuals as "appearances."[578] Clarifying Simmel's approach, Weingartner wrote, "What is represented must itself be considered apart from its being represented."[579] Said differently, the map is not the territory.

## FORMS OF EXPERIENCING AND THEIR SOCIAL ORIGINS

Simmel's conception of forms and "forms of experiencing" modified Kantian epistemology by founding all knowledge in the circumstances of social life. The source of the categories by which we know all things was not, as Kant argued, individual mind. The source was human interaction, or "sociation." The concept of "sociation" included not only reciprocity among individuals, but also shared interests, shared meanings, and unity. Sociation was "the reciprocal influence among parts producing a unity;"[580] a reciprocity that constituted society.[581]

> Sociation is the form (realized in innumerable ways)
> in which individuals grow together into a unity. . .
> [582]

By sociologizing Kantian categories, Simmel attributed to social life a task that was both epistemological and symbolic; and, by so doing, denied to individual mind the task of calling forth nature. Socially based categories, such as "forms of experiencing," shaped "appearing objects" – life's contents – into something new, into things that were more or less than the "appearing objects" themselves. Forms dictated the "appearance" of objects, made them knowable and interpretable to individuals who had achieved sociative unity (*i.e.*, were members of a discursive community). Through processes of sociation, objects were experienced as embodiments of social meanings. Moreover, societal "forms of experiencing" produced <u>shared</u>, or intersubjectively harmonious[583] unified, experiences among members of that community. Such experiences were facilitated by, and expressed through members' compatible interpretations of objects, of others, and of their own talk and actions.

> I said that, in the case of nature, the achieving of the synthetic unity is a function of the observing mind, whereas, in the case of society, that function is an aspect of society itself. To be sure, consciousness of the abstract principle that he is forming society is not present in the individual.[584]

### The Social Origins Of Societal Forms

> Society exists where a number of individuals enter into interaction.[585]

Forms, originating in interactions among members of a society, and subsequently replayed in interactions,[586] range "all the way from the momentary getting together for a 'walk' to the founding of a 'family.'"[587] Virtually unlimited in application, all aspects of the world become possible "objects of experience," as Oakes remarked, when "constituted by some form or forms."[588] Social interactions serve many purposes: religious, erotic, those expressed in marriage, friendship, play, defense, instruction, *etc.* On their own, however, interactions are not social and do not produce unity, or "sociation." To qualify as sociative, they must exhibit transformational properties as societal forms, "within which individuals grow together into a unity" and realize their interests.[589]

Sociative unity requires that the meanings of life's contents be shaped by forms, *i.e.,* given meanings, and are shared by members of a community, *i.e.,* when some measure of intersubjective agreement and harmony has been achieved. Members of a community agree on the constituted "appearances" of objects, gestures, and interactions. The raised fist shaped by the play form is not misunderstood as threatening but rather is experienced as "playful." In the context of the political demonstration, the raised fist is "resolute;" in a bar room dispute, "threatening."

SOCIOLOGY'S SUBJECT MATTER

Simmel took pains to define a <u>unique</u> subject matter for sociological inquiries, a unit of analysis that would not be subject to reductionist criticisms. Sociology's subject matter was abstract but not metaphysical. Not individualistic, it was rooted in sociations that produced a wide variety of symbolic forms that shape our experience of life's contents by adding something to them.

**Abstract, not concrete, not individual, but social**

> Sociology thus is founded upon an abstraction from
> concrete reality.[590]

Simmel's approach to sociology's subject matter did not deny a concrete reality inhabited by concrete, acting individuals – the so-called real world of "appearing things." But by insisting that individuals did not constitute sociology's subject matter, Simmel was clear: the subject matter of sociology was abstracted from, but was <u>not</u> the actual concrete behavior of individuals.

> Existence, we hear, is an exclusive attribute of individuals, their qualities and experiences. 'Society' by comparison, is an abstraction.[591]

In a critical appraisal of what might be gained from observing individuals, Simmel wrote, "We cannot determine what a person wants, thinks, and feels by observing him. On the contrary, the observable is only a bridge and a symbol."[592] He thus underscored the observable in its capacity as a sign, something standing for something else. In support of his point, Simmel suggested that we "consider how frequently our own past remains completely unintelligible to us. . ."[593] Thus, he concluded that sociology's subject matter cannot "be defined from the individual considered in isolation."[594]

Simmel further complicated sociological inquiry. "Society," he insisted (in contrast to individuals) "is no real object."[595] He likened the abstract character of the subject matter of sociology to Gothic architecture, which, he wrote, was an "intellectual phenomenon."[596] It was an abstraction, not a given reality. As with sociology, an inquiry into Gothic style is not encompassed by descriptions of particular cathedrals or palaces. The careful distinction Simmel drew between attributes of individuals and what could by analytically be <u>abstracted</u> from interactions among them was not without its critics. Weber, *e.g.,* who otherwise appreciated Simmel's approach to interpretation, took exception to his idea of interaction, noting it was too broad and abstract.[597]

**Not metaphysical.**

> The first difficulty which arises if one wants to
> make a tenable statement about the science of soci-
> ology. . . is that its claim to be a science is not un-
> disputed. [598]

The first criticism leveled at Simmel's abstract project for sociology was that it was metaphysical. Simmel, however, envisioned sociology's subject matter to be epistemological and symbolic, not metaphysical. Through bypassing individual mind, he founded the categories by which we know and experience the world in "sociation," *i.e.*, in <u>social</u> interaction and all the products of it – embodiments of socially originating meanings, not in <u>individual</u> productions and constructions. Kaern called attention to the way in which Simmel's constructionist position made him "realize that humans do not only analyze the world, they also create it."[599]

> Sociology thus emerges as the epistemology of the
> special social sciences, as the analysis and systemi-
> zation of the bases of their forms and norms.[600]

Thus it is wrong, analytically speaking, to assert individuals *qua* individuals produce categories – the societal forms – that serve to shape their experiences of the world. "Forms of experiencing," with their origins in "sociations," shape individual experience. In Oakes' assertion that "a form has both an epistemological and an ontological status" there is the suggestion that societal forms, such as conflict, marriage, play, coquetry, or adventure, <u>constitute</u> the conditions "under which the world can be experienced and conceived in a certain way. . ."[601] Some talk or act might be experienced as "hostile" when shaped by the conflict form, or as part of marital "privilege" when shaped by the marriage form, or merely "playful" when shaped by the play form. Sociology "will thus become a special science in the same sense (in spite of all obvious differences in method and result) as epistemology."[602] It is through form that life's contents attain significance and meaning, transcending particular subject matters in other social sciences.

Life's contents always unfold according to the form they occupy – and are thus experienced as "playful," "adventurous," or "threatening," Therefore, Simmel's sociological analyses were not preoccupied with descriptions of life's contents, norms, culture, *etc.* , as found in anthropology and other social sciences. Instead, he concentrated on how social life and fields of inquiry produced symbolic frameworks that shaped the meaning and significance of those contents. Sociological interest was not in the contents of secrets, play, adventures, *etc.*, but rather in an examination of the part played by societal forms in shaping society's members experience of any of life's content as secrets, play and adventures.

**Reality**

> It [life] can enter reality only in the form of its antithesis, that is, only in the form of form.[603]

The meaning of "forms of experiencing" was not fulfilled by a mere list of interactions those forms governed. No matter whether forms are conceived in terms of institutional arrangements (such as marriage or the family); or in terms of such interactions as subordination or conflict; or as "forms of experiencing," (such as adventures); much more is involved; namely, the experience of life's contents as "real," and the notion of that reality as symbolic form.[604] Simmel's examination of the epistemological implications of sociology's subject matter led to a consideration of assumptions about what is real. For those taking the world for granted – the naïve – "experience and practice is reality as such." For them, the consequence is that "the phenomena of the world exist as perceivable and manageable facts."[605] Echoing sentiments expressed by Husserl, Schutz, James, and others, Simmel hastened to add that that so-called "'real' world, however, is only one of many possible ones."[606] Different worlds, he emphasized, such as the worlds of art and religion, *e.g.*, could very well be made up of the same materials – *i.e.* contents – albeit , differently shaped in accord with <u>alternative</u> forms and different presuppositions.

Different "realities" exist for differently organized individuals with different needs. Socially constructed realities prevail because conditions of social life require different actions, *i.e.*, actions based on different considerations.[607] Schutz, expressing a similar idea, noted that different considerations produced different "interpretative schemes," "provinces of meaning,"[608] or "meaning-contexts,"[609] so that, *e.g.,* the spelling bee, the dinner party, or the drinking party invoke different considerations and different meanings. For Simmel, life's contents were <u>formed</u> in different ways and <u>meant</u> different things. The same content, *i.e.,* can take on myriad "appearances," embodying meaning or significance that is aesthetic, playful, or spiritual. Consequently, *descriptions* of images on glass buildings (discussed earlier) were not an issue for sociology; sociological interest was in the societal influences that shaped those images' significance and their being experienced as *religious* images, *art* images, or *chemically* induced images. Moreover, as Oakes pointed out, one property of forms is that they are incomparable or incommensurable, with the result that the understanding – or interpretation – employed in one (chemistry) is often inappropriate to another (religious). [610]

## Not ontological, meaning is added: sociation

How can the same material – that is, any of life's contents – be differently experienced? Simmel's answer was that forms symbolically shape life's contents, not literally but figuratively, via metaphorical <u>additions</u> to them. What is added, however, is not merely descriptive; it is transformational. In some cases, that which is added has the potential to challenge the authority of sense impressions. Experiencing subjects – in a manner suggestive of what was earlier discussed as constitutive activities – experience worlds through the influence of one or another societal form. Socially produced "objects" and "realities" are taken for granted.[611] Individuals do not usually work through the meaning of a window as this or that, but experience it – see it – directly and unquestionably as a design imperfection; or a religious image, a disruption causing highway congestion, or perhaps, nothing at all. What was added to life's contents serves to re-present "appearing things" in terms of what they signify, or stand for – their formed and mediated "appearances." Striking the same chord in his discussion of historical significance in relationship to added materials, Simmel noted that if something is important, then importance must be "ascribed" or "attached" to it, because the historian is interested in it.[612]

"Forms of experiencing" shape sense experiences, imposing on them symbolic themes and significations. Thus life's contents are experienced as embodiments of meaning. Simmel was not taken in by assurances provided by so-called evidence of the senses.

> Sense impressions, toward which we are simply receptive, are not yet knowledge, and the complex of the contents of sense impressions is not nature. On the contrary, these impressions must be given forms and connections which not inherent in them but which are imposed on them.[613]

By imposing something symbolic onto life's contents, "forms of experiencing" convincingly shape an individual's experience of those contents as "playful," "secrets," "fashionable" or not, or "adventures." Play form, *e.g.*, adds something to a raised fist that precludes its consideration as a real threat. Bateson, *e.g.*, identifying that "something" as *metanarrative*, wrote that "signals exchanged in play" make it clear that gestures "are in a certain sense untrue or not meant." [614] A cocked fist, *i.e.*, is not an authentic threat! Examples of life's contents thus rendered "untrue" are plentiful, and include not only actions and gestures in play form and in fooling around, but also talk, *e.g.*, exchanged in the "dozens" and debates. Simmel observed that play form is also exhibited in the sociology of sex: "the play-form of eroticism is coquetry," an interaction, we recognize as one in which the female is able "to stop short of a decision." [615]

Any and all of life's contents can be variously shaped by different societal forms. No necessary one-to-one relationship exists between a particular content and a particular societal form. "Forms of experiencing" provide for alternative interpretations, so that the same gesture interpreted as "threatening" due to the figurative operation of one interactive form, such as a domestic conflict, can be alternatively interpreted as "playful" in another. The same "appearing" words directed at someone else's mother, assuming an "appearance" of "playfulness" in the competitive play form "the dozens," are profoundly offensive when shaped by any another form.[616] "Appearing" objects, such as nuclear weapons, assume the "appearance" of – or are interpreted as – deterrents to warfare, on the one hand, or, on the other, as weapons of mass destruction. It seems clear from a consideration of Simmel's forms that competing interpretations of gestures as hostile or not, or sexual acts as playful or dutiful, cannot be based upon a consideration of content alone. Because content can be variously shaped, clues as to what talk, objects, and actions stand for, and their interpretation, must be sought in the form that metaphorically adds to, or imposes meaning onto, that content.

> Clearly, in either case there occurs a process which
> we inject into reality, an ex-post-facto intellectual
> *transformation* of the immediate given reality. Be-
> cause of constant habit, we achieve this almost

automatically. We almost think it is no transformation at all, but something given in the order of
things.[617]

"The forest is objectively always the same," Simmel wrote, although aspects of it – for example, significance for different groups – vary, becoming
"objects of special interest" to "a hunter, a proprietor, a poet, a painter, a civic of-
ficial, a botanist, and a tourist."[618] Even though forms metaphorically carve up
reality, Simmel cautioned, "that reality has no regard to these boundary lines."
"Forms of experiencing" shape our experience of the world, not the volcanic natural forces that alter its face. Ontology is not at issue here, and one might say of
Simmel the same thing Carrier wrote about Kenneth Burke: "He does not reject
the existence of the objective world, he just denies that we can have unmediated
access to it." [619]

> Supreme contrast between the world as content, as
> existence determined in itself -- but not apprehen-
> sible by us in its immediacy -- on the one hand,
> and, on the other, the fact that this world is never-
> theless made apprehensible in that it is articulated in
> a diversity of forms. . . [620]

SIMMEL'S FORM AND CONTENT: The Struggle Met

That we apprehend the world through a diversity of forms suggests a
situation involving both simultaneity and potential conflict. Simultaneity is impli-
cated because forms require content. Forms that are "severed from all content can
no more attain existence than a spatial form can exist without a material whose
form it is."[621] But when institutional arrangements, such as play, sociability, marriage, family, *etc.*, emerge – through sociation – as forms, conditions are ripe for
the figurative struggle between life's contents and their "appearances" (as em-

bodiments of institutional constraints).[622]

> Life as such is formless, yet incessantly generates
> forms for itself. As soon as each form appears,
> however, it demands a vitality which transcends the
> moment and is emancipated from the pulse of life.
> For this reason, life is always in a latent opposition
> to the form.[623]

Simmel often alluded to struggles between life and form, between "appearing things" and their "appearances." Articulating a "Heraclitean ontology," [624] Simmel wrote that "life as such is formless."[625] "Forms of experiencing," in opposition to formless life, necessarily achieve autonomy, are lifted out of the flux of life, and are freed of their material with its inherent gravity.[626] Life perceives form as something imposed or forced upon it.[627] This means that interactions of all types – courtship, educating, recreating, *etc.*, originally free and spontaneous – are captured in inescapable symbolic containers, and transformed by autonomous societal forms into meaningful, perhaps obligatory, dutiful institutionalized routines.[628] Accordingly, life struggles against form --striving for a return to spontaneity-- but is defeated in that struggle. Form prevails, and, moreover, has the power to present itself as truth.

> Life wishes here to obtain something which it can-
> not reach. It desires to transcend all forms to appear
> in its naked immediacy.[629]

One illustration of the struggle between life and form is the way in which free and formless productive work, when shaped by a 9 to 5 regime, comes to signify "tasks," "chores," "tedium," "duties," "responsibilities," or merely a means to some other end. Sexual activity also illustrates Simmel's point. Once free and unencumbered, it acquires myriad meanings when shaped by one or another form, and then is experienced as "adulterous," "work," "promiscuous," "amorous," "ar-

duous," "virtuous," "dutiful," "financial," "perverse," or "criminal." The outcomes of those struggles and contradictions between life and form are predictable.
Societal form trumps content.

> The forms themselves, however, deny this contra-
> diction: in their rigidly individual shapes, in the
> demands of their imprescriptible rights, they boldly
> present themselves as the true meaning and value of
> our existence.[630]

SIMMEL'S FORM AND CONTENT: Some Criticisms

> Even in sculpture the tangible piece of marble is not
> the work of art.[631]

Simmel's forms – societal forms and "forms of experiencing" – have been
subjected to various interpretations. Some writers, unfortunately, cloud both the
meaning of forms and their sociological implications. Some found too much ambiguity and too little systemization in Simmel's theory.[632] Kaerns recalled how
Stark, *e.g.,* accused Simmel of pushing a "moonshine of pure forms," in his capacity as a "tautology-monger."[633] Simmel was faulted for failing to present an
"explicit classification" of his forms, although others have done so for him.[634] The
absence of a classificatory scheme has been regarded as an omission wholly incompatible with "formal" theory.[635] These criticisms misread Simmel's intention
by presuming he was more interested in developing formal theory as a social calculus than developing sociology as an epistemology. Simmel's "formal" theory
was criticized because it neither referred to, nor was based upon, factual matters
or experience. Ironically, Simmel's "forms of experiencing," conceived constitu-
tively, do precisely that: they symbolically shape and give meaning to (thus constituting) individual experience. The criticism, of course, is based on the meaning
of experience, in the sense of "empirical," that is, in quantitative terms. It harkens

back to the belief that sociology's unit of analysis should be countable objects, and to the questions raised in the "two sociologies" debate, about experience, its interpretation, and facticity.[636]

That debate created a wide divide. One side regards objects – "appearing things" – and evidence of the senses as reliable, empirically relevant indicators of countable experiences. The other advocates a qualitative and interpretative approach. Admittedly, Simmel's "forms of experiencing" have little to do with the "experience" of raw "appearing things." They have much more to do with the societal forces that shape – or cook – those "appearing things," namely, what they mean or signify. Some clarification of what Simmel had in mind was offered by Aronowitz, who wrote, "His [Simmel's] is the attempt to articulate what life is like: not as seen, but as lived," or, said differently, as lived, experienced, and interpreted as "appearances."[637]

Arguably, Simmel's style – his "intellectual virtuosity" – led "to the interpretation that labeled it negative, destructive, and dilettantish."[638] Simmel, indeed, wrote and lectured on an astonishing variety of topics, some of which are not ordinarily included in the sociological *oeuvre*: adventures, art, actors, ruins, fashion, handles, philosophy, religion, the face, society, play, discretion, secrecy, the stranger, subordination under a variety of social circumstances, the metropolis and mental life, dyads and triads, discretion, lies, sociability, fashion, conflict, architecture and the ruin, money and value, and more. [639]His virtuosity has been regarded as an indication of unsystematic thought, producing "fragmentary and incomplete materials."[640] It has also been interpreted as indicating a lack of commitment, or, even worse, as an expression of escapism. Frisby, *e.g.* likened Simmel to a *Flaneur*, pejoratively characterizing him as a retreatist, or escapist.

But not all of his interpreters agree. In Simmel's defense, Spykman wrote that characterizations of Simmel's work as "fragmentary" were unfair. They misrepresented Simmel's "great volume on sociology," *e.g.,* in which he explicitly set out to illustrate different applications of "its methods to different phenomena within the field."[641] Simmel often intended, *i.e.,* to be more illustrative than systematic. Sorokin's dismissal of Simmel's forms as total failures (noted earlier) was characterized by Tenbruck as "hasty."[642] Weinstein and Weinstein, and other writers, defended Simmel's virtuosity.[643] Some went so far as to lament the fact that his wide-ranging interests, expressed in what was termed an impressionistic sociology, were not well represented in American sociology.[644]

SIMMEL'S FORM AND CONTENT: Disassembled

In a typical analysis, Simmel would disassemble sociological phenomena "by scientific abstraction" into two qualitative factors that he termed form and content.[645] Some topics he examined in this way were secrecy,[646] general (social) types[647] play,[648] the adventure,[649] super-ordination,[650] the stranger,[651] fashion,[652] *etc.* With this approach, he set aside exclusive concern for descriptions of the contents of play, secrets, or adventures in order to examine their properties as societal forms. Sociological interest in a smile, *i.e.,* how one interprets and then acts toward another's smile, is not limited to physical descriptions: how far lips were pulled back over teeth, how much of the teeth or gum line showed, or how eyes crinkled and sparkled. Shaped by one or another form, smiles might signify (and thus inform) a variety of interpretations: joy, subordination, sweet revenge, irony, or the sale of a used car. While the physical description of it might not change, what the smile *stands for*, and how the smile is interpreted, are variously shaped by something added to crinkled eyes and bare teeth. The smile of a subordinate means something different from a mother's smile, the smile of the winner of the spelling bee, or the smile of a lover. Consider how the well-intended smile of someone sitting across the table with remnants of food between his teeth or on his beard is usually experienced, simply, as disgusting![653]

In several places, Simmel illustrated how form shaped content with the use of examples from geometry.[654] Cubes, *e.g.*, can be examined in two ways, formally or concretely. When considered formally, cubes can be differentiated from spheres, squares, triangles, and circles, each having different geometric properties. Considered concretely, cubes can be composed of very different materials, such as wood, ivory, clay, water, aluminum, *etc.* When materials are formed into cubes, they become wooden, ivory, or clay dice, just as water, when frozen, is shaped into ice cubes. These materials, when shaped into spheres, become more or less successful bowling balls. In any of their concrete representations – shaped by the cube form – something is added to otherwise shapeless pieces of wood, hunks of clay, ivory, or water, by configuring them into six sided figures that are then used as six sided dice or ice cubes.

Similarly, societal forms figuratively add something to life's contents, shaping their "appearances," *i.e.,* one's experience of the raised hand as "friendly" or "threatening." But whereas physical materials are more easily grasped in their transformations by geometrical forms such as cubes, the symbolic shaping of life's contents by societal forms is less transparent. The application of Simmel's distinction between form and content does, however, illuminate some otherwise puzzling aspects of social life. Why, *e.g.*, hostile, threatening actions or gestures – such as raised fists – are not experienced as threatening in play settings. Or, why the contents of sex acts are variously experienced as "duty," "boring," "adventurous," "rape," "financial transactions," or "work."[655] Or why bits of information (content, again) that are commonplace in one context become secrets in another. Form also impacts fashion, as Simmel observed, women who would not likely wear low-cut dresses at "an intimate personal and friendly meeting with one or several men," would do so "without any embarrassment at a larger party."[656] The difference between their selection of an "appearing thing," such as a low-cut dress, is linked to the form that shapes its <u>meaning</u>, its different "appearances" in each situation.

## SIMMEL'S FORM AND CONTENT: Examples

It was Simmel's gift to us that he not only conceptualized the part played by social life (through forms and "forms of experiencing") in the production of differences between "appearing things" and their "appearances," but he also <u>applied</u> systematically that abstract conceptual system of thought in analyses of sociological phenomena. The following sections illuminate how different "forms of experiencing" shape life's contents ("appearing things") into the "appearance" of "adventures," "secrets," "strangers," and "general types."

### The Adventure

> Itself is a specific organization of some significant meaning.[657]

The adventure, Simmel wrote, "in its specific nature and charm," is a "form of experiencing."[658] It is not <u>produced</u> by life's contents, nor does it "consist in a substance which is won or lost, enjoyed or endured."[659] Content is seized as a component of the adventure because the "form of experiencing" transforms the meaning of "mere experience into adventure."[660] With this departure from common sense, Simmel emphasized an adventure's formal properties – not "formal" in the sense of a calculus, but as a "form of experiencing." He opposed the view that life's contents, for example: moguls, river rapids, party favors, drugs, beer, or people, determined adventures. The experience of an adventurous dinner, *e.g,* does not consist in food consumed and enjoyed (or the size of the bill); an adventurous courtship does not consist in a person won; an adventurous ski run does not consist in moguls enjoyed or endured; and a climbing adventure does not consist in trials endured on the mountain. Contents depend upon societal "forms" to transform them symbolically into secrets, play, or adventures.[661]

Curiously, on the one hand, any of life's content can be symbolically shaped to stand for, and subsequently be experienced, as an adventure. On the other, even so-called high-risk activities do not, on their own, constitute adventures. A trek up the mountain or a float through the river rapids might be adventurous, but each, regarded through the prism of a different form, could also be experienced as necessitous work, boring, merely a game, or frightening. Adventures are not necessarily risky. They are neither physically nor pharmaceutically produced solely because of associated adrenaline rushes, alcohol, or drug euphoria. While altered states can accompany – or even promote – symbolic transformations of life's contents into adventures, those adventures do not consist simply in enduring or consuming the intoxicant. Because form shapes content by adding something symbolic to it, any and all of life's content is potentially adventurous. At the same time, it is potentially a religious experience, an educative experience, self-growth experience, an aesthetic experience, or an experience to scare one out of one's wits.

Simmel's analysis of the adventure advanced the essential distinction between content and form, between things that "appear" and our experience of them – their meaning – as adventures. The transformational properties of "forms of experience" shape interpretations of life's content as adventurous or not because the elements of adventure, Simmel said, "in some measure reside in everything."[662] All of life's contents are potentially adventurous. Just as hunks of ivory are shapeless and not dice until they are cubed, life's contents – amusement park rides and attractions, floating the rapids, visiting a supermarket, sex acts, rain delays, mountain climbing, washing dishes or even bathrooms – are not adventures until they have been symbolically shaped. Sexual acts, *e.g.*, are symbolically shaped adventures in the case of seduction, which Simmel termed the quintessential adventure. But, in writing "a love affair, even if short-lived, is by no means always an adventure," he intimated something had be added to life's content to shape it adventurous.[663] Bear in mind that any form, according to Simmel, "can be taken on by an undetermined number of experiences;" and, by the same token, "the meaning of no single part of life is exhausted by its belonging in that context."[664] Even though we generally understand sexual adventures in terms of erotic experiences, the same physical acts can also be symbolically shaped and experienced as economic transactions, necessitous work as in the case of the working prostitute, duty, promiscuity, sin, or play. Finally, in a creative stretch of the imagination, Borges reported a fictional anthropological account of a tribal elder who interpreted both copulation and mirrors as abominations, "because they increase the number of men."[665]

Simmel abstracted formal properties from particular adventures. As one of "the great forms in which we shape the substance of life," the adventure synthesizes, compromises, and antagonizes "life's fundamental categories."[666] He represented those formal, fundamental, and abstract categories in terms of three oppositional pairs: activity-passivity, chance-necessity, and certainty-uncertainty. Adventuring unfolds as the adventurer antagonizes goals by figuratively setting one content against another. This is made possible by symbolically representing life's content as goals, the certain attainment of which (for example, successfully negotiating the rapids in one canyon) is symbolically juxtaposed or set against the uncertain passage through the rapids in the next canyon. Juxtaposing uncertain goals (goals that have yet to be attained) and the certainty of goals already attained constitutes adventuring, whatever the content. Contrariwise, to attain a goal without defining another, uncertain one, ends the adventure.

Adventures are also constituted by form when life's contents, symbolically represented as goals, are <u>compromised</u>, *e.g.,* when adventurers change goals in face of <u>chance</u> events that present obstacles, *e.g.* Goals then are either redefined downward – the adventurer will settle for less – or redefined upwards into the realm of uncertainty. An unexpected snowstorm requires climbers to camp at a lower elevation than planned, settling for the attainment of a less desirable goal.

<u>Synthesizing</u> is different from compromising. Synthesizing entails the symbolic blending of life's contents by incorporating <u>chance</u> events into the central and <u>necessitous</u> meaning of a socially governed activity. Here Simmel introduced the idea of passivity-activity, one of life's fundamental categories, to distinguish between events that conquer us and those that we conquer. With the dualism, chance-necessity, Simmel established symbolic boundaries around social activities by sorting life's content into two categories: whether they are necessitous – central and essential to social definitions of the activity – or exogenous, exemplified by such content as the rain delay at the outdoor concert or ball game, an ant invasion at the picnic, a lost child at the beach, or lightning on the golf course.

With that abstract conceptual scheme in hand, Simmel analytically disassembled a sociological adventure into two parts: a "form of experiencing" and <u>content</u>. Just as design makes the use of the material it shapes more important than the material itself, so the "form of experiencing" symbolically shapes life's contents into an adventure. Briefly, a Simmelian adventure entails juxtaposing, or antagonizing goals (re-presentations of life's content) that are more or less certain of attainment into conquerable opportunities or obstacles that are not; meanwhile synthesizing what is central and necessitous to a socially defined activity with what is peripheral to it. [667]

178

## Secrets

Although secrets always have some sort of content, no laundry list, no matter how complete, can reveal the properties of secrets. The reason is that any aspect of life's content – running the gamut from the trivial to the profound – is potentially a secret. "For Simmel," Helle observed, "the secret is first and foremost the activity of keeping a secret."[668] Some people keep secret their age, their weight, religion, food preferences, sexual experience (or the lack thereof), sexual preference, incompetence, preparation or lack thereof, criminal or bad habits, or race; some manage to hide their inability to read and write, making their illiteracy a secret; and some keep their marital status (in a singles bar) a secret.

Clearly nothing about life's content on its own qualifies it as a "secret." The essentially social character of secrets is illustrated by an aphorism attributed to Benjamin Franklin: three, he said, can keep a secret, if two of them are dead. Simmel's more stringent variation on that theme was that "a secret that two know is no longer a secret."[669] The potential for life's content to serve as a "secret" is realized in interaction, not the character of the content. For Simmel, descriptions of the contents of secrets altogether miss the mark. It was not the "appearing thing," such as the infidelity, the inability to read or write, or the alcoholism, *e.g.*, that constitute the secrets, but rather, the secret form that shaped it.[670]

## The Stranger

To emphasize his interest in leaving psychological and descriptive concerns behind, Simmel conceived "the stranger," not only as a social type, but also, and more significantly, as a "specific form of interaction."[671] Disavowing any dependence on personal characteristics in an analysis of strangers, Simmel wrote that "strangers are not really conceived as individuals, but as strangers of a particular type."[672] Notwithstanding racial, sex, or ethnic differences among participants in interactions, "strangers," considered from a sociological viewpoint, are not individuals with particular "appearing" attributes. Rather they are participants in social interactions whose "appearances" are symbolically formed to reveal consistent properties *qua* strangers.

Mistakenly, some substantive treatments of Simmel's general types, particularly the "stranger," stress individual characteristics.[673] Personal attributes, however, do not constitute "strangers" any more than the contents of secrets make "secrets." Societal form qualifies individuals – whatever their personal attributes – for the interactional benefits and disadvantages enjoyed by strangers. Benefits include objectivity and freedom, nearness and remoteness, and an unusual degree of openness from others.[674] "Strangers," Simmel wrote, belong to the group at the same time they are beyond it, partly outside, but also confronting it; they synthesize nearness and distance, and because of their objective "appearance," they receive confidences not otherwise shared among members of the group. The "stranger" is "not tied down in his action by habit, piety, and precedent."[675] It bears repeating that benefits do not accrue because of personal characteristics. Instead, the "stranger," an interactional general type, is constituted by the form that symbolically shapes any configuration of personal attributes. One only need recall the Western film cliché, delivered from one look-alike cowboy to another, "New in town, stranger?"

GENERAL TYPES

"Forms of experiencing" not only contain meanings that institutionalize interactions, they figuratively transform the contents of interactions into what experiencing subject consider "real." And not only real, but "unquestionably plausible," as Schutz pointed out.[676] Perhaps surprisingly, social objects, others, whom we encounter and cast into <u>types</u>, are no exception to the influence of symbolic transformations. Something is figuratively <u>added</u> to them.

Our experience of others – how we see them (and ourselves, for that matter) – is not simply a product of raw sense experience. Others are <u>first</u> classified according to a general type, and <u>then</u> meanings accompanying that general type-form are figuratively added to what they say and do. Thus do we "know" others, who Simmel maintained, are experienced by us not *qua* individuals, but as general types. Expressed differently, "appearing things" – others – are figuratively and symbolically transformed into interpretative characters. Then, the meanings of what individuals *qua* types say and do take on "appearances" – are interpretable as, and come to stand for, the typical talk and actions of a general type. "Seen" in light of their symbolic "appearances" – so-called interpretative characters – individuals *qua* types assume the patina of truth and reality. Every glimpse of their talk, behavior, and gestures bears meaning contained in the type, in the sense that Husserl employed "meaning more." Just as <u>two dots</u> on landed dice mean something more than what is meant in the moment, namely, that roll means that "I lose," the "meaning more" of tears, frowns, raised hands of "friends," are experienced as friendly, while those of "foes" are experienced as fake, or threatening.

Some general types are based on physical attributes, such as epilepsy, age, height, hair color, or handedness. What those physical attributes signify or mean is socially produced. Consider the general social type based upon physical evidence of epileptic seizure; historically, afflicted individuals have been variously cast as "possessed," "spiritual," "holy," or "ill." Other general types are associated with social attributes, such as wealth, sex, gender, and power. Even generational membership has been typed: yuppies, baby-boomers, X-ers and Y-ers. Whether types are founded on social or physical attributes, general typing <u>fills out</u>

limited perceptions of whole individuals, and successfully shapes their "appearances" as interactional participants and interpretative characters. The map is not the territory, however, and through those symbolic representations (or "appearances"), one might agree with Simmel that "man distorts the picture of another."[677]

In classrooms, doctors' offices, church, *etc.* , societal forms produce a cast of likely interpretative characters. Due to typing, interpretations of others are <u>not</u> necessarily dependent on their personal attributes – as "appearing things." Because our experiences of others are shaped by "appearances," *i.e.,* as products of typing, general types call attention to a curious kind of objectification. Individuals are not seen, heard, or "grasped" according to their whole individuality, but, instead, according to type.[678] Literally, the authority of sense experience of others is diminished by general typing: sense experience is subordinate to form.

> In order to know a man, we see him not in terms of his pure individuality, but carried, lifted up or lowered, by the general type under which we classify him.[679]

If individuals are not "seen" in terms of their individuality (*i.e.*, not apprehended as "appearing things" in light of individual attributes, but are instead either "lifted up" or "lowered" into "appearances" determined by a general type), then it follows that interactions with them are based upon something more than sense impressions alone. General-typing, consistent with the place of forms in social life, <u>adds</u> something of consequence: individuals are constituted not *qua* individuals but as types. Typing adds to sense impressions a symbolic framework that represents their talk and actions as if that talk and action were the talk and action of particular (and figurative) general types. General typing is an efficacious interpretative framework within which the talk and actions of individuals <u>stand for</u>

182

something <u>else</u>. "The mind," Kaern wrote in his discussion of typifications, "works independent of external reality . . . in its capacity to treat the objects to be known-and-discovered [things as well as people] as-if they were what they are not."[680] Simmel elucidated this concept: symbolic representations of individuals' talk and actions figuratively <u>raise</u> or <u>lower</u> their "pure individuality."

Because of the *metanarrative* associated with a particular general type, the talk and actions of another is experienced as "playful" or "secretive," his or her smile is an act of "subordination" or "insubordination." General typing helps answer the question of why, on the one hand, the actions of someone who is interpreted as a general typed "good person" are figuratively <u>raised up</u> and seen as "good" actions, and her criticisms as "friendly" and "helpful," while, on the other hand, similar talk and actions of someone else, who is interpreted as a general typed "bad person," are <u>lowered,</u> and then seen as "troublesome" or "damaging." To figuratively "raise up" or "lower down" suggests that something rather insistent is facilitating a reconciliation between the interpretative character and her talk and actions. Family squabbles among siblings, lovers' quarrels, marital partners' arguments as to what the in-laws are up to, and our colleagues' comments at faculty meetings all illustrate typical situations in which talk and actions are "seen" and "heard" in support of different and prefigured interpretative characterizations.

What is remarkable about interpretative characterizations is how they persist in face of evidence to the contrary. The FBI, *e.g.*, over the course of several years, targeted the wrong man, their own agent Brian Kelley, as a spy for Russia. (CBS Broadcasting Inc. 2002) To prove Kelley's guilt, his accusers administered a lie-detector test. Kelley passed "with flying colors." Instead of accepting the test results as evidence of his innocence, his accusers interpreted them in the context of his alleged interpretative character saying, "He's the ice man. He's the perfect spy. He can beat the polygraph." Next, they mounted a "flag operation," in which an FBI agent appeared at Kelley's home pretending to be a Russian intelligence officer with an offer to help him leave the U.S.A., safely, with a passport and money. Even though Kelley reported that visit to his superiors (who had set up the operation), his report did not establish his innocence. Again his accusers said. "Oh, my God, he's perfect. He's a brilliant spy. He knew it was a ruse." Then, Kelley was called in for an interview and confronted with "evidence" of which he knew nothing – his supposed KGB code name. His innocent countenance, however, was interpreted as evidence of how "perfect" a spy he was, so well trained in skillful denial.

Then he was shown a map of a park in which document exchanges – "drops" – were made with the Russians. It turned out to be a map he had once used to sketch his jogging routes through the park. Fifth, a tape recording of a spy talking to his Russian handler surfaced. When his accusers listened to it, allegedly someone who knew Kelley said it was clearly not Kelley's voice. But, "he's too smart to place the call himself." More than two years later the real spy, a mole, was taken into custody and Kelley was fully exonerated.

Examples of how typing informs interpretations overrun everyday life. Not uncommonly, around the dinner table, the "meaning more" of actions of a general typed "good" sibling – the youngest? – are typically experienced and interpreted by the parents as "good," while the actions of a "troublesome" sibling, are "bad;" at a department meeting, points made by a colleague wearing the interpretative mantle of "friendly" team player type, are "important, significant and telling," while similar points made by non team players are "trivial and repetitive." General typing adds meaning to the content of interactions just as other societal forms shape life's contents into secrets and adventures: when threatening actions are interpreted as acts of play, when smiles symbolize and are interpreted as subordinate acts, and when actions are interpreted as acts of lovers.

General typing typically transforms our experience of individuals into symbolically laden interpretative characters. Each of us creates an Other, Kaern noted, "out of the empirical bits and pieces that he know of him," but not as-if he were those bits and pieces.[681] We make a whole out of him by subordinating him under a type. Simmel's approach to societal forms in general, and general types in particular, contravened common sense by asserting that individuals' talk, actions, and gestures were not first "seen" or heard (*i.e.*, as items of sense experience) and then judged or interpreted as such. He proposed something different: the talk and actions of others are "seen" according to how their talk and actions were first "lifted up" or "lowered" by an interpretative framework, *i.e.*, by the general type.[682]

Common sense often confuses "appearing things" and their "appearances," when words and actions, *e.g.,* are regarded as intrinsically "good," "bad," "impolitic," or "rude." "Rude" actions lead to judgments that the actor is a "rude" person, while "kind" actions lead to judgments of the actor as a "kind" person. To take actions and talk for granted presumes the "appearing thing" is unquestionably plausible and, in no way – or, at best, in a very limited way – enhanced by socially inspired typing associated with interpretative characterizations.

Types and their meanings reside in the public domain, readily available for both imputations and adoptions, and general types are plentiful. Klapp listed more than 800 types and interpretative characters.[683] In the single category of "villains," he found: desperado, rebel, flouter, rogue, troublemaker, oppressor, authoritarian, selfish, grabber, intruder, monster, sneak, and traitor.

Typing is useful and valuable insofar as individuals who lack personal experience about particular "appearances," namely, how to interact with particular types, find guidance in the subculture's stock of social knowledge, and act in relatively smooth fashion towards dentists, police, and teachers upon encountering them for the first time. Hoboes negotiated a world of relative strangers with guidance about social types found in hobo signs.[684] Individuals can find guidance about how to carry on as a particular type, *e.g.* adopt the characteristics of a type into which they have been fitted as if into a shell. Such imputational guidance is also found in a subculture's stock of social knowledge, films, TV, and novels. Davies, *e.g.*, described how a young lawyer dipped into fiction for details on his profession:

> Actors deficient in observation and resource adopted this stock character of the lawyer, and he was to be seen in hundreds of plays. And Matthew Snelgrove, whose professional and personal character was being formed about the turn of the century, seized upon this lawyer-like shell eagerly, and made it his own. Through the years he perfected his impersonation until . . . he was not only a lawyer in reality, but also a lawyer in a score of stagey mannerisms . . . Mr. Snelgrove had become the prisoner of a professional manner . . .[685]

The practical usefulness of knowledge about general types is shown in the following account of how effectively typing contributes to smoothing out some rather complicated transactions in everyday life. Anyone caught up in pedestrian traffic in a large city will recognize the usefulness of the following guidance on crossing intersections in NYC:

> You are a biker, a blader, or a pedestrian. You must remain true to type, because all the people with whom are intersecting are making calculations based on the standard intersection behavior exhibited by your type. New Yorkers know that a man riding a bicycle for work --the dreadlocked deliv-

ery-man in the Day-Glo lycra and wraparound
shades--is going to behave differently from a man
riding a bicycle to work, like Mr. Businessman over
there, with his cuffs nearly gartered in metal ankle
clips. The guy pushing a rack of clothes (a moving
obstacle indigenous to the garment district) is going
to keep pushing --head down, hardly looking, hur-
rying restlessly through the jammed traffic-all the
way through the jammed traffic--all the way
through the intersection, and you can plot your
course accordingly.[686]

In his effort to de-individualize and de-psychologize sociology's subject
matter, Simmel recommended the study of forms and "forms of experiencing."
His effort made individual experience interpretatively accessible by objectifying
the societal forces that help individuals make sense of (interpret) not things themselves – *i.e.,* life's raw contents – but their "appearances." Why chads, for example, are experienced as "pregnant" or "hanging." "Appearing" life's contents,
on their own, *e.g.,* are neither dull nor adventurous. Their "appearance" as adventures is shaped by "forms of experiencing" – symbolic transformations, or the
figurative rendering of those contents. Simmel conceived of "forms of experiencing" as symbolic forces rooted and replayed in sociation, namely, in the circumstances of social life.

Of sociological interest – in terms of the interpretative refrain set forth by
Simmel – were not "counselors'" contradictory raw "yes" or "no" replies to questions, but what those replies meant to students in the social context of university
counseling sessions – their "appearances." Similarly, what smiles mean in this or
that context, that is, their interpretations as expressions of love or subordination;
why gestures appear to be threatening in a moment of hostility, but not in play;
and the way general typing adds something to our sense experience of others, so
as to guide and shape our interpretations of what they say and do. With the con-

cept of societal "forms of experiencing," Simmel substituted objective interpretative schemes for subjective ones, freeing meanings from their dependence on purely subjective individualistic factors and from *Verstehen,* with its reliance on individual motives and intentions.[687]

---

[1] Garfinkel, *Studies in Ethnomethodology,* pp. 76-103

[2] Ibid., p. 80

[3] Ibid., p. 89

[4] Ibid., p. 91

[5] Ibid., p. 92

[6] Bourdieu, *The Logic of Practice,* p. 53.

[7] Pressler and Dasilva (1996:6-7) listed different "interpretative" projects. In addition to texts, reproductive interpretation "such as in the reproductive performance of a piece of music or a play, and pragmatic interpretation, as is found in the application of a general law to a specific case."

[8] According to Palmer (1969:7) the "deciphering" process is the focus of hermeneutics. The relationship between hermeneutics and sociology are discussed in Wolff (1991). See, also Pressler and Dasilva (1996).

[9] Since then, hermeneutics, as Palmer pointed out (1969:33), developed along six different lines. He termed them biblical exegesis, philological, scientific, geisteswissenschaftliche, existential and cultural. Geisteswissenschaftliche refers to the discipline devoted to the understanding of the arts. Human actions and writings.

[10] Oakes, in his "Introduction" (Simmel 1980:3-92), presented an extensive review of interpretations, particularly Simmel's approach to the variety of interpretations in the arts, music, painting, theater, etc., which, Oakes noted, is an "aspect of Simmel's hermeneutic" and consequence of Simmels "theory of forms (Simmel 1980:74).

[11] Schutz, (1971:61)

[12] American Record Guide, p.22.

[13] See, Simmel (1980), for Oakes discussion of Simmelian interpretations in the context of music performances, acting, etc..

[14] Pareto, *The Mind and Science, Vol. I: Non-Logical Conduct,* pp. 329-330.

[15] Peterson, "Discourse and Display: the Modern Eye, Entrepreneurship and the Cultural Transformation of the Patchwork Quilt," pp. 461-490.

[16] Tobin and Dobard, *Hidden in Plain View, a Secret Story of Quilts and the Underground Railroad.*

[17] Barthes, *Mythologies,* p. 19.

188

There are, of course, other interpretations of Barthes essays. See, *e.g.*, Berman 1988:147-148).
In the cultural arena sociologists have been well represented by Denzin's film interpretations (*e.g.*, 1989; 1991; 1993).

[19] Wittgenstein (1970:29e) speculated about a man without acquaintance with music who, upon hearing someone playing a reflective piece of Chopin, "is convinced that this a language and people merely want to keep the meaning secret from him"?

[20] Laffey, "Inside Dope: Scenes from the Life of an Officer on the Narcotics Beat," p. 30.

[21] Robertson, "20th Century American Art: The Ellsworth Collection," p. 216.

[22] Gadamer, *Truth and Method*, p. 158.

[23] Hirsch, *Validity in Interpretation*.

[24] Sontag, *Against Interpretation*, p. 6.
In a similar vein, Hirsch's (1967) argued that an author's intentions were the norm for clarification of the meaning of a text.

[25] Sontag, *Against Interpretation*, pp. 6-7.

[26] Sontag, *Against Interpretation*, p. 8. They are interpretations based on social allegory, psychoanalytic allegory (fear of father) and third, religious allegory.

[27] Gadamer, *Truth and Method*, p. 42.

[28] Ronen, "The Real as Limit to Interpretation," p. 122-123.

[29] Ibid., p. 123.

[30] Debunking was followed by efforts to limit interpretations, as found, *e.g.*, in loyalty oaths taken by priests: "I accept without equivocation the doctrinal content of the faith as passed downh in unbroken sequence from the apostles through the orthodox fathers, always with the same meaning and the very same interpretation of that meaning...."

[31] Debunking was followed by efforts to limit interpretations, as found, *e.g.*, in loyalty oaths taken by priests: "I accept without equivocation the doctrinal content of the faith as passed down in unbroken sequence from the apostles through the orthodox fathers, always with the same meaning and the very same interpretation of that meaning...."

[32] Pareto, *The Mind and Society, Vol. I: Non-Logical Conduct*, pp. 208-209.

[33] Goldberg , *Bias*, p. 5.
As is shown in later chapters, many sociologists questioned the independence, suggested by Goldberg's quote, between sense experience and discourse.

[34] Ricoeur, *Freud and Philosophy: An Essay on Interpretation*, p. 33.

[35] Ricoeur (1970:5-6) distinguished between dream images and what the dreamer says about them: "it is not the dream as dreamed that can be interpreted, but rather text of the dream account."

[36] "Hidden," "inaccessible" or "proper" more concisely stated as "inaccessible to the consciousness of the dreamer" or "unconscious" (Freud 1943:102). Hidden feelings and thoughts have to be flushed from the unconscious with the aid of free association, dream analysis and other psychoanalytic techniques developed by Freud and others. 'Interpretation' means discovering a hidden meaning " (Freud 1943:78).

[37] Freud, *Interpretation of Dreams*, p. 3.

[38] Freud, *A General Introduction to Psychoanalysis*, pp. 136-139.

[39] Freud, *Interpretation of Dreams*, p. 12.

[40] Wittgenstein, *Lecture & Conversations on Aesthetics, Psychology, and Religious Belief*, p. 43.

[41] Freud, *An Outline of Psychoanalysis*, p. 49.

[42] In later chapters that difference is referred to as "appearing objects" and the appearance" they take.

[43] Freud, *A General Introduction to Psychoanalysis*, p. 101.

[44] Freud, *Psychopathology of Everyday Life*, p. 63.

[45] Ibid., p. 95.

[46] Marx, *Points on the Modern State and Civil Society*, pp. 399-402.

[47] Remmling, *Road to Suspicion: A Study of Modern mentality and the Sociology of Knowledge*, p. 145.

[48] Levy, *Realism: An Essay in Interpretation and Social Reality*, p. 72.

[49] Marx, *Writings of the Young Marx on Philosophy and Society*, p. 404.

[50] Ibid., p. 409.

[51] Ibid., p. 409.

[52] Ibid., p. 409, 414.

[53] Remmling, *Road to Suspicion: A Study of Modern mentality and the Sociology of Knowledge*, p. 184. My emphasis.

[54] Marx, *A Contribution to the Critique of Political Economy*, p. 11.

[55] Durkheim, *The Elementary Forms of the Religious Life*, p. 62.

[56] Popular music examined as early as 1941 by Adorno (1941).

[57] Personal computers and CD burning has threatened this control.

[58] Marx, *A Contribution to the Critique of Political Economy*, p. 11.

[59] Merton, *Social Theory and Social Structure*, p. 73.

[60] See, Radcliffe-Brown (1952) and Smith (1894) for examples of anthropological "functionalism.'

[61] Turner (1974) traced functionalism from the organismic analogy, through anthropological influences to Parsons (1968) and Merton (1968).

[62] Malinowski, *A Scientific Theory of Culture and Other Essays*, p.168.

[63] Ibid., p. 83.

[64] Weber, *The Theory of Social and Economic Organization*, p. 102.

[65] Ibid., p. 103.

[66] But even then, Weber conceded that "This is only the beginning of sociological analysis as here understood" (1964:103).

[67] Giddens, *New Rules of Sociological Method: A Positive Critique of Interpretative Sociologies*, p.113.

68 See Swingewood (1991) for a discussion of the history of functionalism in terms of functional systemic unities.

[69] Malinowski, *A Scientific Theory of Culture and Other Essays*, p. 168.

[70] Frazer, *The New Golden Bough*, p. 602.

[71] Service, *A Profile of Primitive Culture*, p. 17.

[72] Frazer, *The New Golden Bough*, p. 479.

[73] Ibid., pp. 463 – 466.
See Fernandez-Armesto (2002) for some accounts of contemporary cannibalism.

[74] Service, *A Profile of Primitive Culture*, p. 256.

[75] See Fernandez-Armesto (2002) for some accounts of contemporary cannibalism.

[76] See, James Pritchard (1973)..

[77] Durkheim, *The Elementary Forms of the religious Life*, p. 484.
The opposite sentiment is expressed by Ogden Nash, in poem that begins:
> The more I grow less young,
> The more I grow bewildered by my mother tongue.
> There are words that bring me up short, subpoena-like,
> Because they look different but they turnout to mean alike
> (Nash 1962:159).

[78] Train, *Valsalva's Maneuver: Mots Justes and Indispensable Terms.*

[79] Dated meanings in the English language appear in the Oxford Dictionary.

[80] The three streams of interpretative social theory (or their roots) are noted by Giddens (1976:23-24): (1) Weber's *Verstehen* (subjectively meaningful action) stems from Geisteswissenshaften,

hermeneutics, 18th century philosophy, an interpretative sociology, emphasizing the differences between physical and social sciences. (2) later Wittgenstein, Winch and others in social science (3) Phenomenology, centrally through Schutz and Husserl, the former also indebted to Weber. Garfinkel joins Schutz and Wittgenstein.

[81] Giddens, *New Rules of Sociologica method: a Positive Critique of Interpretative Sociologies,* p. 23.

[82] Brown, "Symbolic Realism and Sociological Thought: Beyond the Positivistic-Romantic Debate," p. 38.

[83] Interpretation and interpretative theory played a part in several of their disagreements.

[84] Simmel, "The Field of Sociology," p. 4.
Detailed discussions of the emergence and development of sociological theory are found in Turner and Beeghley (1981). Sociology's origins have been open to a variety of interpretations. Recently, Burawoy (2004:103) wrote "In its origins, sociology was stimulated by moral commitment. Thus, Marx, Weber, and Durkheim were all driven by an appraisal of the malaise of modernity...."

[85] This not to say that sociology has established a firm claim. Watson (2000), *e.g.,* reviewing interpretive sociology in sociology, characterized interpretation as peripheral to a discipline that is still marginal.

[86] Durkheim, Simmel, and Weber are usually referred to the founders of modern sociology, while Plato and Aristotle lay claim as the so-called fathers of the science of society. Comte, as noted elsewhere, coined the word "sociology" circa 1839.

[87] Durkheim, *The Rules of the Sociological Method,* p. 38.

[88] Weber, *Rational and social Foundations of Music,* p. 68.

[89] In his earlier writings, *e.g.,* The Rules, Durkheim, as Mestrovic (1989) suggested, tended to criticize Kantian positivistic doctrines.

[90] Simmel's debt to Kant is discussed in Wolff (1974:35-36).

[91] Lukes (1973: 235) wrote: "Durkheim had by the time of his latest writing come very close to maintaining that symbolic thought is a condition of and explains society."

[92] Durkheim, *The Rules of the Sociological Method,* p. 13.

[93] Dukheim, *Sociology and Philosophy,* p. 26.

[94] The ways Simmel employed "forms" are discussed in Levine (1959); distinctions between content and forms, in Weingartner (1959).

[95] Simmel, "The Field of Sociology," p. 13.

[96] Lichtblau (1991) discussed theoretical links between Weber and Simmel.

[97] The collectivist/individualist dispute is still carried on, see Berger 2003.

[98] Eldridge, *Max Weber: The Interpretation of Social Reality,* p. 25.
For more on Weber's "entirely negative" view of Durkheim's The Rules, see Segre (1986-87). For a comparison of their methods, see Morrison (1998).

[99] Sociology's departure from conceptual reliance on individuals as units of analysis has been met with more than moderate skepticism, prompting Douglas to observe that while "every thinking sociologist agrees...in principle" that "reality is socially constructed," the question remains "but how far dare they follow it? (Douglas 1973:9-10).

[100] Gerth and Mills, *From Max Weber: Essays in Sociology,* p. 55.

[101] Some writers (Maguire 1983) believe that sociology, especially the "interpretive sociologies" have neglected the study of individuals as active agents. Others, such as Denzin (1986) argue that aspects of the domain of "critical interpretive sociology" is best achieved through analyses of the arts, biographies, *etc.*

[102] Corning, "Durkheim and Spencer," p. 337.

[103] Post, "Floyd Allport and the Launching of Modern Social Psychology."

[104] Douglas, *How Institutions Think,* p. 10.

[105] Lukes, *Emile Durkheim: His Life and Work. A Historical and Critical Study,* p. 314.

[106] This is not to say that Durkheim has not been without defenders. Some counter arguments are presented in Chapter X, below.

[107] Durkheim, *The Rules of the Sociological Method*, p. 103, and *Sociology and Philosophy*, p. 17.

[108] Lukes, *Emile Durkheim: His Life and Work. A Historical and Critical Study*, p. 314.

[109] Ibid., p. 52.

[110] Durkheim, *The Rules of the Sociological Method*, p. 34.

[111] Simmel, "The Field of Sociology," p. 13.

[112] Ibid., p. 24.

[113] Sorokin, *Contemporary Sociological Theories*, p. 501.

[114] Another view of Simmel's contributions in found in Levine, *et al.*, (1976a; 1976b).

[115] Oakes, *Essays on Interpretation in Social Science*, p. 10.

[116] Levine, "The Structure of Simmel's Thought," p. 19.

[117] Simmel, "The Field of Sociology," p. 4.

[118] An argument has been made for a third approach in sociology, the historical.

[119] Lundberg, "The Postulates of Science and Their Implications for Sociology," p. 45.

[120] Weber, *The Theory of Social and Economic Organization*, p. 74.

[121] Glassner and Moreno, *The Qualitative-Quantitative Distinction in the Social Sciences*.

[122] Brown, "Symbolic Realism and sociological Thought: Beyond the Postivistic-Romantic Debate," p. 16.

[123] Haritos and Glassman, "Emile Durkheim and the Sociological Enterprise," p. 72.

[124] It should not be overlooked that "countable" implies acceptance of the assumption that "present values and social structure are taken as given, out-there-to-be-discovered facts" (Brown and Lyman 1978:9).

[125] Tiryakian, *Sociologism and Existentialism*, p. 17.

[126] Ibid., p. 34.

[127] Just one example of which is phenomenological sociology, which, according to Brown (1978:165) includes "such American social scientists as W. I. Thomas, Cooley, and G. H. Mead, in addition to the European school influences directly by Max Weber, are all representatives of the phenomenological standpoint."

[128] Giddens, *New Rules of Sociological method: A Positive Critique of Interpretative Sociologies*, p. 14.

[129] For a discussion of the many different understandings of positivism in sociology, see Halfpenny (1982).

[130] Drawn from *The Encyclopaedia Britannica*. 1910-1911 (6:815-824).

[131] Giddens, *New Rules of Sociological method: A Positive Critique of Interpretative Sociologies*, p. 14.

[132] See, *e.g.,* H.P. Rickman (1988).

[133] Remmling, *Road to Suspicion: A Study of Modern Mentality and the Sociology of Knowledge*, p. 78.

[134] Giddens, *New Rules of Sociological Method: A Positive Critique of Interpretative Sociologies*, p. 55.

[135] Dilthey, "The Dream," p. 41.

[136] Remmling, *Road to Suspicion: A Study of Modern Mentality and the Sociology of Knowledge*, p. 78.

[137] Brown, "History and Hermeneutics. Wilhelm Dilthey and the Dialectics of Interpretive Method," p. 38.

[138] Levy, *Realism: An Essay In Interpretation and Social Reality*, p. 27.

[139] Remmling, *Road to Suspicion: A Study of Modern Mentality and the Sociology of Knowledge*, p. 78.

[140] As shown in the letter in which he advocated exorcising such collectivist ideas. See Chapter X. For a recent review of the collectivist individual dispute in the context of a mystery story, see Berger, 2003.

[141] Weber, *The Theory of Social and Economic Organization*, p. 89.

[142] Not all writers would agree. Morrison, 1998, p. 486, e.g. said, "Weber repealed the investigative prohibitions of scientific methodologies by essentially steering sociology in the direction of interpretive practices."

[143] Legal training was of two types: training for ca career in the law or for a bureaucratic career. Weber trained for the latter.

[144] Discussions of Weber's life and ieas, and in some instances, of the cultural background factors that influenced him, can be found in Alexander (1982), Bendix (1960), Collins (1986), Coser (1971), Gerth and Mills introduction to Weber (1957), and Pampel (2000).

[145] Hilbert (1992, p. 142), e.g., noted, "Weber's discussion of bureaucracy is one of the most widely cited in sociological literature."

[146] Weber, *The Theory of Social and Economic Organization*, p. 88.

[147] Ibid., p. 101.

[148] Ibid., p. 101.

[149] Ibid., 102.

[150] Ibid., 101.

[151] Weber, *From Max Weber: Essays in Sociology*, p. 55.

[152] Weber (1981) essayed some conceptual distinctions between sociology, psychology, and the law.

[153] Weber, *The Theory of Social and Economic Organization*, p. 108.

[154] Eldridge, *Max Weber: The Interpretation of Social Reality*, p. 17.

[155] Weber, *The Theory of Social and Economic Organization*, p. 109.

[156] Ibid., p. 109.

[157] Concepts of "types" are not without critics. Lewis (1975) cautioned the reader that typologies are man made; that types are not natural; they do not reveal universal essences; should not be used predicatively; and should be used as open ended abstractions. Understanding, for Weber, included the interpretative grasp of the meaning present in any of the following contexts: "(a) as in the historical approach, the actual intended meaning for concrete individual action; or (b) as in cases of sociological mass phenomena the average of, or an approximation to, the actual intended meaning; or (c) the meaning appropriate to a scientifically formulated pure type (an ideal type) of a common phenomenon." (Weber, 1964, p. 96)

[158] Weber, *The Theory of Social and Economic Organization*, p. 107.

[159] Ibid., p. 114.

[160] Ibid., p. 88.

[161] Ibid., p. 109.

[162] Ibid., p. 95.

[163] Ibid., p. 95.

[164] The "laws" of logic that involve interpretations of history, social life, and individual experience *in conceptual experiments* should not be confused with the kinds of general laws that Comtean sociology would have argued operated to make social behavior understandable. Comte structured an approach to positivism based on his view that the universe is not composed of a multitude of individuals each with his own volition, but as an ordered organism governed by necessary laws.

[165] Weber, *The Theory of Social and Economic Organization*, p. 95.

[166] Hughes (1958, p. 195) pointed out that Dilthey did not have a quarrel with science or the scientific method, he simply aimed to "dispel the current confusion of the world of nature with the world of human activity."

[167] Pressler and Dasilva (1996, p. 4) wrote, "to the program of the natural sciences, Weber added a significant requirement, the demand for undertaking a process of interpretations, which is called for by virtue of the fact that we are dealing with human phenomena – thus advocacy for an interpretative sociology."

[168] The article from which the quote is drawn is entitled, "Critical Studies in the Logic of the cultural Sciences." (Weber, 1949, pp. 113 – 188)

[169] Levy, *Realism: An Essay in Interpretation and Social Reality*, p. 17.

[170] Weber, *The Methodology of the Social Sciences*, p. 171.

[171] Ibid., p. 171.

[172] Ibid., p. 171.

[173] Wells and Loftus, *Eyewitness Testimony: Psychological Perspectives*.

[174] Weber, *The Methodology of the Social Sciences*, p. 171.

[175] Ibid.

[176] Ibid., p. 177.

Essays on *Verstehen's* past and future prospects, in addition to Abel's critique, can be found in Truzzi (1974). Weber's contribution to interpretive theory in the U.S.A. was discussed by Kivisto and Swatos (1990).

[177] Weber, *The Theory of Social and Economic Organization*, pp. 98-99.

[178] Weber, *The Methodology of the Social Sciences*, pp. 177-178.

[179] Ibid., p. 178.

[180] Ibid., p. 179.

[181] Ibid., p. 180.

[182] Ibid., p. 180.

[183] Ibid., p. 181.

[184] Ibid., pp. 178-179.

[185] Abel, "The Operation Called *Verstehen*," (1948).

[186] Ibid.

Truzzi, *Verstehen: Subjective Understanding in the Social Sciences*, (1974).
Berger and Luckman (1966, p. 15) reserved a place for subjective meanings in the "constitution of reality."

[187] Weber, *The Theory of Social and Economic Organization*, p. 89.

[188] Ibid., p. 90.

[189] Ibid., p. 95.

[190] See Schutz's detailed discussion of Husserl's intersubjectivity, *Collected Papers I: The Problem of Social Reality*, pp. 51-91. Other critics merely call attention to Weber's failure to make clear the relationship between the meanings of an action for the actor and the observer (Levy, 1981, p. 29). Schutz contended that Weber's failure to make this distinction produces "many ambiguities" (1967, p. 151).

[191] Weber, *The Methodology of the Social Sciences*, p. 110.

[192] Weber, *The Methodology of the Social Sciences*, p. 78.

[193] Ibid., p. 79.

[194] James, *Pragmatism: A New Name for Some Old Ways of Thinking*, p. 172.

[195] Weber, *The Theory of Social and Economic Organization*, pp. 88-89.

[196] Weber, *The Methodology of the Social Sciences*, p. 180.

[197] Ibid., p. 178.

[198] Garfinkel, *Studies in Ethnomethodology*, p. 36.

[199] Schutz, *Collected Papers I: The Problem of social Reality*, p. 98.

[200] Weber, *The Theory of Social and Economic Organization*, p. 94.

[201] Levy, *Realism: an Essay in Interpretation and Social Reality*, p. 28.

[202] Berger and Luckmann, *The Social Construction of Reality*, pp. 80-81.

[203] Schutz, *Collected Papers II: Studies in Social Theory*, p. 326, and Schutz, *Collected Papers I: The Problem of Social Reality.*

[204] Giddens, *Modernity and Self-Identity*, p. 172.

[205] Garfinkel, *Studies in Ethnomethodology*, p. 272.

[206] Ibid., pp. 272-273.

[207] Abel, "The Operation Called *Verstehen*," p. 687.

[208] Weber, *the Methodology of the Social Sciences*, p. 178.

[209] Fulbrook, "Max Weber's 'Interpretive Sociology," (1978).

[210] Velarde-Mayol, *On Husserl*, p.1.

[211] Schutz, *Collected Papers I: the Problem of Social Reality*, p. 99. Not only are there difficulties posed by special terms in phenomenological literature, but, as Schutz observed there is also some tendency to substitute "slogans."

[212] Scanlon, "Review of Sokolowski's *Introduction to Phenomenology*," (2002).

[213] Even though the idea is traceable to Medieval times, Husserl adapted Brentano's approach, with some differences. These differences are discussed in several places, see, Morrison (1970) and Verlarde-Mayol (2000).

[214] Sokolowski, *Introduction to Phenomenology*, (2000).

[215] Husserl, *The Idea of Phenomenology*, p. 37.

[216] Husserl, *Cartesian Meditations*, p. 39.

[217] To which a skeptical student of his replied, you cannot even do it once.

[218] Husserl, *Cartesian Meditations*, p. 33.

[219] Ibid., p. 33.

[220] Every perceived noema contains a rigidly defined core which is immediately given in experience. At the same time, it also refers to not immediately given aspects, considered its "internal horizon" (Gurwitsch 1967:143). There is also its "external horizon" that refers to perceptible objects appearing as figures as backgrounds. More on horizons appears in the chapter on Schutz.

[221] Husserl, "The Thesis of the Natural Standpoint and Its Suspension," pp. 33-34.

[222] Husserl, *Cartesian Meditations*, p. 65.

[223] The word phenomenon, from the Greek, means "appearance."

[224] Husserl, *Cartesian meditations*, pp. 152-153.

[225] Natanson (1973:93) outlined three ways to understand "constitution" as used by Husserl: (1) "a logic of building a meaning," found in experience; (2) "a self-generating dynamic of consciousness (object constitutes itself); (3) "the constitutive process is one of world-creation." Levy (1981:12) drew a distinction between constitution as a "constitution of meaning rather than, in the literal sense, a construction of reality...."

[226] But individual mind does not engage in constitutive activities on its own. It benefits from, and depends on, the indispensable aid of anonymously prefigured communities of significations and meanings "by virtue of which such and such objects and categories of objects exist..." (Husserl 1973:75-76).

[227] Natanson, *Literature, Society, and the Social Sciences*, p. 165.

[228] Giddens, *New Rules of Sociological method: a Positive Critique of Interpretative Sociologies*, p. 165.

[229] Kockelmans, "Husserls Pheonomenology and 'Existentialism,'" p. 34.

[230] Gurvitsch, "Intentionality, Constitution, and Intentional Analysis," p. 129.

[231] Schutz, *Collected Papers III: Studies in Phenomenological Sociology*, p. 28.

[232] Velarde-Mayol, *On Husserl*, p. 24.

[233] In the sense of "building meaning." (Natanson 1962:93)

[234] Husserl, *Cartesian Meditations*, p. 42.

[235] Velarde-Mayol, *On Husserl*, p. 33.

[236] Husserl, *Cartesian Meditations*, p. 65.

[237] Husserl, *The Idea of Phenomenology,* p. 9, and Morrison, "Husserl and Brentanon on Intentionality," p. 41.

[238] Husserl, *Cartesian Meditations,* p. 37.

[239] Husserl, "The Thesis of the Natural Standpoint and its Suspension," pp. 70-71.

[240] Commenting on the senses, Husserl noted how all too easy it is to imagine how they fail to provide valid knowledge of the world, as in dreams or what he termed "illusion[s] of the senses" (Husserl 1973:17). Again, Husserl echoed Heraclitus: "the senses are bad witnesses."

[241] Husserl, *Cartesian Meditations,* p. 39.

[242] Ibid., p. 39.

[243] Ibid., p. 39.

[244] Ibid., p. 33.

[245] What Husserl (1973:41) termed "a noetic-neomatic unity."

[246] Husserl, *Cartesian Meditations,* p. 46.

[247] Ibid., p. 46.

[248] Ibid., p. 33.

[249] Husserl, "the Thesis of the Natural Standpoint and Its Suspension," p. 71.

[250] Berger and Luckman, *The Social Construction of Reality: A Treatise in the Sociology of Knowledge,* p. 79.

[251] Morrison, "Husserl and Brentano on Intentionality," p. 43.

[252] Ibid., p. 39.

[253] Levy, *Realism: An Essay in the Interpretation and Social Reality,* p. 9.

[254] Husserl, *The Idea of Phenomenology,* pp. 9-10.

[255] Husserl, "The Thesis of the Natural Standpoint and Its Suspension," p. 71.

[256] Husserl, *Cartesian Meditations,* p. 33.

[257] Perhaps "free floating anxiety" is one exception, or perhaps it suggests that the "something" is everything.

[258] Banks, "The Caul," p. 37.

[259] Wittgenstein, *Philosophical Investigations 3$^{rd}$ Edition,* p. 193.

[260] Giddens, *Modernity and Self-Identity: Self and Society in the Late modern Age,* p. 127.

[261] Simmel, "The Adventure," p. 402.

[262] Kockelmans, "Theoretical problems in Phenomenological Psychology," p. 34.

[263] Husserl, *the Idea of Phenomenology,* p. 35.

[264] Husserl, "The Thesis of the Natural Standpoint and Its Suspension," p. 76.

[265] Husserl, *Cartesian Meditations,* p. 25.

[266] Ibid., p. 26.

[267] Ibid., p. 35.

[268] Husserl, "The Thesis of the Natural Standpoint and Its Suspension," p. 78.

[269] Mead, *Mind, Self, and Society, Vol. 1,* pp. 89-90.

[270] Husserl, *Cartesian Meditations,* p. 153.

[271] That prefigured meanings and significations reside in social or discursive communities is easily and frequently overlooked. In part, because of naivete, and, in part, to the trust one tends to place in the "correct depiction of reality" represented by the world view (Orleans 1991:176).

[272] Husserl, *Cartesian Meditations,* p. 35.

[273] Husserl, "The Thesis of the Natural Standpoint and Its Suspension," p. 68.

[274] Lauer (Husserl 1965:159, fn 15) translated *Einstellung,* Husserl's term, as "attitude." Husserl, *Phenomenology and the Crisis of Philosophy,* pp. 81-82, 85.

[275] Velarde-Mayol, *On Husserl,* p. 42.

[276] Kockelsmans, "Theoretical Problems in Phenomenological Psychology," p.28. This assumption, roaming without consquence, ignores what Husserl expressed as the codetermination through which intentionalities are constituted (Husserl 1931:57-59).

196

[277] Husserl, *Cartesian Meditations*, p.9.

[278] Ibid., p. 9. Husserl, *Ideas General Introduction to Pure Phenomenology*, p.111.

[279] Husserl, *Cartesian Meditations*, p. 18.

[280] Bierce, *The Devil's Dictionary*, p.20.

[281] Husserl, "The Thesis of the Natural Standpoint and its Suspension," p. 72.

[282] Schutz, *The Phenomenology of the Social World*, p. 85.

[283] Husserl, "The Thesis of the Natural Standpoint and Its Suspension," p. 72

[284] Velarde-Mayol, *On Husserl*, p. 76.

[285] Pressler, *Sociology and Interpretation: From Weber to Habermas*, p. 96, and Natanson, *Anonymity: A Study in the Philosophy of Alfred Schutz*, p. 141.

[286] Natanson, *Literature, Philosophy, and the Social Sciences*, p. 38.

[287] Husserl, *Cartesian Meditations*, p. 130. There is little agreement that Husserl satisfactorily answered the question about transcendental intersubjectivity.

[288] The intersubjective world is experienced by each member of the discursive community "more or less" perfectly. (Husserl 1973:131)

[289] Husserl, *Cartesian Meditations*, p. 108.

[290] Ibid., p. 108.

[291] Ibid., p. 108.

[292] Ibid., p. 125.

[293] Tiryakian, "Sociology and Existential Phenomenology," p. 197.

[294] Schutz, *The Phenomenology of the Social World*, p. 184

[295] Ibid., p. 25.

[296] Schutz noted that "while I know he is angry, I remain in the dark as to what that anger means to him subjectively." (Schutz 1967:26). Phillipson (1972:88) more generally observed that the unique perspecitive the other has on te world "is always beyond our grasp."

[297] Schutz, *The Phenomenology of the Social World*, p. 134.

[298] Garfinkel, *Studies in Ethnomethodology*, p. 272.

[299] Schutz, *Collected Papers I: The Problem of Social Reality*, p. 326. The term 'taken for granted' .... means to accept until further notice our knowledge of certain states of affairs as unquestionably plausible (Schutz 1971a:326). Giddens (1976:127) characterization was "what other people appear to do, and who they appear to be, is usually accepted as the same as what they are actually doing and who they actually are." As Natanson pointed out (1973:14), "the phenomenologist believes that essences do not lurk somehow behind or within objects but are the object grasped in its intentional character, grasped *as* being this or that.

[300] Schutz, *Collected Papers I: The Problem of Social Reality*, p. 36.

[301] Berger and Luckman, *The Social Construction of Reality*, p. 44·

[302] Schutz, *The Phenomenology of the Social World*, p. 10.

[303] Ibid., p. 86.

[304] Ibid., p. 21.

[305] Ibid., pp. 28-29.

[306] Ibid., p. 116.

[307] This is not to say that projects might not be changed. Eldridge (1971:29) wrote, "it is recognized by Collingwood that purposes may change as the activity proceeds but 'the purpose is always in advance of the act.'" This position is roughly equivalent to Schutz's treatment of projects and 'in-order-to' motivation."

[308] Schutz, *The Phenomenology of the Social World*, p. 91.

[309] Ibid., p. 91.

[310] Ibid., p. 92.

[311] Levy, *Realism: An Essay in the Interpretation and Social Reality*, p. 41.

[312] Schutz, *The Phenomenology of the Social World*, p. 39.

[313] Ibid., p. 59.

[314] Levy, *Realism: An Essay in the Interpretation and Social Reality*, p. 41.

[315] Schutz, *The Phenomenology of the Social World*, pp. 39-40.

[316] Pressler and Dasliva, *Sociology and Interpretation: From Weber to Habermas*, p. 20.

[317] Levy, *Realism: An Essay in the Interpretation and Social Reality*, p. 18.

[318] Schutz, *The Phenomenology of the Social World*, p. 9.

[319] Ibid., p. 7.

[320] Weber, *From Max Weber: Essays in Sociology*, p. 55.

[321] Schutz, *The Phenomenology of the Social World*, p. 13.

[322] In a shift from philosophy to sociology (Giddens 1976:33), Schutz introduced "trustworthy *recipes* for interpreting the social world" (Schutz 1971b:95). See, also, Costelloe (1996). Natanson (1998) discussed the shift, differently, in terms of the relationships among sociology, theory, method, demography the natural attitude and the phenomenological attitude.

[323] Pressler and Dasliva, *Sociology and Interpretation: From Weber to Habermas*, p. 20.

[324] Husserl, *Ideas*.

[325] Schutz appears to have used "attitude" and "standpoint" interchangeably. "In everyday life," he said "occupying as I do the position of the *natural attitude* (or *standpoint)...* " (Schutz 1967:36).

[326] Schutz, *Collected Papers I: The Problem of Social Reality*, p. 115.

[327] Husserl, *Cartesian Meditations*, p. 55.

[328] Giddens, *New Rules of Sociological Method: A Positive Critique of Interpretative Sociologies*, p. 27.

[329] Ibid., p. 27.

[330] Schutz, "Phenomenology and the Social Sciences," p. 471.

[331] Schutz, *The Phenomenology of the Social World*, p. 13.

[332] Schutz, *Collected Papers III: Studies in Phenomenological Sociology*, pp. 2-3.

[333] In his studies of "flow experience," Csikszentmilhaly (1993) included reports of mothers experiencing "flow" when teaching their children. He characterized the flow state as a loss of self consciousness (1993:178).

[334] To avoid terminological confusion it should be noted that the concept of "intentionality" in phenomenological sociology is different from common sense or psychological "intention." It does not mean "I really intended to get snow tires on my car before the first snow, but something came up" or, "although I intended to cut the wood in preparation for winter, I couldn't because my chainsaw broke down." Schutz's usage is also different from the use of "intentional" as an irreducible attribute of an individual's psychological state of mind.

[335] Schutz, *The Phenomenology of the Social World*, p. 40.

[336] Swingewood, *A Short History of Sociological Thought*, p. 268.

[337] Giddens, *New Rules of Sociological Method: A Positive Critique of Interpretative Sociologies*, p. 25.

[338] Schutz, *The Phenomenology of the Social World*, p. 102.

[339] Schutz, *Collected Papers I: The Problem of Social Reality*, p. 102.

[340] Schutz, *The Phenomenology of the Social World*, pp. 46-47.

[341] Gurwitsch, "On the Intentionality of Consciousness," p. 129.

[342] Although Cooley used different terminology, one is reminded of the "looking glass self."

[343] Schutz, *The Phenomenology of the Social World*, pp. 34-35, 42.

[344] Schutz, *Collected Papers I: The Problem of Social Reality*, p. 110. Schutz (1971c:28) noted that "Husserl calls these environmental objects upon which a new intentional meaning has been bestowed "founded objects."

[345] Natanson, *Literature, Philosophy and the Social Sciences*, p. 165.

[346] Schutz, *Collected papers I: The Problem of Social Reality*, p. 110.

[347] Schutz, *collected Papers III: Studies in Phenomenological Sociology*, p. 87.

[348] Levy, *Realism: An Essay in the Interpretation and Social Reality*, p. 9.

[349] Husserl, *Ideas*, pp. 9-10.

[350] Schutz, *Collected Papers I: The Problem of Social Reality*, p. 297.

[351] There are alternative interpretations of "thumbs up" and "thumbs down." The definitive Eleventh Edition of the *Encyclopaedia Britannica* (1910:64) included two: "If the spectators were in favour of mercy, they waved their handkerchiefs; if they desired the death of the conquered gladiator, they turned their thumbs downwards." And, in the same place: "those who wished the death of the conquered gladiator turned their thumbs towards their breasts, as a signal to his opponents to stab him; those who wished him to be spared, turned their thumbs downwards, as a signal for dropping the sword."

[352] The shared character is suggested by Schutz (1967b:123), in saying: "A meaning is connected with a sign insofar as the latter's significance within a given sign system is understood both for the person using the sign and for the person interpreting it."

[353] Schutz, *The Phenomenology of the Social World*, p. 120.

[354] Husserl, *Ideas*, p. 71.

[355] Harris, "The Social Construction of Equality in Everyday Life," pp. 374-375.

[356] Husserl, *Cartesian Meditations*, p. 108.

[357] Schutz, *The Phenomenology of the Social World*, p. 51.

358 Ibid., pp. 46-47.

[359] Schutz, *Collected Papers I: The Problem of Social Reality*, p. 210.

[360] Schutz, *The Phenomenology of the Social World*, p. 52.

[361] Ibid., p. 40.

[362] See, *e.g.*, Lakoff and Johnson (1980), and Schon (1979).

[363] Lakoff and Johnson, *Metaphors We Live By*, pp. 7-8.

[364] Ricoeur, *Interpretation Theory, Discourse and the Surplus of Meaning*, p. 51.

[365] Schutz, *Collected Papers II: Studies in Social Theory*, pp. 135-136.

[366] Fine, "Wittgenstein's Kitchen: Sharing Meaning in Restaurant Work."

[367] Tiryakian, "Sociology and Existential Phenomenology," p. 205.

[368] Schutz, *The Phenomenology of the Social World*, p. 125.

[369] Laza, "Gender, Discourse and Semiotic: The Politics of Parenthood Representations," p. 376. For Mead (1974:89-90) "a universe of discourse is simply a system of common or social meanings."

[370] Pendergast and Pendergast, *International Dictionary of Films and Filmmakers, Vol. I.*, p.1124.

[371] Compare Denzin (1986) and the use of life stories.

[372] Beggan and Allison, "The Playboy Rabbit is Soft, Furry, and Cute: Is it Really the Symbol of Masculine Dominance of Women," p. 366.

[373] As Fine pointed out (1995:255), "attached" meanings include metaphors that are used to discuss the taste, smell, texture, or looks of food.

[374] Schutz, *Collected Papers I: The Problem of Social Reality*, p. 34.

[375] Ibid., 230.

[376] Schutz, *The Phenomenology of the Social World*, p. 85.

[377] Ibid., p. 85.

[378] Ibid., p. 85.

[379] Themes either actively or passively evoke interests. In its passive modality, "theme" refers to receptivity (Schutz 1971c:98), how an object adverts, or directs our attention to something. Passive themes waken a more fleeting interest than "themes" in the active mode. Active themes more broadly evoke interest. They involve "taking part" in an activity (Schutz 1971c:98).

[380] Schutz, *Collected Papers III: Studies in Phenomenological Sociology*, p. 125.

[381] Schutz (1971b:11) wrote of action being determined by the project of the actor. "The project

is the intended act imagined as already accomplished, the in order-to motive is the future state of affairs to be realized by the projected action."

[382] Schutz, *Collected Papers II: Studies in Social Theory,* p. 81.

[383] Ibid., p. 78.

[384] Ibid., p. 78.

[385] Schutz, *The Phenomenology of the Social World,* p. 85.

[386] Husserl, *Cartesian Meditations,* p. 71.

[387] Fernandez-Armesto (2002) included a chapter on the attachment of symbolic meaning to food.

[388] See Zborowski (1953). Other writers, *e.g.,* McCullock (1993) maintained that not all states of mind have intentional objects, including so-called sensational states or bodily feelings in that category.

[389] Schutz, *The Phenomenology of the Social World,* p. 125.

[390] Ibid., p. 85.

[391] Giddens, *New Rules of Sociological Method: A Positive Critique of Interpretative Sociologies,* p. 113.

[392] The implication, for interpretative sociology is, of course, that a naive interpretation of others talk and actions is only one possible interpretation.

[393] Expressed by Tudor (1976), everyday life is constituted by meanings actors ascribe to it. "Our first outlook upon life is that of natural human beings... 'from *the natural standpoint'*" (Husserl 1967:101).

[394] Schutz, *The Phenomenology of the Social World,* p. 36.

[395] Walsh, "Sociology and the Social World," p. 27.

[396] Schutz, *Collected Papers II: Studies in Social Theory,* p. 21.

[397] Schutz, *Collected Papers I: The Problem of Social Reality,* p. 326.

[398] Silverman, "Some Neglected questions about Social Reality," p. 166.

[399] Schutz, *Collected Papers I: The Problem of Social Reality,* p. 342.

[400] Those glimpses have been termed "vulgar," or "naive." At the natural standpoint, experiencing subjects assume their minds can roam through the world at will and consider it or parts of it without changing its objective nature, ignoring what Husserl expressed as the codetermination through which intentionalities are constituted.

[401] Schutz, *Collected Papers II: Studies in Social Theory,* p. 21.

[402] Schutz, *Collected Papers I: The Problem of social Reality,* p. 13.

[403] According to Pressler and Dasliva (1996:6), "the goal of interpretive science is to reach intersubjective understanding of symbol systems...."

[404] Garfinkel, *Studies in Ethnomethodology,* pp. 35, 75.

[405] Schutz, *Collected Papers III: Studies in Phenomenological Sociology, "* p. 77.

[406] Ibid., p. 80.

[407] Ibid., p. 82.

[408] Schutz, *The Phenomenology of the Social World,* p. 99,

[409] Giddens called attention to how Schutz achieved an intersubjective understanding "through discourse," detaching *Verstehen* from the Cartesian individualism in which it was grounded ...." (Giddens 1976:62).

[410] Husserl, *Cartesian Meditations,* p. 130.

[411] Schutz, *Collected Papers III: Studies in Phenomenological Sociology,* p. 82.

[412] Schutz, *Collected Papers I: The Problem of Social Reality,* p. 13.

[413] At the same time that members of society learn a set of typical recipes, they may develop low tolerance or an aversion for alternative meanings and interpretations. The latter are often embodied in cultural proscriptions and taboos, and consist of atypical solutions to atypical practical and theoretical problems, for example, sexuality in the family, food objects, *etc.* They are also products of learning and training, a trained incapacity.

[414] Lengermann, "Intersubjectivity and Domination: a Feminist Investigation of the Sociology of Alfred Schutz," p. 27.

[415] Schutz, *Collected Papers III: Studies in Phenomenological Sociology*, p. 125.

[416] Schutz, *Collected Papers II: Studies in Social Theory*, p. 233.

[417] Ibid., p. 233.

[418] Natanson, *Edmund Husserl: Philosopher of Infinite Tasks*, p. 111.

[419] Schutz, *Collected Papers II: Studies in Social Theory*, p. 233.

[420] Schutz, *Collected Papers I: The Problem of Social Reality*, p. 348.

[421] Schutz, *Collected Papers II: Studies in Social Theory*, p. 73.

[422] Wittgenstein, *Zettel*, p. 39.

[423] Schutz, *Collected Papers II: Studies in Social Theory*, p. 57.

[424] Schutz, *Collected Papers III: Studies in Phenomenological Sociology*, p. 97.

[425] Schutz, *Collected Papers I: The Problem of Social Reality*, pp. 347-348.

[426] Schutz, *Collected Papers II: Studies in Social Theory*, p. 237.

[427] Klapp, *Heroes, Villains, and Fools*, p. 11.

[428] Schutz, *Collected Papers II: Studies in Social Theory*, p. 47.

[429] Ibid., p. 45.

[430] Schutz, *Collected Papers III: Studies in Phenomenological Sociology*, p. 95. See Klapp (1962), for an extended discussion of popular social types.

[431] Berger and Luckman, *The Social Construction of Reality*, p. 29.

[432] Denzin (1989:32), *e.g.,* defined meaning "in terms of the intentions and actions of a person."

[433] Schutz, *The Phenomenology of the Social World*, p. 184.

[434] Schutz acknowledged that some ambiguity --in regards to classification and constitution-- was introduced by inner horizons. "The constituents of socially approved knowledge refer both to classificatory elements such as Sumner's folkways and mores, and to situations constituted as such in accordance with Thomas' theorem" (Schutz 1971a:348).

[435] Manning, "Metaphors of the Field: Varieties of Organizational Discourse," p. 227.

[436] Klapp, *Heroes, Villains, and Fools.*

[437] Natanson, *Edmund Husserl: Philosopher of Infinite Tasks*, p. 14.

[438] Berger and Luckman, *The Social Construction of Reality*, p. 29.

[439] Simmel, "The Stranger," p. 407.

[440] Emerson, "Behavior in Private Places: Sustaining Definitions of Reality in Gynecological Examinations."

[441] Reiss, "The Social Integration of Queers and Peers."

[442] Ricoeur, *Interpretation Theory: Discourse and the Surplus of Meaning.*

[443] Silverman, "Methodology and Meaning," p. 192.

[444] Natanson (1962:165) wrote, "such American social scientists as W. I. Thomas, Cooley, and G. H. Mead, in addition to the European school influences directly by Max Weber, are all representatives of the phenomenological standpoint," if intentionality is taken as the proper locus for the understanding of social action..."

[445] Silverman, "Methodology and Meaning," p. 189.

[446] Alexander (1989:4) separated Durkheim's earlier and later interests.

[447] Mestrovic, *Durkheim and PostModern Culture*, p. 74.

[448] Durkheim, *The Elementary Forms of the Religious Life*, pp. 28-29.

[449] Berlin, *The Age of Enlightenment: the 18th Century Philosophers*, p. 180.

[450] Durkheim, *The Elementary Forms of the Religious Life*, p. 26.

[451] Durkheim distinguished between the container and what it contains. His terms can be interpreted to constitute the symbolic elements present in "moulds," "collective representations," etc.

[452] Ibid., pp. 31-32.

[453] Ibid., pp. 25, 491-493, 484.

[454] Ibid., p. 492.

[455] Ibid., p. 488.

[456] Hund, "Socialism and Philosophy," p. 215.

[457] Hilbert, "Ethnomethodological Recovery of Durkheim," p. 346.

[458] Bordieu, "Social Space and Symbolic Power," p. 34.

[459] Mestrovic, *Durkheim and PostModern Culture,* p. 14.

[460] Haritos and Glassman, "Emile Durkheim and the Sociological Enterprise," p. 72.

[461] Karady, "Durkheim, Social Sciences, and the University: The Balance Sheet of a Semi-Failure."

[462] Durkheim, *The Rules of the Sociological Method,* p. 104.

[463] Durkheim, *Sociology and Philosophy,* p. 29.

[464] Durkheim, *The Rules of the Sociological Method, p. 103.*Turner (1974:313) wrote, "Thus, since at least the time of Durkheim, sociologists have felt confident that society is a real entity, *sui generis.* Yet they have not pursued this insight into the nature of society...."

[465] Durkheim, *The Elementary Forms of the Religious Life,* p. 492.

[466] See, *e.g.,* Fine's (1995) examination of the establishment of meaning in the interactional context of a restaurant.

[467] Hund, "Are Social Facts Real," p. 273. Durkheim also viewed language as "a system of collective representations that can be treated as social facts." (Mestrovic 1992:73)

[468] Perinbanayagam, "The Definition of the Situation: An Analysis of the Enthnomethodological and Dramaturgical view," p. 537.

[469] See, e.g., Hawkins (1980) and Turner (1974:18) who stated, "it is not surprising that Emile Durkheim's early works were heavily infused with organismic terminology."

[470] Durkheim, *The Elementary Forms of the Religious Life,* p. 31.

[471] Fine, "Wittgenstein's Kitchen: Sharing meaning in Restaurant Work," p. 266.

[472] Durkheim, *The Elementary Forms of the Religious Life,* pp. 31-32.

[473] Durkheim, *The Rules of the Sociological Method,* p. 34.

[474] Durkheim, *The Elementary Forms of the Religious Life,* p. 22.

[475] Hilbert, *The Classical roots of Ethnomethodology: Durkheim, Weber, and Garfinkel,*p. 68.

[476] Durkheim, *The Elementary Forms of the Religious Life,* p. 486.

[477] See, e.g., Douglas (1986); Knapp (1985); and Allport's protest again the group mind which was reviewed by Post (1980). A review of early criticism appears in Lukes (1973), particularly, Chapter 25.

[478] Douglas, *How Institutions Think,* p. 10. Mestrovic (1992:78) attributed part of the controversy surrounding Durkheim's definition of a "social fact" to the translation of the French word *fait* into "fact" instead of "act."

[479] Durkheim was careful to qualify his usage: "When we said that obligation and constraint are the characteristics of social facts we had no intention of giving a summary explanation of the later. We wished simply to point out a convenient sign by which the sociologist can recognize the facts falling within his field (Durkheim 1953:25, fn#1).

[480] Durkheim, *Sociology and Philosophy,* p. 25, footnote #1.

[481] Corning, "Durkheim and Spencer," p. 337.

[482] In the "Author's preface to second edition," *The Rules of the Sociological Method,* p. xli.

[483] Interpretations of "social facts" develop along several lines. First, and least controversial, are "social facts" when put to actuarial use. Davis (1978), *e.g.,* discussed what "social facts" can be learned from social surveys. Hund (1982:272) asked, rhetorically, "For what are social rules if not social facts?" Ritzer (2000:76) pointed out that Durkheim differentiated two types: material and nonmaterial social facts "with the heart of his sociology... in the study of nonmaterial social facts."

[484] Full agreement, however desirable, might not indicate a successful theory. Davis (1986), *e.g.,* argued that successful theories not only address the concerns of the day, but are also <u>ambiguous</u>.

202

[485] Davis, "That's 'Classic!' the Phenomenology and Rhetoric of Successful Social Theories."

[486] Hilbert, "Ethnomethodological Recovery of Durkheim."

[487] Vogt, "Early French Contributions to the Sociology of Knowledge."

[488] Hund, "Are Social Facts Real?" p. 274.

[489] Durkheim , *The Rules of the Sociological Method,* p. 29.

[490] Durkheim, *Suicide,* p. 51.

[491] Ibid., p. 51.

[492] Ibid., pp. 309-310.

[493] Ibid., p. 307.

[494] Durkheim, *Sociology and Philosophy,* p. 112.

[495] Ibid., p. 35.

[496] Ibid., pp. 25-26.

[497] Ibid., pp. 25-25.

[498] Rawls, "Durkheim's Epistemology: The Neglected Argument."

[499] Mestrovic, *Durkheim and PostModern Culture,* p. 73. Mestrovic (1987) discussed discussed anomie – normlessness – as a social fact. Durkheim used the analogy himself, noting (1938:2) that "The system of signs I use to express my thought, the system of currency I employ to pay my debts, ... function independently of my own use of them."

[500] Durkheim, *The Elementary Forms of the Religious Life, p.* 490.

[501] Mestrovic, *Durkheim andPostModern Culture,* p. 9.

[502] Turner, "Using Classical Theorists to Reconceptualize Community Dynamics."

[503] Perinbanayagam, "The Definition of the Situation: An Analysis of the Ethnomethodological and Dramaturgical View," p. 536.

[504] Schutz and Luckman (1973:173-174) noted "in the case of Durkheim, it seems that interpretation is significant, particularly since his model calls for a fundamental rupture between the subject and the object, thus putting the burden of interpretation-explanation in the consciousness of the subject. However, for Durkheim the question is not *per se* a major concern. Interpretation itself, *i.e.,* must be explained sociologically. Thus instead of interpretation being the rule, the issue is shifted into the domain of epistemology."

[505] Mestrovic (1992:73-74) also saw social facts as "symbols, representations of a veiled, underlying reality that must be deciphered and interpreted, not regarded as hard facts."

[506] Mestrovic, *Durkheim and PostModern Culture,* p. 74. Durkheim occasionally used the term "interpretation" and often made use of similar terms, *e.g.,* discussing religion and mythology he wrote, "It is only by regarding religion from this angle that it is possible to see its real significance..." (1965:467); or in noting that ethnographers and sociologists are generally satisfied with the native's explanation of the source of rites of mourning --the obligation-- when they say that the dead want to be lamented, he pointed out an alternative: "but this mythological interpretation merely modifies the terms of the problem, without resolving it...."(1965:443). Moving on to the desire for surviving memory, he noted that this "classic interpretation appears still more unsustainable.....(1965:444).

[507] Levi-Strauss, "French Sociology," p. 518.

[508] As used here, the term "realities" does not include subjective elements. Instead, as Schutz (1971:207) indicated in his use of "provinces of meaning," "it is in the meaning of our

[509] This is especially true later in his career.

[510] Among certain peoples, after --sometimes, before-- the birth of his child, the father takes to his bed and receives the attention typically shown women at their confinements. One interpretation held that the custom, originating in matriarchal societies where descent and inheritance are reckoned through the mother alone, arose in the father's desire to emphasize his ties with the child (*Encyclopaedia Britannica* 1910:338).

[511] Durkheim, *The Elementary Forms of the Religious Life,* p. 23.

[512] Ibid., p. 492.

[513] Durkheim, *The Rules of the Sociological Method*, p. 45.

[514] Durkheim, *Suicide*, p. 45.

[515] Durkheim, *The Elementary Forms of the Religious Life*, p. 30.

[516] Segre (1986-1987) wrote of Weber's "entirely negative" judgment of Durkheim, a judgment based mainly on Durkheim's *Rules*.

[517] Durkheim, *The Rules of the Sociological Method*, p. 45.

[518] Ibid., p. 103.

[519] Durkheim, *Suicide*, pp. 38.

[520] Ibid., p. 38.

[521] Durkheim, *The Elementary Forms of the Religious Life*, p. 491.

[522] Ibid., p. 490.

[523] Durkheim, *The Rules of the Sociological Method*, pp. 105-106.

[524] Durkheim, *The Elementary Forms of the Religious Life*, pp. 481,483.

[525] Rose (1988:25) examined Old English definitions of the word "things" and found that "Of all things, a thing was an assembly, a court, a meeting: Old English thingan expressed to 'negotiate things.'" Rose proposed "that a thing is whatever has been negotiated by an assembly of people."

[526] Durkheim, *The Rules of the Sociological Method*, p. 17.

[527] Ibid., p. 13.

[528] Durkheim, *The Elementary Forms of the Religious Life*, pp. 23-24.

[529] Durkheim, *Suicide*, p. 309.

[530] Durkheim, *The Elementary Forms of the Religious Life*, p. 488.

[531] Durkheim, *Sociology and Philosophy*, p. 34.

[532] Hilbert, "Ethnomethodological Recovery of Durkheim," p. 347.

[533] Durkheim, *Sociology and Philosophy*, pp. 25-26.

[534] Durkheim, *The Rules of the Sociological Method*, p. lvi.

[535] Durkheim, *The Elementary Forms of the Religious Life*, p. 492.

[536] Ibid., p. 24.

[537] Hund, "Are Social Facts Real?" p. 273.

[538] Durkheim, *Sociology and Philosophy*, p. 59.

[539] Durkheim, *The Elementary Forms of the Religious Life*, p. 261. Durkheim's emphasis.

[540] Tiryakian (1962:34) noted "the meaning of objects does derive from properties inherent in them. But rather from their being symbols of the collective representations of society."

[541] Durkheim, *The Elementary Forms of the Religious Life*, p. 144.

[542] Durkheim, *Sociology and Philosophy*, p. 86.

[543] Ibid., p. 87.

[544] Durkheim, *The Elementary Forms of the Religious Life*, p. 156.

[545] Durkheim, *The Rules of the Sociological Method*, pp. 35-36.

[546] Durkheim, *Sociology and Philosophy*, pp. 94-95.

[547] Durkheim, *The Elementary Forms of the Religious Life*, p. 481.

[548] Ibid., p. 481.

[549] Ibid., p. 26.

[550] Ibid., p. 484.

[551] Ibid., p. 264.

[552] Alexander 1986, 1989; Bourdieu 1989; Byrne 1976; Coenen 1981; Hill 1973; Lukes 1973; Remender 1973; and Stone and Farberman 1967, to name just a few.

[553] Giddens (1982:36), addressing the issue of the "duality of structure," suggested that "the structural properties of social systems are both medium and outcome of the practices that constitute those systems."

204

[554] Stone and Farberman (1967:154) observed, "the metaphor of society as container cannot be maintained, for Durkheim begins to see the contained as creator of the container."

[555] Durkheim, *The Elementary Forms of the Religious Life,* p. 261.

[556] Durkheim, *The Rules of the Sociological Method,* p. 70.

[557] Scaff (1988).

[558] Lukes, *Emile Durkheim: His Life and Work. A Historical and Critical Study,* p. 235.

[559] And there are several (Jones 2001).

[560] Durkheim, *The Rules of the Sociological Method,* p. xliii.

[561] Durkheim, *The Elementary Forms of the Religious Life,* p. 460.

[562] Simmel, "The Problem of Sociology," p. 311. Introductions to Simmel thought appear in Coser (1965), Featherstone (1991), Frisby (1981), Levine (1959;1965), Spykman (1964) and Pampel (2000), and Levine et al. (1976) for an examination of Simmel;s influence on American sociology.

[563] Burawoy (2004:103) wrote that "sociology as a science came of age... during the first half of the twentieth century."

[564] Simmel, "The Field of Sociology," p. 4.

[565] Simmel, "Superiority and Subordination as Subject-Matter for Sociology," p. 167.

[566] Levine, "The Structure of Simmel's Social Thought," p. 59; and Frisby, *Sociological Impressionism: a Reassessment of Georg Simmel's Social Theory,* p. 81. Levine (1965:98) cited three broad categories: social processes, social types and developmental patterns. Oakes (1977:23-24) listed seven "definitive properties of forms": (1) they involve categories, taxonomies, language or conceptual schemes that represent the world; (2) these representations have epistemological status, making possible certain kinds of knowledge and experiences; (3) forms have metaphysical status, asserting ontological existence of aspects of the world as constituted by a particular form (what defines any form is immanent to the form, i.e.,forms are not dependent upon the content they shape); (5) forms are incommensurable, the properties of one cannot be linked to properties of others; (6) no form is complete and exhaustive of the world and its contents; (7) forms are hierarchically related.

[567] Simmel, "The Adventure." Arguable, much of what is said of "forms of experiencing" also holds true for other Simmelian forms.

[568] Husserl, *The Idea of Phenomenology,* p. 9.

[569] Morrison, "Husserl and Brentano on Intentionality," p. 9.Oakes classification of the three (specific) referents in Simmel's use of of form, all of which, it turns out, are easily contained in phenomenological thought: forms (1) the constitutive categories themselves; (2) their constitutive processes; and (3) constitutive products.

[570] Weingartner, *Experience and Culture: The Philosophy of Georg Simmel,*p. 625.

[571] Kaern, "The World as Human Construction," p. 79.

[572] Weingartner, *Experience and Culture: The Philosophy of Georg Simmel,* p. 5.

[573] Backhaus, "Georg Simmel as an Eidetic social Scientist," p. 98.

[574] Oakes, *Essays on Interpretation in social Science,* pp. 63-64.

[575] Kaern, " The World as Human Construction," p. 75. Spykman (1964:214) defined the task of sociology, as envisioned by Simmel, as finding "the laws or, avoiding all metaphysical implications, to find phenomenological relationships with sufficiently high degrees of correlation to give a high probability of repitition." Hardin, Power, and Sugrue (1986) included Mead as well as Garfinkel, Schutz, Husserl, and Cicourelin a phenomenological approach to sociology. Also, see Backhaus (1998).

[576] Owsley and Backhaus, "Simmel's Four Components of Historical Science."

[577] Simmel, "The Number of Members as Determining the Sociological form of the Group. I," p. 324.

[578] As Harre (1983:20) pointed out individuals' acts and interpretations of the social and physical world are "prefigured in collective actions and social representations."

[579] Weingartner, *Experience and Culture: The Philosophy of Georg Simmel*, p. 23.

[580] Simmel, "The Problem of Sociology," p. 314.

[581] Spykman, *The Social Theory of Georg Simmel*, p. 31.

[582] Simmel, "The Problem of Sociology," p. 315.

[583] Not Simmel's terms, but he (1904a:491) did assert that society requires some "quantitative relation of harmony and disharmony."

[584] Simmel, "How is Society Possible?" p. 341.

[585] Simmel, "The Problem of Sociology," p. 314.

[586] Giddens (1982:36) addressed the same issue: "By the 'duality of structure' I refer to the essentially recursive character of social life: the structural properties of social systems are both medium and outcome of the practices that constitute those systems." Berger and Luckman (1966:17) make a slightly different point: "it is precisely the dual character of society in terms of objective facticity *and* subjective meaning that makes its reality *sui generis*...." Simmel's words (1968:392) were "Life must either produce forms or proceed through forms."

[587] Simmel, "The Problem of Sociology," p. 314.

[588] Oakes, *Essays on Interpretation in Social Science*, p. 8.

[589] Simmel, "The Problem of Sociology," p. 315.

[590] Simmel, "The Field of Sociology," p. 11.

[591] Ibid., p. 4.

[592] Oakes, *Essays on Interpretation in Social Science*, p. 99.

[593] Ibid., p. 180.

[594] Simmel, "The Field of Sociology," p. 13.

[595] Ibid., p. 4.

[596] Ibid., p. 5. Oakes (1977:2) suggested that "Simmel favors metaphors taken from the textile industry," such as fabrics or webs.

[597] Lichtblau (1991:42) pointed out that Weber had already observed that Simmel clearly separated the objective interpretation of the meaning of a statement from the subject interpretation of the motives of a person. See Lichtblau (1991) for a full discussion Simmel's and Weber's approach to interaction and interpretation.

[598] Simmel, "The Field of Sociology," p. 3.

[599] Kaern, "The World as Human Construction," p. 76.

[600] Simmel, "The Field of Sociology," p. 24.

[601] Oakes, *The Problems of the Philosophy of History: An Epistemological Essay*, p. 19.

[602] Simmel, "The problem of Sociology," p. 318. This is not to say that there was universal agreement that he achieved his goal.

[603] Simmel, *The Conflict in Modern Culture and Other Essays*, p. 392.

[604] Boella, "Visibility and Surface: The Possible and the Unknown in GeorgSimmel's Concept of Form."

[605] Simmel, "Sociology of Religion," p. 3.

[606] Ibid., p. 4.

[607] Ibid., p. 4.

[608] Schutz, *Collected Papers I: The Problem of Social Reality*, p. 230.

[609] Schutz, *The Phenomenology of the Social World*, p. 125.

[610] Oakes, *Essays on Interpretation in Social Science*, p. 21.

[611] One is reminded here of Husserl, who, Alexander (1989:38) said, "showed that the objectivity of social life -- its 'realness' vis-à-vis the actor -- rests upon the actor's ability to bracket, to make invisible to his own consciousness, his intentional creation of objectivity."

[612] Simmel, *The Problems of the Philosophy of History: an Epistemological Essay*, p. 163.

[613] Simmel, "On the nature of Philosophy," p. 291.

[614] Bateson, *Steps to an Ecology of Mind,* p. 183. In a remarkably similar way Simmel (1977:171) identified one sense in which history had meaning: "Consider history as a function of metatheoretical interests, interests that provide a foundation for historical theory."

[615] Simmel, "Sociability: An Eample of Pure, or Formal, Sociology," pp. 50-51.

[616] There is a way of thinking about the dozens as a competitive game, the objective of which is to elevate content above play form in order to crack the other player, evidenced by his getting angry, hostile, abusive or embarrassed. Since it is only a game, whatever is said (content) ought to be subordinated to form and therefore not taken as real (cited example of the raised fist). The object of the game is to transcend the game itself, so to speak. To lose the game is to take what is said as real. As Simmel pointed out 1964b:52) "For conversation to remain satisfied with mere form it cannot allow any content to become significant in its own right," which of course signals the end of sociability.

[617] Simmel's emphasis.

[618] Simmel, "A Chapter in the Philosophy of Value," p. 579.

[619] Carrier, "Knowledge, Meaning, and Social Inequality in Kenneth Burke," p. 48.

[620] Simmel, "On the Nature of Philosophy," p. 288.

[621] Simmel, "The Problem of Sociology," p. 315.

[622] Simmel, "The Field of Sociology," p. 8.On the contrary, Levine (1959:23) suggested that Simmel was more interested in the interactional aspects of subject matter than the symbolic, which institutional analyses presumes.

[623] Simmel, *The Conflict in Modern Culture and Other Essays,* pp. 376-377.

[624] Oakes, *Essays on Interpretation in Social Sciences,* p. 47.

[625] Simmel, *The Conflict in Modern Culture and Other Essays,* p. 376.Si

[626] Simmel, "Sociability: An Example of Pure, or Formal, Sociology," p. 43. Weingartner(1962:54) "....contents are formed in one of many possible ways. In being formed, they become objects and independent of the process of life itself."

[627] Simmel, *The Conflict in Modern Culture and Other Essays, p. 377.*

[628] See Oakes(1980:41-45) for a discussion of Hesse's novel *The Glass Bead Game* and Simmel's distinction between subjective and objective culture.

[629] Simmel, *The Conflict in Modern Culture and Other Essays,* p. 393.

[630] Ibid., p. 392.

[631] Simmel, "The Ruin," p. 259.

[632] Oakes (1980:10) considered Simmel's theory to be "systematically ambiguous."

[633] Oakes, *The Problems of the Philosophy of History: An Epistemological Essay,* pp. 23-24.

[634] Levine, "The Structure of Simmel's Social Thought," p. 98.

[635] See Tenbruck (1965) for a review of Simmel's formal theory and its critics.

[636] Schutz and Luckmann (1973:173) did not include Simmel in the interpretative tradition in sociology because they believed the question of interpretation for Simmel was grounded in his philosophy, thus emphasizing a formal approach.

[637] Aronowitz, "The Simmel Revival: a Challenge to American Social Science," p. 17.

[638] Weingartner, *Experience and culture: The Philosophy of Georg Simmel,* pp. 7,9.

[639] See Levine (1965) for a list of subjects.

[640] Frisby, *Sociological Impressionism: A Reassessment of Georg Simmel's Social Theory,* p. 86.

[641] Spykman, *The Social Theory of Georg Simmel,* p. 93.

[642] Tenbruck, "Formal Sociology," p. 78.

[643] Weinstein and Weinstein, "Georg Simmel *Flaneur Bricoleur,*" pp. 152-153.

[644] Aronowitz, "The Simmel Revival: A Challenge to American Social Science," p. 94.

[645] Simmel, "The Problem of Sociology," p. 316.

[646] "How is Society Possible?"

[647] Ibid.

[648] "The Field of Sociology."
[649] "The Adventure."
[650] "Superiority and Subordination as Subject-Matter for Sociology."
[651] "The Stranger."
[652] "Fashion."
[653] Miller (1997:4) discussing pea soup on a beard, noted that the same soup as in the bowl, on the beard is disgusting because of what it means: it represents a character defect, or a moral failure. Also see Kolnai (2003), who drew on Husserl in a discussion of emotions of aversion such as fear, contempt, and disgust.
[654] Simmel, "Superiority and Subordination as Subject-Matter for Sociology," p. 168, and "The Problem of Sociology," pp. 320-321.
[655] Reiss, "The Social Integration of Queers and Peers," p. 64.
[656] Simmel, "Sociability: An Example of Pure, or Formal, Sociology," p. 46.
[657] Simmel, "the Adventure," p. 246.
[658] Ibid., p. 253.
[659] Ibid., p. 257.
[660] Ibid., p. 258.
[661] Wanderer, "Simmel's Forms of Experiencing as Symbolic Work."
[662] Simmel, "The Adventure," p. 256.
[663] Ibid., p. 251.
[664] Ibid., p. 250.
[665] Borges, "Tlon, Uqbar, Orbus Terius," p. 3.
[666] Simmel, "The Adventure," p. 247.
[667] Simmel employed dualisms repeatedly, as, e.g., in his analysis of fashion (1904b:134) which combines "union and segregation...."
[668] Helle, "The Secret in the Work of Georg Simmel."
[669] Simmel, "The Sociology of Secrecy and of Secret Societies," p. 471.
[670] In subsequent sociological analyses Simmel analyzed the social consequences of secrets, whether their content "embraced the highest values...." or "moral badness." (Simmel 1906:463)
[671] Simmel, "The Stranger," p. 402.
[672] Ibid., p. 407.
[673] Levine (1977) pointed out that the stranger has been subjected to several misinterpretations, as "marginal man," "outsider, etc.
[674] Simmel, "The Stranger," pp. 404-405.
[675] Ibid., p. 405.
[676] Schutz, Collected Papers I:The Problem of Social Reality, p. 326.
[677] Simmel, "How is Society Possible?" p. 345.
[678] Lichtblau, "Causality or Interaction? Simmel, Weber, and Interpretive Sociology," p. 52.
[679] Simmel, "How is Society Possible?" p. 343.
[680] Kaern, "The World as Human Construction," p. 78. Kaern (1990:77) in his discussion of "As-if" includes typifications and uses the example of fruit which make it possible to place apples and oranges in the same type "fruit" "as if they were the same although they are not."
[681] Kaern, "The World as Human Construction," p. 93.
[682] Compare Wittgenstein's (1964:193e) observation, "so we interpret it, and see it as we interpret it," and Lippman's (cited in Sandstrom, et al. 2003:47) similar sentiment, "for the most part, we do not first see and then define, we define first and then see."
[683] Klapp, Heroes, Villains, and Fools.
[684] Wanderer, "Hobo Signs: Embodied Metaphors and Metonymies."
[685] Davies, The Salterton Trilogy: Leaven of Malice, p. 30.
[686] THE NEW YORKER, "How to Intersect Without Really Trying," p. 70.

208

---

[687] Lichtblau, "Causality of Interactin? Simmel, Weber and Interpretive Sociology," p. 52. Simmel's contribution to interpretative theory was discussed in Lichtblau (1991:40), who noted that "quite early Weber credited Simmel with the achievement of having worked out 'by far the most logically developed approaches to a theory of 'interpretation. . .'" Not surprisingly, Weber accused Simmel of turning problems of being into problems of meaning. Oakes wrote that "Simmel's various contributions to the problem of interpretation appear in a variety of writing published between 1892 and 1918, "but he never attempted to articulate these views into a systematic theory of interpretation..." (Simmel 1980:57)

# BIBLIOGRAPHY

Abel, T. "The Operation Called *Verstehen*." *Readings in the Philosophy of the Social Sciences*. Eds. H. Feigl and M. Brodbeck. New York: Apple-Century-Crofts, Inc., 1948.

Adorno, T. W. "On Radio Music." *Studies in Philosophy and Social Science*. New York: Institute of Social Research 9 (1941):17-48.

Alexander, J. 1986. "Rethinking Durkheim's Intellectual Development, II: Working Out a Religious Sociology." *International Sociology* 1.2 (1986):189-201.

Alexander, J. *Structure and Meaning: Rethinking Classical Sociology*. New York: Columbia University Press. 1989.

*American Record Guide*. March/April, 1999.

Aronowitz, Stanley. "The Simmel Revival: A Challenge to American Social Science." *The Sociological Quarterly* 35.3 (1994):397-414.

Backhaus, Gary. "Georg Simmel as an Eidetic Social Scientist." *Sociological Theory* 16.3 (1998):260-281.

Banks, Russell. "The Caul." *The Angel on the Roof: The Stories of Russell*. New York: Harper Collins Publishers, 2000.

Barthes, Rolande. *Mythologies*. New York: Hill and Wang, 1972.

Bateson, G. *Steps To An Ecology Of Mind*. New York: Chandler Publishing Co., 1972

Bash, Harry H. "A Scatter of Sociologies: Vertical Drift and the Quest for Theoretical Integration in Sociology." *The Living Legacy of Marx, Durkheim & Weber*, ed. by Richard Altschuler. New York: Gordian Knot Books, 1998.

210

Beggan James, K. and Scott T. Allison. "The Playboy Rabbit is Soft, Furry, and Cute: Is this Really the Symbol of Masculine Dominance of Women?" *Journal of Men's Studies* 9.3 (2001):341-370.

Bendix, Reinhard. *Max Weber: an Intellectual Portrait*. New York: Doubleday & Co., 1960.

Berger, Arthur A. *Durkheim is Dead*. Walnut Creek, CA: Altamira Press, 2003.

Berger, P.L. and T. Luckman. *The Social Construction of Reality: A Treatise in the Sociology of Knowledge*. Garden City, N.Y.: Doubleday and Co., Anchor Books, 1966.

Berlin, I., editor. *The Age of Enlightenment: The 18th Century Philosophers*. New York: New American Library, 1958.

Berman, Art. *From the New Criticism to Deconstruction*. Urbana and Chicago: University of Illinois Press, 1988.

Bierce, Ambrose. *The Devil's Dictionary*. Mount Vernon, N.Y.: The Peter Pauper Press, 1958.

Boella, Laura. "Visibility and Surface: The Possible and the Unknown in Georg Simmel's Concept of Form." *Social Science Information* 25.4 (Dec. 1986): 925-943.

Borges, J.L. "Tlon, Uqbar, Orbis Terius." *Labyrinths: Selected Stories & Other Writings*. Ed. by D.A. Yates and J.E. Irby. New York: New Directions, 1964.

Bourdieu, Pierre. *The Logic of Practice*. Stanford, California: Stanford University Press, 1990.

Bourdieu, Pierre. "Social Space and Symbolic Power." *Sociological Theory* 7.1 (1989):14-25.

Brown, Richard H. "Symbolic Realism and Sociological Thought: Beyond the Positivistic-Romantic Debate." *Structure, Consciousness, and History*. Eds. R.H. Brown and S.M. Lyman. London: Cambridge University Press, 1978.

Brown, Richard H. "History and Hermeneutics. Wilhelm Dilthey and the Dialectics of Interpretive Method."*Structure, Consciousness, and History*. Eds. R.H. Brown and S.M. Lyman. London: Cambridge University Press, 1978.

Burawoy, M., et al. "Public Sociologies: A Symposium from Boston College." *Social Problems* 51.1 (2004):103-130.

Byrne, N.T. "Emile Durkheim as Symbolic Interactionist," *Sociological Symposium* 16 (1976):25-43.

Carrier, James G. "Knowledge, Meaning, and Social Inequality in Kenneth Burke." *American Journal of Sociology* 88.1 (1982):43-61.

Coenen, H. "Developments in the Phenomenological Reading of Durkheim's Work," *Social Forces* 59.4 (1981):951-965.

Collins, Randall. *Weberian Sociological Theory.* Cambridge:Cambreidge University Press, 1986.

Corning, P. "Durkheim and Spencer." *British Journal of Sociology* 33.3 (1982):359-382.

Coser, Lewis A. *George Simmel.* Englewood Cliffs, New Jersey: Prentice Hall, 1965.

Coser, Lewis A. *Masters of Sociological Thought.* New York: Harcourt Brace Jovanovich, 1971.

Costelloe, Timothy M. "Between the Subject and Sociology: Alfred Schutz's Phenomenology of the Life-World." *Human Studies* 19.3 (1996):247-266.

Csikszentmihalyi, Milhaly. *The Evolving Self: A Psychology for the Third Millennium.* New York: HarperCollins Publishing, 1993.

Davies, Robertson. *The Salterton Trilogy: Leaven of Malice.* Penguin Books, 1980.

Davis, J.A. "Teaching Social Facts with Computers," *Teaching Sociology* 5.3 (1978):235-258.

Davis, M.S. "That's 'Classic!' The Phenomenology and Rhetoric of Successful Social Theories." *Philosophy of the Social Sciences* 16.3 (1986):285-301.

Denzin, Norman K. *Interpretive Interactionism.* Newbury Park, California: Sage Publications, Inc., 1989.

Denzin, Norman K. "Interpretive Interactionism and the Use of Life Stories." *Revista Internacional de Sociologia* 44.3 (1986):321-337.

Denzin, Norman K. "Interpreting the Lives of Ordinary People: Sartre, Heidegger and Faulkner." *Life Stories /Recits de Vie* 2 (1986):6-20.

Denzin, Norman K. "Reading Tender Mercies: Two Interpretations." *Sociological Quarterly* 30.1 (1989): 37-57.

Denzin, Norman K. "Paris Texas and Baudrillard on America." *Theory, Culture and Society.* 8.2 (1991):121-133.

Denzin, Norman K. "Rain Man in Las Vegas: Where Is the Action for the Postmodern Self?" *Symbolic Interaction*, 16.1 (1993):65-77.

Dewey, John. *Intelligence in the Modern World: John Dewey's Philosophy.* Ed. by J. Ratner. New York: Modern Library, 1939.

Dilthey, W. "The Dream." *Philosophy of History in Our Time.* Ed. by H. Meyerhoff. New York: Doubleday Anchor Books, 1959.

Douglas, M. *How Institutions Think.* Syracuse, N. Y.: Syracuse University Press, 1986.

Douglas, M. *Rules and Meanings.* Baltimore, Maryland: Penguin Books Ltd., 1973.

Durkheim, Emile. *The Division of Labor in Society.* Trans. By George Simpson. New York: The Free Press, 1964.

Durkheim, Emile. *The Division of Labor in Society.* Trans. by W.D. Halls. New York: The Free Press, 1984.

Durkheim, Emile. *Education and Sociology.* New York: The Free Press, 1956.

Durkheim, Emile. *The Elementary Forms of the Religious Life.* Trans. by J.W. Swain. New York: The Free Press, 1965.

Durkheim, Emile. *The Rules of the Sociological Method.* Glencoe, Illinois: The Free Press, 1938.

Durkheim, Emile. *Sociology and Philosophy.* Trans by D.F. Pocock. Glencoe, Illionois: The Free Press, 1953.

Durkheim, Emile. *Suicide.* Trans. by John A. Spaulding and George Simpson. Glencoe, Illinois: The Free Press, 1951.

Durkheim, Emile and M. Mauss. *Primitive Classification*. Trans. by R. Needham. Chicago: The University of Chicago Press, 1963.

Eldridge J.E.T. *Max Weber: The Interpretation of Social Reality*. New York: Charles Scribner's Sons, 1971.

Emerson, Joan P. "Behavior in Private Places: Sustaining Definitions of Reality in Gynecological Examinations." *Recent Sociology*. Ed. by P. Dreitsel. New York: Macmillan, 1970.

*The Encyclopaedia Britannica. Eleventh Edition. Volume VII.* New York: The Encyclopaedia Britannica Company, 1910.

Featherstone, Mike, 1991. "Georg Simmel: An Introduction." *Theory Culture & Society* 8.3 (1991): 1-16

Fernandez-Armesto, Felipe. *Near a Thousand Tables: A History of Food.* New York: The Free Press, 2002.

Fine, Gary A. "Wittgenstein's Kitchen: Sharing Meaning in Restaurant Work." *Theory and Society* 24 (1995):245-269.

Fish, Stanley E. *Is There a Text in this Class? The Authority of Interpretive Communities*. Cambridge, Massachusetts: Harvard University Press, 1980.

Fernandez-Armesto, Felipe. *Near A Thousand Tables: A History of Food.* New York: The Free Press, 2002.

Frazer, Sir James George. *The New Golden Bough.* Ed by T.H. Gaster. New York: Criterion Books, 1959.

Freud, Sigmund. *An Outline of Psychoanalysis*. Trans. by J.Strachey. New York: W. W. Norton & Company, Inc, 1949.

Freud, Sigmund. *A General Introduction to Psychoanalysis*. Trans. by J. Riviere. Garden City, New York: Garden City Publishing Company Inc., 1943.

Freud, Sigmund. *Psychopathology of Everyday Life.* Trans. by A. A. Brill. New York: The New American Library A Mentor Book, 1956.

Freud, Sigmund. *The Interpretation of Dreams.* Trans. by A.A. Brill. New York: Carlton House, no date.

Frisby, D. *Sociological Impressionism: A Reassessment of Georg Simmel's Social Theory*. London: Heinemann, 1981.

Fulbrook, Mary. "Max Weber's 'Interpretive Sociology': A Comparison of Conception and Practice." *The British Journal of Sociology* 29.1 (1978): 71-82

Gadamer Hans-Georg. *Truth and Method, 2nd rev*. New York: The Continuum Publishing Co., 2000.

Garfinkel, Harold. *Studies in Ethnomethodology*. Englewood Cliffs, New Jersey: Prentice-Hall, Inc., 1967.

Gerth, H.H. and C. W. Mills. *From Max Weber: Essays in Sociology*. London: Lowe and Bydone Ltd., 1957.

Giddens, Anthony. *Central Problems in Social Theory*. Berkeley and Los Angeles: University of California Press, 1979.

Giddens, Anthony. *Modernity and Self-Identity: Self and Society in the Late Modern Age*. Stanford, California: Stanford University Press, 1991.

Giddens, Anthony. *New Rules of Sociological Method: A Positive Critique of interpretative Sociologies*, London: Hutchinson, 1976.

Giddens Anthony. *New Rules of Sociological Method: A Positive Critique of Interpretative Sociologies*. New York: Basic Books, 1976.

Giddens, Anthony. *Profiles And Critiques In Social Theory*. Berkeley and Los Angeles: University of California Press, 1982.

Glassner, Barry and Jonathan D. Moreno. *The Qualitative-Quantitative Distinction in the Social Sciences*. Boston: Kluwer Academic Publishers, 1989.

Goldberg, Bernard. *Bias*. Washington, D.C.: Regency Publishers, Inc., 2002.

Gurwitsch, A. "Intentionality, Constitution, and Intentional Analysis." *Phenomenology: The Philosophy of Edmund Husserl and Its Interpretation*. Ed. By J.J Kockelmans. Garden City, New York: Doubleday & Co. Inc., 1967.

Gurwitsch, A. "On the Intentionality of Consciousness." *Phenomenology: The Philosophy of Edmund Husserl and Its Interpretation*. Ed. by J. J. Kockelmans. Garden City New York: Doubleday & Co. Inc., 1967.

Halfpenny, Peter. *Positivism and Sociology: Explaining Social Life.* London: George Allen & Unwin, 1982.

Hardin, Joseph B., Martha Bauman Power, and Noreen M. Sugrue. "The Progressive Concretization of Phenomenological Sociology." *Studies in Symbolic Interaction* 7 (1986):49-74.

Haritos, Rosa, and Glassman, Ronald M. "Emile Durkheim and the Sociological Enterprise." *The Renaissance of Sociological Theory.* Ed by Henry Etzkowitz and R. M. Glassman. Itasca, Illinois: F.E. Peacock Publishers, Inc., 1991.

Harris, S.R. "The Social Construction of Equality in Everyday Life." *Human Studies* 23 (2000): 371-393.

Hawkins, M. J. "Traditionalism and Organicism in Durkheim's Early Writings," *Journal of The History of The Behavioral Sciences* 16.1 (1980):31-44.

Helle, Horst. 2002. "The Secret in the Work of Georg Simmel." www.horsthelle.com/**simmeld**.html.

Hilbert, Richard A. *The Classical Roots of Ethnomethodology: Durkheim, Weber, and Garfinkle.* Chapel Hill:The University of North Carolina Press, 1992.

Hilbert, Richard A. "Ethnomethodological Recovery of Durkheim." *Sociological Perspective* 34.3 (1991):337-357.

Hill, S. "Professions: Mechanical Solidarity and Process or: How I Learnt to Live with a Primitive Society." *Australian and New Zealand Journal of Sociology* 9.3 (1973):30-37.

Hirsch, E.D. Jr. *Validity in Interpretation.* New Haven: Yale University Press, 1967.

Hughes, H. Stuart. *Consciousness and Society.* New York: Alfred A. Knopf, Inc., 1958.

Hund, J. "Are Social Facts Real?" *British Journal of Sociology* 33.2 (1982):270-278.

Hund J. "Sociologism and Philosophy." *British Journal of Sociology* 41.2 (1990):197-224.

Husserl, Edmund. *Cartesian Meditations.* Trans. By D. Cairns. The Hague: Martinus Nijhoff, 1973.

Husserl, Edmund. *Ideas. General Introduction to Pure Phenomenology.* Trans. By W.R. Boyce Gibson. London: George Allen & Unwin Ltd., 1931.

Husserl, Edmund. *Ideas.* Trans. by W.R. Boyce Gibson. New York: Humanities Press, 1967 (1931).

Husserl, Edmund. *The Idea of Phenomenology.* Trans. By William P. Alston and George Nakhnikian. The Hague: Martinus Nijhoff, 1964.

Husserl, Edmund. *Phenomenology and the Crisis of Philosophy.* Trans. by Quentin Lauer. New York: Harper Torchbook, 1965.

Husserl, Edmund. "The Thesis of the Natural Standpoint and Its Suspension." *Phenomenology: The Philosophy of Edmund Husserl and Its Interpretation.* Ed. by J.J. Kockelmans. Garden City, New York: Doubleday & Co. Inc., 1967.

James, W. *Pragmatism: A New Name for Some Old Ways of Thinking.* New York: Longmans, Green and Co., 1943.

Jones, Susan S. *Durkheim Reconsidered.* Cambridge, UK: Polity, 2001.

Kaern, Michael. "The World as Human Construction." *Georg Simmel and Contemporary Sociology.* Eds. Michael Kaern, Bernard S,. Phillips and Robert S. Cohen. The Netherlands: A. A. Dordrecht, Kluwewar Academic Publishers, 1990.

Karady, Victor. "Durkheim, Social Sciences, and the University: The Balance Sheet of a Semi-Failure." *Revue francaise de Sociologie* 17.2 (1976):267-311.

Kivisto, Peter annd William H. Swatos, Jr. "Weber and Interpretive Sociology in America." *The Sociological Quarterly* 31.1 (1990):149-163.

Klapp, O. E. *Heroes, Villains and Fools.* Englewood Cliffs, N.J.: Prentice Hall Inc., 1962.

Knapp, P. "The Question of Hegelian Influence upon Durkheim's Sociology," *Sociological Inquiry* 55.1 (1985):1-15.

Kockelmans, Joseph. J. "Husserl's Phenomenology and 'Existentialism.'" *Phenomenology: The Philosophy of Edmund Husserl and Its Interpretation.* Garden City, New York: Doubleday & Co. Inc., 1967.

Kockelmans, Joseph J. "Theoretical Problems in Phenomenological Psychology." *Phenomenology and the Social Sciences Vol. I.* Edited by M. Natanson. Evanston, Ill. Northwestern University Press, 1973.

Kolnai, Aurel. *On Disgust.* Open Court Publishing Company, 2003.

Laffey, Marcus. "Inside Dope: Scenes from the Life of an Officer on the Narcotics Beat." *The New Yorker* February 1, 1999.

Lakoff, George and Mark Johnson. *Metaphors We Live By.* Chicago and London: University of Chicago Press, 1980.

Laza, M. "Gender, Discourse and Semiotic: The Politics of Parenthood Representations," *Discourse and Society* 11.3 (2000): 373-400.

Lengermann, P. "Intersubjectivity and Domination: A Feminist Investigation of the Sociology of Alfred Schutz." *Sociological Theory* 13.1 (1995): 25-36.

Levi-Strauss, C. "French Sociology." *Twentieth Century Sociology.* Ed. By G. Gurvitch and W. E. Moore. New York: The Philosophical Library, 1945.

Levine, Donald N. "Simmel at a Distance: On the History and Systematics of the Sociology of the Stranger." *Sociological Focus* 10.1 (1977):15-29.

Levine, Donald N. "Some Problems in Simmel's Work." *George Simmel.* Ed. by Coser. L.A. Englewood Cliffs, New Jersey: Prentice Hall, 1965.

Levine, Donald N. "The Structure of Simmel's Thought." *Essays on Sociology, Philosophy & Aesthetics by Georg Simmel et al.* Ed. by K.H. Wolff. New York: Harper Torchbooks, 1959.

Levine, Donald N., Elwood B. Carter and Eleanor Miller Gorman. "Simmel's Influence on American Sociology I." *American Journal of Sociology* 81.4 (1976):813-845.

Levine, Donald N., Elwood B. Carter and Eleanor Miller Gorman. "Simmel's Influence on American Sociology II." *American Journal of Sociology* 81.5 (1976):1112-1132.

Levy, David J. *Realism: An Essay in Interpretation and Social Reality.* Atlantic Highlands, New Jersey: Humanities Press, 1981.

Lewis, Tom T. "Ideal Types: Opium of the Social Scientists." *ETC* 32.3 (1975):287-304.

Lichtblau, Klaus. "Causality or Interaction? Simmel, Weber and Interpretive Sociology." *Theory Culture & Society* 8.3 (1991): 33-62

Lundberg, G. "The Postulates of Science and Their Implications for Sociology." *Philosophy of the Social Sciences*. Ed. M. Natanson. New York: Random House, 1963.

Lukes, S. *Emile Durkheim: His Life and Work. A Historical and Critical Study.* New York: Penguin Books, 1973.

Maffesoli, Michel. "Epistemology of Everyday Life [Toward a Sociological "Formism"]," *Cahiers Internationaux de Sociologie* 30.74 (1983):57-70.

Malinowski, Bronislaw. *A Scientific Theory of Culture and Other Essays*, New York: Oxford University Press, 1960.

Manning, P. K. "Metaphors of the Field: Varieties of Organizational Discourse." *Qualitative Methodology*. Ed. by J.V. Van Maanen. Newbury Park, California: Sage Publications, 1983.

Maquire, Brendan. "Interpretive Scoiology: The Diseased Theoretical Perspective." *Humanity and Society* 7.2 (1983):104-126.

Marx, Karl. "Points on the Modern State and Civil Society. Notebooks of 1844-1845." *Writings of the Young Marx on Philosophy and Society.* Ed. and Trans. by Loyd D. Easton and Kurt H. Guddat. Garden City, N.Y. Doubleday & Co., Inc., 1967.

Marx, Karl. *Capital and Other Writings*. Ed. by Max Eastman. New York: The Modern Library, 1932.

Marx, Karl. *Writings of the Young Marx on Philosophy and Society*. Ed and Trans by Loyd D. Easton and Kurt H. Guddat. Garden City, N.Y. Doubleday & Co., Inc., 1967.

Marx, Karl. *A Contribution to the Critique of Political Economy*. Trans. and ed. by N.I. Stone. Chicago: Charles H. Kerr & Company, 1904.

McCullock, Gary. "The Very Idea of the Phenomenological." *Proceedings of the Aristotelian Society* 93.1 (1993):39-57.

Mead, George H. *Mind, Self, & Society, Vol 1*. Ed by C. W. Morris. Chicago: University of Chicago Press, 1974.

Merton, Robert K. *Social Theory and Social Structure*. New York: The Free Press, 1968.

Mestrovic, Stjepan. *Durkheim and PostModern Culture*. New York: Aldine De Gruyter, Inc., 1992.

Mestrovic, Stjepan. "Durkheim's Concept of Anomie Considered as a 'Total' Social Fact." *British Journal of Sociology* 38.4 (1987):567-583.

Mestrovic, Stjepan. "Searching for the Starting Points of Scientific Inquiry: Durkheim's Rules of Sociological Method and Schopenhauer's Philosophy." *Sociological Inquiry*. 59.3 (1989):267-286.

Miller, William I. *The Anatomy of Disgust*. Harvard University Press, 1997.

Morrison, J.C. "Husserl and Brentano on Intentionality." *Philosophy and Phenomenological Research* XXXI.1 (September 1970):27-46.

Morrison, Kenneth L. "Social Life and External Regularity: A Comparative Analysis of the Investigative Methods of Durkheim and Weber." *The Living Legacy of Marx, Durkheim & Weber*. Ed. by Richard Altschuler. New York: Gordian Knot Books, 1998.

Mulligan, G. and B. Lederman. "Social Facts and Rules of Practice," *American Journal of Sociology* 83.3 (1977):539-555.

Nash, Ogden. *Everyone But Thee and Me*. Boston: Little, Brown and Company, 1962.

Natanson, Maurice. "Alfred Schutz: Philosopher and Social Scientist." *Human Studies* 21.1 (1998):1-12.

Natanson, Maurice. *Anonymity: A Study in the Philosophy of Alfred Schutz*. Bloomington, Indiana: Indiana University Press, 1986.

Natanson, Maurice. *Edmund Husserl: Philosopher of Infinite Tasks*. Evanston: Northwestern University Press, 1973.

Natanson, Maurice. *Literature, Philosophy and the Social Sciences*. The Hague: Martinus Nijhoff, 1962.

*The New Yorker*. "How to Intersect Without Really Trying" in "Talk of the Town." September 18 (2000):70.

Orleans, M. "Phenomenological Sociology." *The Renaissance Of Sociological Theory*. Ed. By H. Etzkowitz & R.M. Glassman. Ithaca, Illinois: F.E. Peacock Publishers, Inc., 1991.

Owsley, Richard and Gary Backhaus. "Simmel's Four Components of Historical Science." *Human Sciences* 26.2 (2003): 209-222.

Palmer, Richard E. *Hermeneutics*. Evanston, Illinois: Northwestern University Press, 1969.

Pampel, Fred. *Sociological Lives and Ideas*. New York: Worth Publishers, 2000.

Pareto, Vilfredo. *The Mind and Society. Volume I: Non-Logical Conduct*. Ed. by Arthur Livingston. New York: Harcourt, Brace and Company, Inc., 1935.

Parsons, Talcott. "Max Weber: 1964-1964." *American Sociological Review*. 30.2 (1965): 171-175.

Parsons, Talcott. *The Structure of Social Action*. New York: Free Press, 1968.

Pearce, F. *The Radical Durkheim*. London: Unwin Hyman, 1989.

Pendergast, Tom and Sara Pendergast. *Dictionary of Films and Film-Makers, Vol. 1, 4th Edition*. Detroit: St. James Press.

Perinbanayagam, R. S. "The Definition of the Situation: An Analysis of the Ethnomethodological and Dramaturgical View." *Sociological Quarterly* 15.4 (1974):521-541.

Peterson, Karen E. "Discourse and Display: The Modern Eye, Entrepreneurship, and the Cutlural Transformatin of the Patchwork Quilt." *Sociological Perspectives*. 46.4 (2003):461-490.

Phillipson, Michael. "Theory, Methodology and Conceptualization." *New Directions in Sociological Theory*. Ed. By Paul Filmer et al. London: Collier-Macmillan, 1972.

Post, D. L. "Floyd Allport and the Launching of Modern Social Psychology," *Journal of the History of the Behavioral Sciences*, 16.4 (1989):369-376.

Pressler, Charles A. and Fabio B. Dasilva. *Sociology and Interpretation: From Weber to Habermas*. Albany, New York: State University of New York Press, 1996.

Pritchard, James. *Introduction to the Physical History of Mankind (4vols) London 1836-49.* Chicago: University of Chicago Press, 1973 (1847).

Radcliffe-Brown, A.R. *Structure and Function in Primitive Society.* Glencoe, Illinois: Free Press, 1952.

Rawls, Anne W. "Durkheim's Epistemology: The Neglected Argument," *American Journal of Sociology* 102.2 (1996):430-482.

Rawls, Anne W. "Durkheim's Epistemology: The Initial Critique, 1915-1924." *The Sociological Quarterly* 38.1 (1997):111-145.

Reiss, A.J. Jr. "The Social Integration of Queers and Peers." *The Other Side.* Ed. by H.S. Becker. New York: The Free Press, 1964.

Remender, P. A. "Social Facts and Symbolic Interaction: A Search for the Key Social Emergent in Durkheim's Approach," *Wisconsin Sociologist* 10.4 (1973):83-94.

Remmling, G. W. *Road to Suspicion: A Study of Modern Mentality and The Sociology of Knowledge.* Appleton-Century-Crofts, 1967.

Rickman, H.P. *Dilthey Today: A Critical Appraisal of the Contemporary Relevance of His Work.* N.Y.: Greenwood Press, 1988.

Ricoeur, Paul. *Freud and Philosophy: An Essay on Interpretation.* New Haven and London: Yale University Press, 1970.

Ricoeur, Paul. *Interpretation Theory: Discourse and the Surplus of Meaning.* Fort Worth, Texas: Texas Christian University Press, 1976.

Ritzer, G. *Sociological Theory.* New York: McGraw-Hill, 2000.

Robertson, Bruce. "20th Century American Art: The Ellsworth Collection," *American Art Review* XI.5 (1984):208-219.

Ronen, Ruth. "The Real as Limit to Interpretation." *Semiotica,* 132.1/2 (2000):121-135.

Rorty, Richard. *Objectivity, Relativism, and Truth.* Cambridge; New York: Cambridge University Press, 1991.

Rose, E. *The Werald*. Boulder, Co.: The Waiting Room Press, 1988.

Rubenstein, D. "Individual Minds and the Social Order," *Qualitative Sociology* 5.2 (1982):121-139.

Sandstrom, Kent L., Daniel D. Martin, and Gary A. Fine. *Symbols, Selves and Social Reality.* Los Angeles: Roxbury Publishing Co., 2002.

Scaff, L.A. "Weber, Simmel and the Sociology of Culture." *Sociological Review,* 36.2 (1988):1-30.

Scanlon. "Review of *Sokolowski's Introduction to Phenomenology.*" *Husserl Studies* 18 (2000):83-88

Schon, D. A. "Generative Metaphor: A Perspective on Problem-Setting in Social Policy." *Metaphor and Thought*. Ed. By A. Ortony. Cambridge: Cambridge University Press, 1979.

Schutz, Alfred. *Collected Papers I: The Problem of Social Reality*. Ed. by M. Natanson. The Hague: Martinus Nijhoff, 1971.

Schutz, Alfred. *Collected Papers. II Studies in Social Theory*. Ed. by A. Brodersen. The Hague: Martinus Nijhoff, 1971.

Schutz, Alfred. *Collected Papers III: Studies in Phenomenological Philosophy*. Ed. by I. Schutz. The Hague: Martinus Nijhoff, 1972.

Schutz Alfred. "Phenomenology and the Social Sciences." *Phenomenology*. Ed. By J.J. Kockelmans. Garden City, N.J.: Doubleday & Co., 1967.

Schutz, Alfred. *The Phenomenenology of the Social World*. Evanston, Illinois: Northwestern University Press, 1967.

Schutz, Alfred and T. Luckman. *The Structures of the Life World*. Trans. by R.M. Zanner and H.T. Englehardt, Jr. Evanston, Illinois: Northwestern University Press, 1973.

Segre, Sandro. "On Max Weber's Awareness of Emile Durkheim." *History of Sociology*:6.7 (1986-1987): 151-167.

Service, Elman R. *A Profile of Primitive Culture.* New York: Harper & Brothers, 1958.

Silverman, David. "Some Neglected Questions about Social Reality." *New Directions in Sociological Theory*. Ed. By Paul Filmer et al. London: Collier-Macmillan, 1972.

Silverman, David. "Methodology and Meaning." *New Directions in Sociological Theory*. Ed. By Paul Filmer et al. London: Collier-Macmillan, 1972.

Simmel, Georg. "The Adventure." *Essays on Sociology, Philosophy & Aesthetics*. Ed. by K.H. Wolff. New York: Harper & Row, 1959.

Simmel, Georg. "A Chapter in the Philosophy of Value." *American Journal of Sociology* V.5 (1900):577-603.

Simmel, Georg. *The Conflict in Modern Culture and Other Essays*. Trans. by K. Peter Etzkorn. New York: Teachers College Press, 1968

Simmel, Georg. *Essays on Interpretation in Social Science*. Trans. and ed. by G.S. Oakes. Totowa, New Jersey: Rowman and Littlefield, 1980.

Simmel, Georg. "Fashion." *International Quarterly* 10 (1904):130-155.

Simmel, Georg. "The Field of Sociology." *The Sociology of Georg Simmel*, trans. and edited by K.H.. New York: The Free Press, 1964.

Simmel, Georg. "How is Society Possible?" *Essays on Sociology, Philosophy & Aesthetics*. Ed. by K.H. Wolff. New York: Harper & Row, 1959.

Simmel, Georg. "The Number of Members as Determining the Sociological Form of the Group. I." *American Journal of Sociology* VIII.1 (1902):1-46

Simmel, Georg. "On the Nature of Philosophy." *Essays on Sociology, Philosophy & Aesthetics*. Ed. by K.H. Wolff. New York: Harper & Row, 1959.

Simmel, Georg. *The Problems of the Philosophy of History: An Epistemological Essay*. Trans. and ed. by Guy Oakes. New York: The Free Press, 1977.

Simmel, Georg. "The Problem of Sociology." *Essays on Sociology, Philosophy & Aesthetics*. Ed. by K.H. Wolff. New York: Harper & Row, 1959.

Simmel, Georg. "The Ruin." *Essays on Sociology Philosophy & Aesthetics*. Ed. by K.H. Wolff. New York: Harper & Row, 1959.

Simmel, Georg. "Sociability: An Example of Pure, or Formal, Sociology." *The Sociology of Georg Simmel*. Trans. and ed. by K.H.. New York: The Free Press, 1964.

Simmel, Georg. "The Sociology of Conflict." *American Journal of Sociology* IX (1904):490-525.

Simmel, Georg. *Sociology of Religion*. Trans. by C. Rosenthal New York: Philosophical Library, 1959.

Simmel, Georg. "The Sociology of Secrecy and of Secret Societies." *American Journal of Sociology* 11.4 (1906):441-497.

Simmel, Georg. "The Stranger." *The Sociology of Georg Simmel*. Trans. and edited by K.H. Wolff. New York: The Free Press, 1964.

Simmel, Georg. "Superiority and Subordination as Subject-Matter for Sociology." *American Journal of Sociology* 2.2 (1896):167-189.

Smith, William Robertson. *Lectures on the Religion of the Semites*. London: Adam and Charles Black, 1894.

Sokolowski, Robert. *Introduction to Phenomenology*. Cambridge: Cambridge University Press, 2000.

Sontag, Susan. *Against Interpretation*. New York: Dell Publishing Co., 1966.

Sorokin, Pitirim. *Contemporary Sociological Theories*. New York: Harper & Brothers, 1928.

Spykman, Nicholas J. *The Social Theory of Georg Simmel*. New York: Russell & Russell Inc., 1964.

Stark, Werner. *The Sociology of Knowledge*. New York: Humanities Press, 1958.

Stone, G. and H. Farberman. "On the Edge of Rapprochement. Was Durkheim Moving toward the Perspective of Symbolic Interaction?" *Sociological Quarterly* 8 (1967):149-164.

Swingewood, Alan. *A Short History of Sociological Thought 2nd Ed*. New York: St. Martin's Press, 1991.

Tenbruck, F.H. "Formal Sociology." *George Simmel*. Ed. by Coser, L.A. Englewood Cliffs, New Jersey: Prentice Hall, 1965.

Tiryakian, E.A. *Sociologism and Existentialism*. Englewood Cliffs, New Jersey: Prentice-Hall, Inc., 1962.

Tiryakian, E.A. "Sociology and Existential Phenomenology." *Phenomenology and the Social Sciences Vol. I*. Ed. by M. Natanson. Evanston, Illinois: Northwestern University Press, 1973.

Tobin, Jacqueline and Raymond G. Dobard. *Hidden in Plain View, a Secret Story of Quilts and the Underground Railroad*. New York: Doubleday, 1999.

Train, John. *Valsalva's Maneuver: Mots Justes and Indispensable Terms*. New York: Harper & Row, 1989.

Truzzi, Marcello. *Verstehen: Subjective Understanding in the Social Sciences*. Menlo Park, California: Addison-Wesley Publishing Company, 1974.

Tudor, Andrew. "Misunderstanding Everyday Life." *The Sociological* Review 24.3 (1976): 479-503.

Turner, Jonathan H. *The Structure of Sociological Theory*. Homewood, Illinois: The Dorsey Press, 1974.

Turner, Jonathon H. "Using Classical Theorists to Reconceptualize Community Dynamics." *Research in Community Sociology* 6 (1996):19-36.

Turner, Jonathan H. and Leonard Beeghley. *The Emergence of Sociological Theory*. Homewood, Illinois: The Dorsey Press, 1981.

Velarde-Mayol, Victor. *On Husserl*. Belmont, California:Wadsworth, 2000.

Vogt, W. Paul. "Early French Contributions to the Sociology of Knowledge," *Research in Sociology of Knowledge, Sciences and Art* 2 (1979):101-121.

Walsh, David. "Sociology and the Social World." *New Directions in Sociological Theory*. Ed. By Paul Filmer et al. London: Collier-Macmillan, 1972.

Wanderer, Jules J. "Simmel's Forms of Experiencing as Symbolic Work." *Symbolic Interaction* 10 (1987):21-28.

Wanderer, Jules J. "Hobo Signs: Embodied Metaphors and Metonymies." *The American Journal of Semiotics*. 17.4 (2001): 131-146.

Watson, Rodney. "'Interpretive' Sociology in Great Britain: The State of the Art." *Revue Suisse de Sociologies* 26.3 (2000):507-529.

Weber, Max. *The City*. Trans. and ed. D. Martindale and G. Neuwirth. New York: Collier Books, 1962.

Weber, Max. *From Max Weber: Essays in Sociology*. Trans. by Eds. H.H. Gerth and C. W. Mills. London: Routledge & Kegan Paul Ltd., 1957.

Weber, Max. *The Methodology of the Social Sciences*. Trans. and Eds. E. A. Shils and H. A. Finch. Glencoe, Illinois: The Free Press, 1949.

Weber, Max. *Rational and Social Foundations of Music*. Carbondale: The Southern Illinois Press, 1958.

Weber, Max. "Some Categories of Interpretive Sociology." Trans. by Edith E. Graber. *The Sociological Quarterly* 22.2 (1981):151-180.

Weber, Max. *The Theory of Social and Economic Organization*. Ed. by Talcot Parsons. New York: The Free Press of Glencoe, 1964.

Weingartner, Rudolph H. *Experience and Culture: The Philosophy of Georg Simmel*. Middletown Connecticut: Wesleyan University Press, 1962.

Weingartner, Rudolph H. "Form and content in Simmel's Philosophy of Life." *Essays on Sociology, Philosophy & Aesthetics by Georg Simmel et al.* Ed by K.H. Wolff. New York: Harper Torchbooks, 1959.

Weinstein, Deena and M. A. Weinstein. "Georg Simmel *Flaneur Bricoleur*." *Theory Culture & Society* 8.3 (1991):151-168.

Wells, Gary L. and Elizabeth F. Loftus. *Eyewitness Testimony: Psychological Perspectives*. Cambridge; New York : Cambridge University Press, 1984

Wittgenstein, Ludwig. *Lecture & Conversations on Aesthetics, Psychology and Religious Belief*. Ed. by C. Barrett. Berkeley and Los Angeles:University of California Press, 1972.

Wittgenstein, Ludwig. *Philosophical Investigations 3rd Ed*. Trans. by G.E.M. Amscombe. New York: The Macmillan Co., 1964.

Wittgenstein, L. *Zettel*. Ed. by G.E.M. Amscombe & G.H. Von Wright. Berkeley and Los Angeles: University of California Press, 1970.

Wolff, Janet. "Hermeneutics and Sociology." *The Renascence of Sociological Theory*. Eds. H. Etzkowitz and R.M.Glassman. Itasca, Illinois: F.E. Peacock Publishers, Inc., 1991.

Wolff, Kurt, H. *Trying Sociology*. New York: John Wiley & Sons Inc., 1974.

Zborowski, Mark. "Cultural Components in Response to Pain." *Journal of Social Issues*. 8 (1953):16-31.

# INDEX

234

Oakes, Phil, 37, 158, 161, 163, 165, 187, 204
obesity, 106
"object as meant," 72, 100
objectification, 61, 100, 181
objectified experience, as ascertained through reflection, 62
objective idealism human, 44
objective validity, 61
objects, 63, 66, 69-70, 72-89, 92, 99-107, 110, 113, 115, 118-129, 132-134, 138, 140, 142, 144-162
observation, 32, 41, 49, 52-54, 63, 91-92, 143, 207
orchestra, interpretation of, 5, 105
"organic impulses," 23
organization, special and temporal, 149
Oriental music, and Western music, 55
originary experience, 97, 117
other, the, 19, 30, 37-39, 45, 119, 125
Paige, Satchel, 79
Pareto, Vilfredo, 7, 12
"party standpoint," 85
passivity-activity, 177
patterns of behavior, 149
perception, 73-76, 130, 152, 181
perceptual sphere, 78-79
Perinbanayagam, R.S., 134- 140
personal consciousness, 99, 71
personality, 57, 131, 135
phantoms, 85, 100
phenomenological *epoche,* 81-82
phenomenological sociology, 69, 95, 97, 107, 115, 129, 191
phenomenology, 67, 69-70, 82, 86, 89, 91, 97, 117, 129
philosophy, and sociology, 21, 43, 83-84, 118, 130, 158, 171
Picasso, Pablo, 76
plausibility, 66, 92, 109, 126, 180, 184, 196

play, 29, 163, 165, 167, 171-172, 174-178, 182, 184, 187
*Playboy* magazine, 106
*Pledge of Allegiance,* 87
political correctness, 112
political power, 112
Polynesia, 25
popular music in American culture, 6, 22
positive sciences, 47, 84
positive stage, 41
positivism, 24, 39-45, 191, 192
power, 13, 18-21, 35, 111-113, 169, 180
pragmatic exigencies, 107, 110, 112, 116, 124-125
preconception, 71, 81, 83-84, 113
preconstructed meaning, 108
predispositions, 71, 138, 142
prefigured knowledge, 65
prepredicated meaning, 108
prepredictative thinking, 121
presumed sharedness, 63
presupposition, 61, 84, 86, 96, 109, 165
"presuppositionless observation," 54
Pritchard, James, 27
production, 19-21, 34, 114
profiling, 77
profit, 12, 19, 22
*Protestant Ethic and the Spirit of Capitalism, The,* 48
"provinces of meaning," 107, 165, 203
"pseudo because-statements," 94
pseudo-motive, 94
psychological considerations, 50
psychological reductionism, 33, 39, 50, 131, 133
psychological reenactment, 45
psychology, 32-33, 40, 50-52, 128, 143-144, 188
qualitative/quantitative debate, 40

types, 14, 47-52, 60, 67, 81, 119, 122-126, 169, 172, 174, 179, 181-187, 192-200
typical behavior, 58, 67, 119, 123, 125
typical precepts for typical behavior, 119, 125
typicality121-122, 125
typifactory schemes, 125
typification, and Intersubjectivity, 116
typifications, 69, 116, 119-128, 182
typing, 51, 77, 181-187
UFO, 71
unconsciousness, 13, 15, 17, 18, 188
Underground Railroad, 8
unit of sociological analysis, 49, 96,
university establishment, 31-32
usefulness, 41, 74, 77, 79, 86, 89, 102, 110, 112, 116, 127, 137, 185
*usual* behavior, 56
value, 58, 61, 74, 77-80, 86, 89, 102, 110, 112-113, 127, 150, 170-171
values, 58, 61, 74, 77-80, 86, 89, 102, 110, 112-113, 127, 150, 170-171
Veblen, Thorsten, 65-66
venting anger, 60
verification, 66
*Verstehen,* 30, 42, 45, 47-48, 53, 58-71, 89, 91, 96-97, 117, 123-124, 190, 200
*Verstehende Soziologie,* 97
Virgin Mary siting, 113
voluntarism, 43
Von Helmholtz, Hermann, 40
Washington, George, 56
wealth, 19, 180
Weber, Max, 23-24, 30-35, 38, 40, 42, 45, 47-68, 70, 81, 89, 91-97, 118, 129, 137, 151, 157, 162, 192
Weber's "Ideal Types," 81
Weingartner, Rudolph, 158-159, 204
"we-ness," 119

West Nile Virus, 59
Western music, 55
whistle-blower, 122, 127
Wittgenstein, Ludwig, 15
"Woman at the Mirror," 76
"Woman With Pigeons," 76
woodchoppers, 51-52, 59-67, 94
words and meaning, 28-30, 92, 114, 130, 134, 167
World War II, 79
world-view, 44-45, 60
Wright, Steven, 117
Wundt, Wilhelm, 40
X-ers, 181
Y-ers, 181
yuppies, 181
Zeus, 4
Znaniecki, Florian, 58